D0733608

SHIPWRECKED!

deadly adventures
and disasters
at sea

Evan Balkan

MENASHA RIDGE PRESS
Birmingham, Alabama

DYinG to EXPlore

Published by Menasha Ridge Press
Printed in the United States of America
Distributed by Publishers Group West
First edition, first printing

Library of Congress Cataloging-in-Publication Data

Balkan, Evan, 1972–
    Shipwrecked! : deadly adventures and disasters at sea / by Evan Balkan.
        — 1st ed.
        p. cm. — (Dying to explore series)
    Includes bibliographical references and index.
    ISBN-13: 978-0-89732-653-7
    ISBN-10: 0-89732-653-9
    1. Shipwrecks. 2. Adventure and adventurers. I. Title.
    G525.B256 2008
    910.4'52—dc22
                                2008026581

Text and cover design by Travis Bryant
Cover photo by Rick Rusing/VEER
Indexing by Cindy Coan

Menasha Ridge Press
P.O. Box 43673
Birmingham, Alabama 35243
www.menasharidge.com

TABLE OF CONTENTS

TABLE OF CONTENTS *(continued)*

Dedicated to the memory of John Robert Harrington,
who knew some ripping good yarns.

Greenland
Arctic Circle

EUROPE

NORTH
AMERICA

Tropic of Cancer

Atlantic Ocean

Equator

*Pacific
Ocean*

SOUTH
AMERICA

Equator

Tropic of Capricorn

Antarctic Circle

1 *Peggy*

2 *Essex*

3 *Mignonette*

4 *Nottingham
    Galley*

5 *Francis Mary*

6 *Stirling Castle*

7 *Batavia*

8 *Medusa*

9 *Karluk*

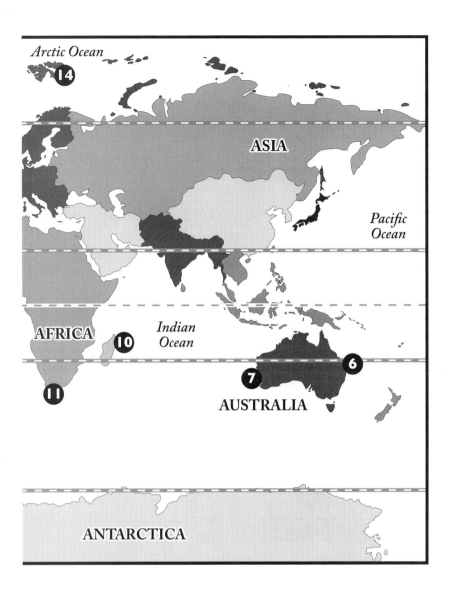

About the Author

Evan Balkan teaches writing at the Community College of Baltimore County. His fiction and nonfiction, mostly in the areas of travel and outdoor recreation, have been published throughout the United States, as well as in Canada, England, and Australia. A graduate of Towson, George Mason, and Johns Hopkins universities, he is also the author of *Vanished! Explorers Forever Lost,*

60 Hikes within 60 Miles: Baltimore, and *Best in Tent Camping: Maryland* (all published by Menasha Ridge Press). He lives in Lutherville, Maryland, with his wife, Shelly, and daughters, Amelia and Molly.

Preface

Since human beings first lashed together the trunks and branches of trees, tested their buoyancy on a body of water, set a tentative foot on the result and pushed off, there have been great rewards. And great dangers. The only way to ensure a safe voyage was to remain in port.

But that doesn't speak to the imagination. There were whole worlds out there, after all—and they screamed for exploration. There were food sources, too. And new lands to conquer. There was money to be made. What stood between this shore and the next was a limitless swelling wilderness of water. We can imagine early humans cupping their hands to their eyes and staring out over that vast swell, scared of what lived within but pulled nevertheless by what lay beyond.

As the centuries passed, humans became especially adept at creating efficient vessels. From the tiniest kayak carrying the solitary hunter to do battle with a whale, to the floating cities that carry goods all over the world—the earth's major waterways are pocked with boats. But all the carriers on the planet congregated in one ocean would barely make a dent in its vastness. Indeed, if the ship fails, there's hardly a more helpless feeling. But when the vessel begins to sink, often that is only the beginning of the story.

Through the last half of the second millennium, the printed word allowed dissemination of incredible tales of shipwreck and their aftermath. Not surprisingly, there was a great hunger for such stories. They were so dramatic as to be almost unbelievable. Today's modes of concentrated conveyance also sometimes give us tragedy, of course. And their calamity is no less severe. But today's air crashes, for example, are more efficient, leaving little chance for escape. When the hold of yesterday's ship began to crack and the saltwater made its way inside, the responses were as varied as the wide spectrum of human emotions. There were bravery and heroism, cowardice and incivility.

But universally, there was horror. The Calcutta lawyer and memoirist William Hickey wrote in 1810, "Death by shipwreck is the most terrible of deaths . . . In a storm at sea, in a miserable cabin on a filthy wet bed where it is as impossible to think as to breathe freely, the fatigue, the motion, the want of rest and food, give a kind of hysteric sensibility to the frame, which makes it alive to the slightest danger. If we look round at the miserable group that surround us, no eye beams comfort, no tongue speaks consolation, and when we throw our imagination beyond—to the death-like darkness, the howling blast, the raging and merciless element—surely, surely it is the most terrible of deaths!"

This book presents fifteen such tales of the "raging and merciless element," spanning the end of the seventeenth century to the beginning of the twentieth, and covering almost every corner of the world.

A note about the organization of this book: *Shipwrecked* was a difficult book to write. That is because as I was researching one wreck, there would inevitably be a reference to another, even more interesting wreck story. This happened so many times that I had to check myself from writing a 10,000-page work covering all the drama of the sea. There are simply too many incredible stories.

Eventually, I settled on the fifteen you'll see here. I grouped them by theme, providing an organizing principle that allowed me some control over the material lest I lose myself once again to all the astonishing drama. Working within a particular frame proved to be something of a check against that impulse. In the end, I settled on five themes, placing three wrecks within each. The five themes are: The Custom of the Sea (Cannibalism); Conflicting Accounts; Incompetence, Disorder, and Evil; On Foreign Shores; and Extraordinary Survival.

No doubt the reader will notice quite a bit of overlap among these categories. For example, the wreck of the *Stirling Castle* off the coast of Australia in 1836 could have logically gone into the On Foreign Shores chapter; there are also hints of cannibalism in that amazing story. However, it is the variation in the accounts of the wreck that makes it resonate even today. Further, the other two wrecks in the Conflicting Accounts chapter (the *Nottingham Galley* and the *Francis Mary*) have tales of cannibalism; however, I reserved the three wrecks in the Cannibalism chapter for those stories that involved the "Custom of the Sea," or the drawing of lots to see who would be killed and then eaten by desperate shipmates. As you will see, it's an important distinction—one that made all the difference to friends and relatives of the shipwreck survivors who were reduced to eating their shipmates to survive. These three tales include the wrecks of the *Peggy*, the *Essex* (inspiration for Herman Melville's *Moby-Dick*), and the *Mignonette*.

The wrecks in the On Foreign Shores chapter include those incredible tales of wide-eyed and often grossly misinformed Europeans finding themselves in lands where images of mythical monsters, animals—and savage people— dominated. There were places often represented on maps by fabulous beasts, and human beings only a rung or two above. For an uninformed European, the prospects were terrifying. And the results were astonishing. Here we have three tales of cultural misunderstanding and hostility, slavery, and even assimilation: these are the wrecks of the *Grosvenor* in southern Africa, the *Commerce* at the western Sahara, and the *Degrave* on the exotic island of Madagascar.

In addition to all the stories of heroism and bravery in the aftermath of a shipwreck, there are also tales of terrible cowardice and mismanagement where dozens or even hundreds of lives ended unnecessarily. Often, the appalling and cowardly decisions led to the wreck themselves, and behavior afterward was even more abysmal. Certainly this is the case for the French frigate *Medusa,* which inspired one of the world's great maritime paintings. Also here are the stories of the *Batavia,* still considered Australia's largest mass murder, and the *Karluk,* stuck deep in the Arctic.

Last, there are some success stories. Even though the ship went down, the unfortunate mariners managed to live through it and the extraordinary ordeal that followed. Here we see maroons (Pedro de Serrano, Alexander Selkirk, and Philip Ashton) scratching out a living on desert isles, dozens of men trudging for years through the terrorizing climate of the Antarctic (the *Endurance,* led by the indomitable Ernest Shackleton), and the story of four Russian men who gave us one of the most amazing—if little-known—survival stories in history.

—Evan Balkan

"THE CUSTOM OF THE SEA": CANNIBALISM

Perhaps no survival accounts excite the Western imagination more than those that involve cannibalism. With a shuddering of revulsion, we have been taught to be repelled by the very thought of it. It's certainly no stretch to say that much of this disgust stems from the deep-seated understanding that faced with the choice of consuming human flesh—of a recent fellow traveler, at that—or die, most of us would choose cannibalism. In other words, appall us though it may, we realize we are a mere survival scenario away from partaking in the great taboo ourselves.

In 1201, an Egyptian doctor, Abd al-Latif, described widespread cannibalism during a famine: "The poor . . . reached the stage of eating little children. The commandant of the city guard ordered that those who committed this crime should be burned alive . . . The corpse was always found to have been devoured by the following morning. People ate it the more willingly, for the flesh, being fully roasted, did not need to be cooked." Once the practice began, the ordinary disgust with which it was once regarded disappeared. Al-Latif continued, "The horror people had felt at first entirely vanished; one spoke of it, and heard it spoken of, as a matter of everyday indifference."

Cases of survival cannibalism—even in societies where the practice is one of the greatest taboos—aren't all that uncommon. The famous stories attending the Uruguayan rugby team in the Andes in 1972 (immortalized in the book and movie *Alive!*) and the Donner party in 1846–47 in the American West attest to this. Those reduced to eating their acquaintances to survive even deserved special sympathy, while the act itself was only whispered about. In the cases of survival cannibalism at sea, those hushed undertones often graduated to open discussion. The men who had undertaken the act were driven to it by extreme desperation. There was one catch, however; there needed to be a lottery.

If each man stood the same chance of drawing the short stick, those who came back home weren't murderers.

At least two thousand years ago, the Roman philosopher Cicero wrote of two men in a boat for whom the circumstance of one eating the other arises. In a meditation on morality, Cicero concludes that "One will give place to the other, as if the point were decided by lot." By the nineteenth century, tales of drawing lots were commonplace, and weren't met with much indignation. That said, acceptance of the practice surely didn't make it very easy for those who were forced to do it, as we shall see in this chapter.

Peggy (1765–66)

The brig *Peggy* sailed from New York in 1765 and reached the island of Faial in the Azores, where it unloaded its cargo and then filled up with wine and brandy for its return trip to North America. The crew left Faial on October 24. They enjoyed five days of good sail before getting battered by a strong storm. It would prove merely a harbinger. For the next month, the *Peggy* endured fierce gales, one coming on top of the previous in rapid and unrelenting succession. By the end of the month, the *Peggy* was still afloat, but she had all of her sails torn off but one, and several leaks were discovered in the hold. By the beginning of December, the weather had improved, but the *Peggy* had been blown far off course, and the damaged state of the ship meant there was little means for steering her aright. The captain, David Harrison, described the ship's wretched condition:

> The conflict which our vessel had so long maintained against waves and winds had by this time occasioned her to leak excessively, and our provisions were so much exhausted that we found it absolutely necessary to come to an immediate allowance of two pounds of bread a week for each person, besides a quart of water and a pint of wine a day. The alternative was really deplorable, between the shortness of our provisions and the wreck of our ship. If we contrived to keep the latter from sinking we were in danger of perishing with hunger, and if we contrived to spin out the former with a rigid perseverance of economy for any time, there was but little probability of being able to preserve our ship. Thus on either hand little less than a miracle could save us from inevitable destruction. If we had an accidental gleam of comfort on one hand, the fate with which the other so visibly teemed gave an instant

check to our satisfaction and obscured every rising ray of hope with
an instant cloud of horror and despair.

Despite their hopeless situation on the open sea, they weren't alone out
there. Other ships skittered along the far horizon, but the relentlessness of the
weather made communicating the *Peggy's* dire situation impossible. Towering
waves kept the *Peggy* from reaching the other ships, and each successive wave
revealed that would-be rescue ships were getting smaller and smaller until they
disappeared altogether.

Now five weeks at sea, their food and water depleted, the crew fell into a
more desperate state, beginning the slow and excruciating process of withering
away from starvation. Despite this, they had to continue to work feverishly at the
pumps just to keep the *Peggy* sailing, so badly damaged was she that neglect would
have meant her sinking. All that was left the men now was the store of wine and
brandy they had picked up in the Azores. The crew, against Captain Harrison's
wishes, broke into the alcohol and consumed it in vast quantities. Their various
states of drunkenness held one thing in common: it made them defiant, mean, and
unwilling to listen to the intended calming entreaties of their beleaguered captain.
It was only the sighting of another ship, on Christmas morning, that allowed the
captain to finally breathe easy. Seeing the sail "suddenly transported [the crew]
with the most extravagant sensations of joy."

There are many accounts of such meetings on the high seas that relate tears
from the eyes of the captain seeing fellow seamen afflicted like those of the *Peggy*.
But the captain of the ship now aside the *Peggy* had an opposite and perhaps
far more common reaction. Crew and captain, contending with limited stores
of their own, often faced the prospect of having to take on and feed an entirely
new crew as a potential death sentence. What if the would-be rescue ship should
fall under the same distress that befell the *Peggy?* What then, with an inflated
crew and limited space? Harrison, though clearly a man who would have helped
had the roles been reversed, nevertheless understood the mean rules of the open
sea. He swore to the opposing captain that if he could take on his crew, the men
of the *Peggy* would not eat any of the food on board. They merely wanted safe
passage home. The captain steadfastly refused, but he did relent on one point: he
would give the crew of the *Peggy* some bread. He merely had to finish his noon
nautical observation first; then he would send the biscuit over.

Harrison, satisfied but extremely exhausted, went belowdecks to rest. He
was soon awakened by his excited crew telling him that the other ship was
sailing away. The other captain had merely used the pretext of an observation

Shipwreck in a Storm. (1629) **Willem van Diest.**

to buy time so he could make his escape. Harrison literally crawled across the deck, watching first the retreating sail of the quick ship and then turning his attention to his deflated crew: "As long as my poor fellows could retain the least trace of him they hung about the shrouds or ran in a state of absolute frenzy from one part of the ship to the other. They pierced the air with their cries, increasing their lamentations as he lessened upon their view and straining their very eyeballs to preserve him in sight, through a despairing hope that some dawning impulse of pity would yet induce him to commiserate our situation and lead him to stretch out the blessed hand of relief."

It wasn't to be; the men watched until the ship disappeared, never to return. If things were desperate before, here they took an even harder turn. According to Archibald Duncan, in his *The Mariner's Chronicle* (G. W. Gorton, 1834), "No language is adequate to describe the despair and consternation which then overwhelmed the crew. Enraged, and destitute of hope, they fell upon whatever they had spared till then." Harrison, however, didn't change his outlook. Desperate, yes. But bitter and contemptuous, as his crew had become—never. In fact, in his subsequent account of the ordeal, *The Melancholy Narrative of the Distressful Voyage and Miraculous Deliverance of Captain David Harrison* (London, 1766), Harrison declines even to name the captain or his ship, writing that he would not offer him up to "universal detestation or infamy . . . to the reader." Instead, he would keep his faith in God's workings upon that man's conscience. But while Harrison maintained his capacity for humanitarianism, his crew had utterly given up. It was time for more bold and decisive action. As far as they were concerned, the good captain would just as soon let them drift forever until each died a slow and agonizing death.

Amazingly, the crew had gone all that time without killing three sources of meat already on board (sources that wouldn't excite revulsion): two pigeons and a cat. But as Duncan noted, they now fell upon what they had previously spared. The birds went first, then the cat soon after. Still angry with their captain, but showing begrudging respect for his position, the crew included Harrison in its division of the beast by tossing him the cat's head. Initially shuddering in disgust at the prospect of consuming the cat head, he soon tried it and thereafter could hardly contain himself: "The piercing sharpness of necessity had entirely conquered my aversion to such food, and the rage of an incredible hunger rendered that an exquisite regale which on any other occasion I must have loathed with the most insuperable disgust." He picked the skull clean, devouring the eyes, leathery tongue and nose, and spongy brain matter, sucking out the minuscule fluid still lingering in the tip of the spinal cord.

The animals provided a reprieve, but it obviously didn't satisfy for long. It had been some eighteen days by this point since they had eaten the last of their store of food. For the next few days, the crew continued to drink and eat whatever was within reach: candles, oil, leather, buttons, until there was literally nothing left. This was December 28. By some miracle, they were all still alive two weeks later; to quote Archibald Duncan, "It is impossible to tell in what manner they subsisted." What is known is that on January 13, the men entered Harrison's cabin, where he lay suffering from a severe case of gout, and trying to stave off the embrace of death by thinking of his family. They had a shocking proposal. Duncan's *Chronicle* recounts the ordeal of the *Peggy* by beginning this way: "Famine frequently leads men to the commission of the most horrible excesses: insensible on such occasions to the appeals of nature and reason, he assumes the character of a beast of prey; he is dead to every representation and coolly meditates the death of his fellow-creature." Sure enough. The men's proposal was simple: they intended (they weren't asking, but rather informing the captain) to draw lots to see who would die so that the rest may feast off him and survive.

Captain Harrison attempted to hold them off. He first appealed to their sense of fraternity, telling the men that they were to regard one another as brothers. If they were to carry through with the terrible deed, they would sink to the level of beasts and forever after resign themselves to the reputation that such a state entailed. His argument didn't work. The men persisted, wild and barely contained in their anger and hunger.

Harrison reminded them that they were desperate and not given toward rational thought because of the deplorable circumstances. Perhaps, but those same deplorable circumstances, they reminded him, meant that the normal hierarchy had been abolished and they would go on without him. For all they cared, he could stay cooped in his cabin and continue his fight with the gout. True, the captain was by this point incapacitated. However, unbeknownst to the men of the crew, he kept a pistol handy in case they tried to drag him out and make him their first victim. The crew, still somewhat torn between a faint sense of duty to their captain (after all, it wasn't his fault they were in this predicament) and fuming at his overt attempts to shame them, returned to his cabin, telling him that they had drawn lots and he would be invited to eat the victim.

The loser, described by Harrison as "that poor Ethiopian," was hardly surprising. The "Ethiopian" was actually a black slave, part of the ship's cargo. Harrison, still belowdecks, didn't witness the drawing of lots, and the time between the crew's stated intention and their return with the slave was just too speedy to believe that the lots weren't fixed—or that they hadn't really been drawn at all. Even writing in 1834, some thirty years before the abolition of slavery, Archibald Duncan noted, "It is more than probable that the lot had been consulted only for the sake of form and that the wretched black was proscribed the moment the sailors first formed the resolution."

The black man burst into Harrison's bunk and pleaded with the captain to save his life. He was dragged off, fighting and pleading all the while. Harrison crawled out only to watch the man momentarily escape to the other side of the deck before he was wrestled down and shot in the head. The fire had been started even before the man was killed.

A crew member, James Campbell, so ravenous and out of his head, immediately began to carve up the body. He cut open the chest and torso and, spotting the liver, reached in and devoured it raw. The rest of the men were more temperate, waiting for the body to be cooked and then savoring their share throughout most of the evening.

By morning, the men, somewhat becalmed by their full bellies, went back to the captain and asked what his orders were for the remaining pieces of flesh. Harrison's only response was to raise his pistol and threaten the asker with a death like that of the slave. The crew members decided to cut the rest of the body into pieces to be parceled out in time. The men got at their grim task, all the while muttering about the self-important captain whose example served to try and shame them when in fact they had only done what they did to save themselves. The truth was, Harrison couldn't have eaten anyway. The odor of the burning man, coupled with his illness and perpetual fear that he would be the next victim, had the effect of completely overwhelming any ravages of hunger. As the men cut and cooked, their captain writhed in agony below, awaiting the next confrontation, sure that if he dared give into the drop of his heavy eyelids, he would either slip into death or be awakened by the bloodthirsty crew. In his semiconscious state, Harrison distinctly heard the men agreeing that the captain should be the next victim; his obstinacy and haughtiness had become a source of great irritation—better him dead than us, they proclaimed. Even with his pistol, he would be hopelessly outnumbered.

Actually, the opportunity to eat another man aside from Harrison did present itself. Three days after eating the slave's raw liver, James Campbell completely lost his mind, no doubt afflicted with the toxins the liver held. His death came only after a period of ranting and raving that made the general conditions on the *Peggy* even worse, if such a thing was possible. When he died, there was little discussion over whether the remaining men should eat him. It was decided that doing so would in turn make them all insane, and so his body was dumped over the side, a meal for the sharks.

Perhaps numbed a bit by this occurrence, the men became much more conciliatory. They had since eaten the last of the slave and after three more days, decided collectively to go ahead and cast lots rather than simply murder the captain. Again, it was not a request, and the captain's name would be added to the lots just like every other man on board. Still, Harrison didn't readily accede, reminding the men that their meal of the slave obviously hadn't sated them and why should they think a new carcass would do the trick? "The poor Negro's death had done them no service as they were as greedy and emaciated as ever," Harrison wrote. Still, they were unrelenting.

Sure that if he didn't oversee the casting of lots, he would be the victim, Harrison wrote each man's name on a slip of paper and put them into a hat. The lot fell to a foremastman named David Flatt. A deep and enduring silence came over the crew. Flatt was easily the most liked among them. Gone was the singular purpose in the killing of the slave. Now, the men seemed suddenly to regret their decision. "The shock of the decision was great," Harrison wrote. He stared at each man's face, noting the despair therein. He made his way back to his bunk, at least somewhat satisfied that his prophecy had come true: this, he reasoned, was the men's just punishment for their barbarism. They would have to dispatch a beloved and competent member of the crew. But Flatt, true to his nature, sought to ease the men of their gnawing consciences. "My dear friends," he addressed them, "all I have to beg of you is to dispatch me as soon as you did the Negro and to put me to as little torture as you can." The men could only nod sheepishly and wipe away their tears. The same man who had executed the slave was chosen to do the deed to Flatt.

In a terribly ironic twist, the men did in fact put Flatt through an unendurable torture, hoping, by contrast, to give him the respect and care they felt he deserved by delaying his execution until the next morning. The crew was certainly familiar with the English sea chantey "Ship in Distress," which upon the subject of cannibalism offers the following stanza:

> Now the lot fell on one poor fellow,
> Whose family was very great,
> Which did the more increase his sorrow,
> for to repent it was too late:
> "I'm free to die, but, messmate brothers,
> unto the top mast head straightway,
> See if you can sail discover,
> whilst I unto the Lord do pray."

Like the unlucky mariner in the song who accepts his fate but asks for more time during which the crew might spot a sail, Flatt accepted his remaining time in the hopes the *Peggy*, too, would find rescue. Flatt, now belowdecks, was painfully aware that every passing moment brought him closer to the appointed execution time of eleven o'clock. In the interim, the men, suddenly very pious and ardent, beseeched Harrison to lead them in prayers, supplicating the heavens for either a ship or success in catching fish at dawn the next morning.

Flatt, facing his own impending murder, slowly went mad. By midnight, he was deaf, and four hours later, in the predawn darkness, he had completely lost his mind. The men debated killing him then to put him out of his misery. But the appointed time of eleven was upheld, on the slim hope that the next few hours would, at last, bring them salvation and allow them to spare poor Flatt. Of course, one must suspect that at least some of this decision was informed by the fear that eating the now raving Flatt would mean a transfer of his insanity.

As it turned out, it made no difference. Like a perfect Hollywood ending, with only an hour or so to spare and a fire going ready to "dress the limbs of the unfortunate victim," the crew spied a sail heading right for them. Even Harrison, so near death himself, felt a surge of renewal and hurried up deck. What they saw turned out to be their rescue ship, the *Susan:* "It is impossible to describe the excess of my transport upon hearing there was a sail at any rate in sight. My joy in a manner overpowered me and it was not without the utmost exertion of my strength that I desired them to use every expedition in making a signal of distress," wrote Harrison. The last of his strength expended, the captain had to be lowered by rope to the rescue ship when it came.

Before this happened, however, there was an interminable pause when the rescue crew stopped just to the leeward of the *Peggy* and stared at the sunken, hollowed faces peering back at them. The men actually engaged in a conversation designed to prove that the crew of the *Peggy* were human beings and not some ghoulish phantoms. The rescuers satisfied, the men were saved. In the rush to get on board, the crew almost left the poor, raving Flatt behind. His last-minute deliverance was nothing short of miraculous, but conflicting accounts make it unclear as to whether Flatt ever actually recovered his senses, or if he spent the remainder of his life completely out of his mind. Archibald Duncan cheerfully reported that "Flatt himself was restored to perfect health after having been so near the gates of death." Harrison, however, recounted that the "unhappy Flatt still continued out of his senses."

The head of the *Susan,* a Captain Evers, provides a nice counterpoint to the unnamed captain that had abandoned the crew of the *Peggy* the previous month. His ship, now laden with seven new and ill men, encountered terrible storms and the *Susan* itself barely made it to land. But they did make it. One more man would die, an Archibald Nicholson, Harrison's first mate, who had apparently so destroyed his stomach with vast quantities of alcohol while on the *Peggy* that his belly wouldn't allow any intake of food. As for Harrison, after managing to imbibe some chicken broth, his attention now turned to basic concerns:

> Having an occasion for a particular indulgence of nature, I thought I should have expired performing it. The pain it gave me was so excruciating to the last degree and the parts were so contracted, having never once been employed for a space of thirty-six or thirty-seven days, that I almost began to despair restoring them to their necessary operations. I was, however, at last relieved by the discharge of a callous lump about the size of a hen's egg, and enjoyed a tranquility of body, notwithstanding all my disorders, with which I was utterly unacquainted for some preceding weeks.

The relief, of course, must have been enormous. But it paled in comparison to the joy at having survived. And for Harrison, he also had the pleasure of surviving with his particular code of ethics intact.

Essex (1819–20)

In the early 1800s, the whaleship *Essex,* out of Nantucket, was just one of an estimated seventy such ships plying the waters of the Atlantic and Pacific, feeding the worldwide demand for whale oil. The *Essex* enjoyed a long and successful history; it was what was known as a lucky ship.

On her 1819 voyage, the man charged with piloting her across the oceans was Captain George Pollard; his first mate was the twenty-two-year-old Owen Chase, Benjamin Franklin's first cousin four times removed. Chase and Pollard had served together on the *Essex* in 1815, though the 1819 voyage would be Pollard's first as captain.

Captain Pollard arrived in Nantucket Harbor on August 12, 1819. Before he left, he received a letter from the owners of the *Essex* wishing him a "short and prosperous voyage." The *Essex* left that day, heading toward the Azores, when a violent storm struck. When it was over, the ship had taken a beating. Though all men were safe, two of the ships' mainsails had been torn to shreds, and two of the whaleboats were lost at sea. A spare boat on deck had been crushed. Pollard declared that the crew would have to return to Nantucket for repairs. However, Chase and Second Mate Matthew Joy convinced Pollard that they should continue on to the Azores, where they'd likely pick up spare boats. Pollard relented.

They did in fact reach the Azores and they did provision the ship; however, they were not able to replenish their whaleboat stock. Thus, when they set off southeast toward the Cape Verde Islands, the crew of the *Essex* didn't have one spare whaleboat. They did manage to pick up another old and leaky whaleboat at Cape Verde, however. They then headed southwest toward the coast of South America. Somewhere between Rio de Janeiro and Buenos Aires, the lookout spotted the *Essex*'s first whale. It had been more than three months since the *Essex* left Nantucket.

The crew climbed into the whaleboats and gave chase. Chase's boat, with steerer Benjamin Lawrence manning the harpoon, reached the whale first. Lawrence steadied himself and prepared to harpoon the gargantuan beast. His arm cocked back, and the crew readied for the resulting wrath of the world's largest animal flailing in a paroxysm of pain and fury. But the harpoon never flew; instead, Lawrence and the other members of Chase's whaleboat found

"His Head half out of water . . . he again struck the ship."

themselves flung into the air, their boat stove in and splintered below them. They could see the retreating lip of another whale's black tail trailing away from their craft. The men clung to the wreck until Pollard came to collect them. It was a terrible disappointment; not only had they failed to take the whale, but they were once again down a boat.

They had better luck a few days later. This time they managed to snare a whale. Though the entire crew had dreamed of this moment, it proved to be an extremely unpleasant spectacle.

A harpoon didn't kill the whale. Rather, it kept the whale in place as it tired itself out trying to escape. The crew then repeatedly stabbed the beast, trying to locate arteries near the lungs so that the whale choked to death on its own blood. The result was a massive pool of red that encompassed the boat and covered everything in a sticky, stinking goo. The noise the animal made was itself horrendous, as the cavernous lungs echoed a gasping fight before the whale finally gave in. It was enough to make green seamen blanch. This occurred even before the work of getting the blubber began. The whale now dead, the crewmen stripped it of its outer skin and layer of blubber underneath. They sent this belowdecks to be cut into small pieces. Then they decapitated the whale, scooping out hundreds of pounds of blubber from within. This process inevitably resulted in a deck covered with greasy oil and blood; it was an altogether nasty affair.

When it came time to melt down the blubber into oil, the fires were fed by pieces of crispy blubber remnants, called cracklings. The stench and the thick black smoke were almost unbearable. A whaler once described the process this way: "The smell of the burning cracklings is too horribly nauseous for description. It is as though all the odors in the world were gathered together and shaken up."

The *Essex* continued on but was battered terribly once again by a vicious storm. When the ship finally rounded the Cape of Good Hope and ventured into the Pacific, it had been five months since the crew left Nantucket. By fall of that year, the crew had reached the Galapagos and filled roughly half its oil capacity. It didn't seem such a great ratio, but they were headed now into the prime whaling grounds of the Pacific. This was very welcome, but the *Essex* had developed a leak. Beaching at the Galapagos for repairs, the men reprovisioned with hundreds of pounds of tortoise meat. Many of the tortoises were brought aboard alive, to be killed later when stocks of food began to dwindle; fifteen-year-old cabin boy Thomas Nickerson estimated the haul at 180 terrapins. Reprovisioned, the *Essex* set off once again, deeper into the Pacific to fill to capacity their remaining empty barrels.

With the storms, it had been an altogether rough voyage. But if anyone on the ship thought things had been trying to this point, nothing in their experience—or their imagination—could prepare them for what came next.

On November 20, the lookout spotted a shoal of whales a few miles away. The *Essex* gave chase and about half a mile from the shoal, lowered the whaleboats. The teams loaded up. Once again, Chase's boat was damaged by the tail flick of an angry whale, its side now sporting Lawrence's harpoon. The men hurriedly stuffed up the hole in the boat and rowed back to the *Essex*. There, Nickerson was at the helm of the ship. He steered the craft toward his captain's whaleboat, now being dragged miles by the harpooned whale. Nickerson and Chase were stopped short by an extraordinary sight. A hundred yards away, an enormous whale, estimated at eighty-five feet long and eighty tons, was gliding slowly toward the ship. All the other whales were fleeing the *Essex*. But this one—the largest any of them had ever seen—kept coming closer. It dove once and then resurfaced less than forty yards away. The great creature stopped for a moment, as if to work up the nerve to do something unprecedented.

It started to swim directly toward the ship. It came faster and faster. The men on board only had time to recover from their absolute stupefaction at what they were seeing before the whale was upon them. Chase recalled: "I ordered the boy at the helm to put it hard up . . . The words were scarcely out of my mouth, before he came down upon us with full speed, and struck the ship with his head . . . The ship brought up as suddenly and violently as if she had struck a rock, and trembled for a few seconds like a leaf."

A whale attack had never been recorded in the history of New England whaling. The men picked themselves up from the deck and looked at each other, dumb with shock. The whale, meanwhile, glided off in a state of disorientation. When Chase spotted it, he "discovered the whale, apparently in convulsions . . . He was enveloped in the foam of the sea, that his continual and violent thrashing about in the water had created around him, and I could distinctly see him smite his jaws together, as if distracted with rage and fury."

Then, as if what had happened wasn't already unthinkable, the whale recovered itself and turned to make yet another attack on the ship. This time the whale moved even faster than before. To Chase, the whale "appeared with tenfold fury and vengeance in his aspect. The surf flew in all directions about him, and his course towards us was marked by a white foam of a rod in width, which he made with continual violent thrashing of his tail; his head was half out of water, and in that way he came upon, and again struck the ship." This time the *Essex* suffered irreparable damage. The jolt was more extraordinary than the first one, and the ship took on water.

There was a chance that the second hit could have been avoided. According to Nickerson, Chase had a perfect opportunity to harpoon the whale but passed because its tail was positioned right under the rudder. He should have taken the chance; in Nickerson's words: "Could he have foreseen all that so soon followed he would probably have chosen the lesser evil and have saved the ship."

By the time Pollard's whaleboat caught up to the *Essex*, all the captain could

Owen Chase

Courtesy of the Nantucket Historical Association, GPN4448

do was sink down, pale and speechless. When the men recovered their senses, there was only enough time to unfasten the remaining whaleboat and throw as many provisions as they could overboard before all leapt in and watched in horror as the *Essex* listed. The whale was by this time only a splotch of white water in the distance. Its revenge was complete, its fury sated. The crew of the *Essex* would kill no more whales.

The twenty men of the *Essex* were alive, but they were now separated from each other in three whaleboats, tethered to the dying hulk of the *Essex*. Worse, they were separated from the rest of humanity. Captain Pollard's quadrant observation put them at latitude 0° 40', longitude 119° 0'—in essence, about as far from inhabited land as it was possible to get on the planet.

The water was working its way through the hull of the ship, destroying everything within. Nickerson wrote: "The casks of oil are continually bursting and flowing out from the hold of the ship filling the whole surface of the deep with the fruits of our labour, as far as the eye can reach . . . Here at one view are our blighted prospects and the reward of our toil scattered to the winds." The waves slopped the oil onto the whaleboats. The men already had cramped conditions; now they had to contend with the slippery conditions. Nickerson called their previous home a "floating and dismal wreck."

The *Essex* was useless; all the men could do now was evenly distribute themselves in the three boats and row for land, thousands of miles away. Pollard proposed making for the Society Islands. But the mates, Chase and Joy, convinced Pollard that the Society Islands were peopled with cannibalistic natives (though they had no real proof to that end). Instead, the mates argued that the whaleboats should sail south for roughly 1,500 miles until captured by trade winds that would take them to the western coast of South America. Pollard relented yet again; Nickerson's rhetorical question summed up this decision best: "How many warm hearts have ceased to beat in consequence of it?"

The men in their whaleboats set off, all turning to watch the receding image of the *Essex* as it still floated, battered and broken, upon the waves. Its complete dissolution was imminent, and the men would have preferred to watch until the bitter end. But as it was, they had lots of ground to cover and rations for much less time than it would take. They said their silent good-byes and, with hearts as heavy as the bloated husk of their beloved ship, turned away, and shuddered with dread at what lay ahead.

Whaleboats, while perfect for speeding up to a whale, were not the vessels people wanted to use to navigate for miles on the open ocean. The boats were only about twenty feet in length and about five feet wide to begin with. And these were terribly overloaded with food rations, tortoises, and water, both freshwater from barrels and seawater that constantly made its way into the boats from cresting waves. Those waves were awful for another reason. They often rose to such a height that each boat would find itself in a valley between them, and thus temporarily lose sight of one another, increasing each man's sense of isolation in a seemingly limitless sea. They continued to sail southward; if they were lucky, they might be spotted by another whaling ship along the way, but in an area so vast, they certainly couldn't pin any hopes on that.

The first problem to afflict the men was painful sores, created by salt and constant moisture, and worsened by the jarring of the wooden boats beneath them. On Chase's boat, sprays of salt water found their way into one of the sacks of hardtack biscuits. Now this important food source was saturated with salt, something that could be deadly to people already in the process of dehydrating. Incredibly, Captain Pollard's boat was attacked again, this time by a killer whale, which took a bite out of the side of the boat. The men could hardly believe it. The prospects for their survival took a downward turn, if that was possible.

And it would only get worse.

Pollard's boat was repaired, but the men on Chase's boat began to suffer terribly from overwhelming thirst. The bread that had been soaked with seawater and left out in the sun to dry now contained excess levels of salt. Eating it started the men down the road toward hypernatremia, characterized by excesses of sodium and attendant electrolyte imbalances.

Nickerson later wrote of mid-December: "Our sufferings during these hot days almost exceed belief and the heart again bleeds at the bare recital." If Nickerson only knew; his ordeal would last another two and a half months.

The three boats had, to this point, managed to stick together—even through howling winds and unyielding storms. On several occasions, however, they got separated during the night only to be reunited in the light of morning or by pistol shot. However, because so much time was often dedicated to finding one another, the men decided that should they get separated again, no measure to reunite would be expended. The implications remained unspoken—none of the boats could reasonably take on any more men, so if one was damaged, the others would have to deny the waterborne men berth on their boat. Instead, they would have to row away and leave them—perhaps even beat them off. Chase wrote: "It appeared to be a universal sentiment, that [taking on men] was calculated to weaken the chances of a final deliverance for some, and might be the only means of consigning every soul of us to a horrid death of starvation."

But for now they were still together, something the men ascribed to providential guidance. They were, however, in bad shape. Nathaniel Philbrick, author of *In The Heart of the Sea* (Penguin, 2001) writes: "Their hair was coming out in clumps. Their skin was burned and covered with sores that a splash of seawater felt like acid burning on their flesh. Strangest of all, as their eyes sunk into their skulls and their cheekbones projected, they all began to look alike, their identities obliterated by dehydration and starvation."

But good news—at last—awaited. After a month apart from the *Essex,* the men sighted land; it was Henderson Island (mistaken by the men's calculations as Ducie Island), one of the Pitcairn Islands. Chase wrote, "It is not within the scope of human calculation, by a mere listener to the story, to divine what the feelings of our hearts were on this occasion." *The South Pacific Handbook,* (Moon, 1986) by David Stanley, describes Henderson today as a pretty inhospitable place: "The interior of the island is a flat coral plateau about thirty meters high but the dense undergrowth, prickly vines, and sharp coral rock make it almost impenetrable."

But it was land, offering a chance to get out of the boats at last. The men staked out the island and found fish and birds to eat, and more importantly, a spring of freshwater revealed during lowest tide. But what Henderson had to offer wasn't, of course, limitless. Within a week, the men of the *Essex* had used up the small island's resources. They determined to set forth for South America once again. But they would be lightened in load; to the surprise of the others, three men—Thomas Chappel, Seth Weeks, and William Wright, one man from each of the three boats—declared that they simply couldn't climb back into the boats for another insufferable journey. Instead, they would stay on Henderson Island and hope that a rescue ship would find them. There was little arguing. After all, three fewer men meant more provisions for those making the journey.

But the parting was excruciating, for everyone involved. When Chase said good-bye to the three men, "They seemed to be very much affected, and one of them shed tears." Those on the boats faced the prospect of more privations at sea, while those who elected to remain behind had now voluntarily abandoned any mode of rescue within their control. All they could do was sit and wait.

Matthew Joy, the *Essex*'s twenty-seven-year-old second mate, was the first to succumb. He had been ill since the stay on Henderson Island, and two weeks later, after being transferred to his captain's boat, Joy died. Soon after, Chase's boat became separated from the others; this time there would be no reunion. These men, who had suffered so terribly, but at least collectively, were now sinking deeper into isolation and deprivation. Worse, their remaining provisions had dwindled drastically. Chase continued to cut rations, to one and a half ounces of bread a day. The decision was stark: either take this reduced ration and hope to survive a few more days and be miraculously rescued. Or give in to their ravages, eat it all, and then slowly wait for death.

Things grew even more desperate. On the night of December 18, the men could hear in the impenetrable darkness of the night and sea, the snorting and spouting of several whales as they alternatively descended on the boat and then swam away, their mighty tails thrashing the water. The men, near death already, could only sit and await the inevitable end. But after a few excruciating hours, the whales swam off.

The boats continued taking on water, and the weak men had to bail just to stay afloat. The effort was too much to bear. But the alternative was worse. Nickerson wrote, "We might at any moment sink beneath this vast extent of ocean leaving scarcely a momentary bubble to mark the spot."

The rationing in Chase's boat wasn't enough for Richard Peterson, a sailor. He died on January 20, exactly two months after the *Essex* sank. On that same day, Lawson Thomas, another sailor on one of the two other boats, died. But whereas Peterson had been committed to the deep, as Joy had weeks earlier, the question on Thomas's boat turned toward cannibalism. The men made the decision: they would eat Thomas's remains.

The scene can scarcely be imagined. One of the men on the boat would have to butcher the body, cut it into manageable pieces, remove the organs, avoid sloshing large quantities of blood inside the boat, and do all this in plain sight of everyone—indeed, considering the cramped quarters, one would have found it impossible to escape the horror. Of course, the prospect of finally eating might have completely overwhelmed the repugnance toward of what was occurring. Thus, the men did the deed, lit a fire on a flat stone in the bottom of the boat, and roasted the organs.

Each of the men partook, so no one could cast a wary eye. Once the line had been crossed, subsequent "feasts" would have been easier to accept. They wouldn't have to wait long. Two days later, the second body was eaten after Charles Shorter, another sailor, died. Within five days, two more sailors died and were eaten. Then the two boats that had been in contact since the sinking parted. No one had the strength to attempt to find one another. Everyone was now alone, bobbing along in a seemingly infinite sea with little but their impending starvation to keep them company. They lacked the strength even to speak to one another.

But on Pollard's boat, Charles Ramsdell, one of only four remaining survivors, managed to say something: he proposed the drawing of lots. They needed to eat someone else; otherwise, they might all succumb sometime during the night. They agreed. The lot fell to Owen Coffin, just a teenager and the nephew of Captain Pollard, who had promised Coffin's mother that he would take extra care in looking out for him. Pollard offered to take the lot for Coffin and declared that the boy could go back on it. But Coffin accepted, muttering, "I like it as well as any other." He gave Pollard a message to deliver to his mother, should he see her again, asked for a few moments of silence, and then lay down in the boat. Another lot, to determine the shooter, fell to Ramsdell, Coffin's friend. Ramsdell, with shaky hand, crawled over to his friend and raised the pistol. "He was soon dispatched," Pollard later reflected, "and nothing of him left."

Another sailor in Chase's boat, Isaac Cole, met an ignominious end. He raved and swore, sprang around the boat asking for all manner of accoutrements of civilization, such as napkins, and then fell into the "most horrid and frightful convulsions." Because the first casualty, Richard Peterson, had been placed into the ocean, there had not yet been any cannibalism in Chase's boat. The men didn't consign Cole to the deep right away. Instead, they waited until morning, when Chase suggested they use his body for sustenance. Again, there was no argument from the others. Chase's version of the event spared no detail, adding that "Humanity must shudder at the dreadful recital." First the crew "separated [Cole's] limbs from his body, and cut all the flesh from the bones; after which, we opened the body, took out the heart, and then closed it again—sewed it up as decently as we could, and committed it to the sea."

The grisly rations did not go far in satisfying the men, even momentarily; each knew the obvious question: who would be next? Chase wrote that he possessed no "language to paint the anguish of our souls . . . We knew not then to whose lot it would fall next, either to die or be shot, and eaten like the poor wretch we had just dispatched."

Meanwhile, back on Pollard's boat, the men, still trying to come to grips with the horror of executing Owen Coffin, now had to contend with yet another death; this time it was the teenager Barzillai Ray. This left only Pollard and Ramsdell. On Chase's boat, there were still three: Chase, steerer Benjamin Lawrence, and Nickerson. Now it looked as if they also would be reduced to two; Nickerson had utterly given up, sinking to the floor of the boat and unable or unwilling to utter a word. Only an absolute miracle would save him.

And then it came: Lawrence espied a sail.

The London ship *Indian* saw the men as well. They were saved, just shy of ninety days since the *Essex* sank. It wasn't a pretty picture. Chase recalled: "We must have formed at that moment, in the eyes of the captain and his crew, a most deplorable and affecting picture of suffering and misery. Our cadaverous countenances, sunken eyes, and bones just starting through the skin, with the ragged remnants of clothes stuck about our sun-burnt bodies, must have produced an appearance . . . affecting and revolting in the highest degree."

Pollard and Ramsdell continued to float on the open sea, scarcely speaking to one another, and devolving more and more into obsession over the litter of bones that decorated their boat. Five days after Chase and Lawrence were saved, Pollard and Ramsdell were met unexpectedly by the horrified faces of sailors from the American ship *Dauphin*. The two men didn't leap for joy and relief; instead, they made mad dashes for the bones that littered the boat, stuffing them into their tattered pockets. So crazed were the two *Essex* survivors that even after rescue, they wouldn't part with their bones, which they sucked for any remnants of marrow. Commodore Charles Ridgely, commander of the U.S. frigate *Constellation,* now docked in Baltimore harbor, reported that the survivors were "ninety two days in the boat & were in a most wretched state, they were unable to move when found sucking the bones of their dead Mess mates, which they were both loth to part with."

All the survivors were eventually taken to Valparaiso, the Chilean port. This is where Ridgely met them, and even a week after their rescue, their appearance had scarcely improved. Ridgely remembered the men this way: "Bones working through their skins, their legs & feet much smaller & the whole surface of their bodies one entire ulcer." After two weeks spent recuperating, four survivors of the *Essex*—Chase, Lawrence, Nickerson, and Ramsdell—boarded the *Eagle,* bound for Nantucket. Pollard followed two weeks later, requiring extra recuperation time, and headed for home aboard the *Two Brothers.*

Another ship, the Australian trader *Surry,* headed for Henderson Island to search for the three maroons left there in January. For four months, Chappel, Weeks, and Wright had managed to subsist on nesting birds, eggs, and shellfish. On April 9, they spied the *Surry;* they, too, were rescued, after 111 days on the island. Though their rescue came after the others, who were now on the way home, it appeared they made a wise decision, sparing themselves the ignominy of having to eat their shipmates.

Sadly, the passengers in the third whaleboat—William Bond, Obed Hendricks, and Joseph West—didn't turn up until almost five years later, three skeletons inside a rotting whaleboat washed upon the shores of Ducie Island, an atoll east of Henderson Island.

There was a certain irony in the men's having resorted to cannibalism. When the *Essex* went down, the captain and mates decided on a longer course toward land than necessary, opting to steer clear of closer islands that they mistakenly believed harbored cannibalistic natives.

The idea of casting lots wasn't anything new or particularly shocking. While no one on Nantucket was quick to celebrate what was to them an embarrassing situation, none of the survivors of the *Essex* hid the fact, and none received any recriminations over it. People on Nantucket understood the necessity. The official port log there recorded the homecoming of the *Essex* survivors and noted neutrally that three of the men had subsisted on "water, crackers, and the body of a shipmate." As sea people, undoubtedly many of those on Nantucket were familiar with "The Ship in Distress," which includes the stanza:

> *Their cats and dogs, O, they did eat them*
> *Their hunger for to ease, we hear,*
> *And in the midst of all their sorrow,*
> *Captain and men had equal share;*
> *But now a scant has come upon us,*
> *A dismal tale, most certainly,*
> *Poor fellows they stood in torture*
> *Casting lots to see who should die.*

There is, of course, no sense of barbarism here; the men are referred to as "poor fellows." Charles Murphey, a Nantucket whaler, wrote a version of "The Ship in Distress" that included details of the *Essex* drawing for lots; again, there were no recriminations involved. Instead, the men were treated as victims themselves. But the Nantucketers were at least disquieted by the whole affair. A. Gustav Kobbé wrote in *Century Magazine* in 1890 in an article called "The Perils and Romance of Whaling" of the arrival of the *Essex*'s first survivors and the silent greeting that awaited them; the crowd that came to the port parted and reverentially let them pass, as if these men were at once tainted, but also due proper space for their travails.

All the survivors had a difficult time coming to grips with what they had been through. A few days after Chase arrived at Nantucket, he was visited by Jethro Macy, the widower of Barzillai Ray's older sister, Lydia. Macy described Chase as deeply affected by all that happened, writing that Chase was a "Man of firm mind and strong constitution of body but whose sufferings have been such that it is impossible for him to talk much about it; even the parts most distant from the worst start the tears, his voice falters and strong efforts mixed with smiles mark his disjointed sentences."

Again, Nantucketers were largely sympathetic. There was one sticky problem, however. While the islanders understood why the men had done what they did, Pollard did cross one taboo; he had eaten his nephew, something a later scholar would term "gastronomic incest." Folks on Nantucket, hardened against the difficult realities of the demands of the sea, were generally forgiving of Captain Pollard and his need to survive in the way he did. Nancy Coffin, mother of Owen, wasn't so magnanimous, however. She had entrusted Pollard with the safety of her son, and while he had tried desperately to safeguard him, the blunt reality was that Pollard was now alive and back on Nantucket, and Owen was not, and part of the reason for that was, of course, because Pollard had eaten the boy. Nickerson later wrote in a letter to Leon Lewis, who hoped to publish Nickerson's account, that the homecoming for Pollard was a difficult one. "On his arrival he bore the awful message to the mother [of Owen Coffin] as her son desired, but she became almost frantic with the thought, and I have heard that she never could become reconciled to the capt's presence."

All who knew the captain well attested to the lifelong torment he felt over the whole affair. A relative of Pollard later claimed that the captain "locked himself in his room and fasted" every year on the anniversary of the *Essex*'s sinking. A midshipman named Charles Wilkes met George Pollard in 1822 and heard the whole horrible story. He was extremely affected, writing, "The Annals of wrecks at sea never has given so disastrous a case; it fairly in contemplation causes one's heart almost to cease beating." Of their ordeal, he added, "They had twice or thrice drawn lots, and intense suffering ensued. I cannot state the narrative of this, it is too horrible to be related as it was told to me." The next April, Pollard met a missionary named George Bennet in the Society Islands; Pollard had by then lost another whaling ship and was an utterly broken man. Upon telling of the horrors after the sinking of the *Essex*, Pollard broke down. He related the execution of Coffin, his plea to switch places with the boy, and the boy's steadfast refusal. Pollard told the rest: "I think, then, another man died of himself, and him, too, we ate. But I can tell you no more—my head is on fire at the recollection; I hardly know what I say."

Nickerson wrote of Pollard after Coffin declined to switch places, "Who can doubt but that Pollard would rather have met death a thousand times . . . None that knew him, will ever doubt."

Mignonette (1884)

Cannibalism at sea wasn't something that necessarily shocked or horrified people in the nineteenth century; they understood the necessity of it. However, what was an essential component in cannibalism at sea was the drawing of lots, even if in the case of the *Peggy*'s first unfortunate victim, the drawing was probably a sham.

According to Neil Hanson, author of *The Custom of the Sea* (John Wiley & Sons, 1999), "Many of the horrors of the Victorian underworld, such as child prostitution, passed largely unnoticed, but the very openness and honesty of seamen who had resorted to *The Custom of the Sea* forced it to public attention. Polite society abhorred the idea of Englishmen practising cannibalism like savages, in defiance of the law and Christian morality. Under the selfless Victorian ideal of service to society and to God, men are expected to die nobly for others, not kill them that they might themselves survive."

The shipwreck of the *Mignonette* stands out in cases of survival cannibalism at sea precisely because of the absence of drawing lots.

In the last half of the nineteenth century, yachting had become popular in England. No fewer than fifty-eight British yacht clubs were in operation in 1884. When John Henry Want, a wealthy Australian lawyer, arrived in England during the previous year, he searched for a British yacht to be delivered to his home in Sydney. When he purchased the *Mignonette,* he commissioned Captain Tom Dudley to sail the vessel to Australia. It was a perfect opportunity for Dudley. He had been considering a move to Sydney, then still a British colony, to start a new life with his family.

Dudley hired a three-man crew: mate Richard Stephens, able seaman Edmund ("Ned") Brooks, and seventeen-year-old ordinary seaman, or cabin boy, Richard Parker. Parker was completely illiterate, unable even to sign his own name on the *Mignonette*'s official documents. His motivation for signing on was to travel and to grow; "I want to go abroad and make a man of myself," he said. Plus, he predicted, "I'll come home a proper seaman, and I'll be able to read and write as well." In the words of someone who knew him, Parker was "honest, civil and obliging, whilst his physique gave promise of becoming a smart man."

Things began propitiously. The crew left England in mid-May and on June 1 reached Madeira, where Dudley cabled his wife: "All is well." They set off quickly, heading into the South Atlantic, where winds were heavy but in their favor. However, by the first week of July, the winds increased and were soon accompanied by a severe storm. On July 5, the sea tossed around them, and soon enough a gale was blowing. Dudley, at the helm, was set to give the

The *Mignonette*, sailing before the wind: how the dinghy was managed during the last nine days.

From the London Illustrated News, *September 20, 1884*

command to turn the ship into the wind in order to tack when he caught sight of a mighty wave "about to break over us . . . I saw all the lee bulwarks was washed away and heard the Mate cry out, 'Her side is knocked in. The boat is sinking.'" Brooks described the wave as "quite half way up to our masthead."

When the wave crashed down, the *Mignonette* "sallied over." The yacht was going down fast. The probable cause was the weak state of the ship's planking at the waterline; apparently, earlier repairs made to the aging yacht had used recycled wood instead of new. Brooks, Parker, and Stephens unlashed the dinghy and got down into it. Dudley stayed on board and even went belowdecks to try to salvage food and water. He managed to save only two tins of turnips before he too got into the dinghy, a cramped vessel at thirteen by four feet, and only twenty inches deep.

All four men were alive. But they were in an unenviable position, caught in a storm in the middle of the ocean. While there were land masses less than seven hundred miles away, the men did not possess the implements necessary to reach them. Their only hope for landfall was to take the currents and prevailing winds to South America, some two thousand miles away. Dudley described a bad sea "like a mountain at times" and "water coming in faster than we could bail it out."

When the storm stopped and the waves finally subsided, the men were able to bail successfully. They took one-hour shifts bailing, steering, or trying to get some rest. One evening, while Dudley was at the helm, he felt a jolt on the underside of the boat. He peered into the inky water and made out a dorsal fin. As the sky lightened, he saw a shark, as long as the dinghy itself, moving back and forth under them. The shark batted its tail against the boat, and seemed ready to strike at any moment. Dudley smashed the water surface with an oar for hours before the shark finally gave up and swam away.

The men had only the turnips, and no fresh water whatsoever. They managed to capture a sleeping turtle and drink its blood. They then subsisted on its meat for almost a week, even when the strips of fat they cut from it had putrefied in the intense sun. By the thirteenth, the men were reduced to drinking their own urine. Stephens later recalled, "We used to sit and look at each other gradually wasting away, hunger and thirst in each face. We were so weak and cramped that we could hardly move." Their skin became so ravaged by the salt and sun that when they bumped against each other in the cramped boat, they screamed in pain. The only source of liquid other than their urine was rainfall, but they were consistently frustrated by the sight of billowing black rain clouds that dissipated without providing relief, or thundered in the distance and never reached them. This proved too much for the young Parker. He began surreptitiously drinking seawater and became violently ill. He was soon afflicted with severe diarrhea, and he lay on the bottom of the boat, groaning. His breath quickened and he became delirious; he appeared on the verge of death.

Parker held on, but barely. He slipped in and out of consciousness, occasionally screaming out, "I want a ship to get on board." The others in the boat began to ruminate on the idea of killing him. Dudley asked the others, "What is to be done? I believe the boy is dying . . . Human flesh has been eaten before." Besides, Parker was the only one of the men who did not have a wife or children. Dudley continued, "I am willing to take my chance with the rest, but we must draw lots." Stephens replied that they should wait to see what morning brought. When dawn arrived, the boy was still alive and no sail had been spied. Dudley and Stephens, by silent consent, agreed that Parker should be killed. Killing him, as opposed to waiting until he died, would mean that his blood, still flowing, could be drunk, essential if the men expected to be kept alive much longer. Besides, the boy was suffering. Dudley considered it an act of mercy to kill him.

He later testified, "For the last three days he lay gasping for breath and his frail frame was all but lifeless when I insisted that we should put an end to his life and drink the drops of blood from his body." But neither Brooks nor Stephens could bring himself to do it, so Dudley took the initiative: "I left to do the horrid deed. I offered up a prayer for to ask . . . that all our souls may be forgiven. I then said, 'Dick your time is come poor boy.' [He] murmured out 'What me, Sir?' and I said 'Yes, my boy.' But he did not move." Dudley then thrust his penknife into Parker's throat and caught the blood in a chronometer case.

The men stripped the body and threw the clothes overboard. They cut Parker open and consumed his heart and liver. Brooks described the scene as a "horrible sight," but admitted that at the moment he didn't think so much of it. It was only later, "when I am by myself I think of it a good deal and my thoughts then of what I have seen and what we went through are very dreadful." Dudley was even more forthright, while defending himself as temporarily insane: "We all was like mad wolfs who should get the most, and for men, fathers of children, to commit such a deed we could not have our right reason." When they threw Parker's head and entrails overboard, it wasn't long before the pieces of carcass were in the center of a frothing pink commotion as sharks fought for the flesh.

While Brooks claimed that Stephens ate very little, never able to completely reconcile himself to the whole affair, Dudley and Brooks "partook of it with quite as much relish as ordinary food." The men ate the body for four days before a passing ship, the bark *Moctezuma*, rescued them. The captain of the *Moctezuma* described what he saw in the dinghy as a "frightful spectacle," and the survivors, "living skeletons." The men had sailed more than one thousand miles for three weeks in their dinghy, a solid rate, but one that had covered only half the distance they needed to reach land. It had been the body, Brooks claimed, that had saved them: "I feel quite sure had we not that awful food to exist upon not a soul would have lived until we were rescued."

Aboard the *Moctezuma*, the men slowly recovered strength. However, their limbs had become so contorted by their painful positions on the cramped dinghy, that it was weeks before they could even walk. When they returned to England, they gave statements on the wreck and subsequent sufferings, including all the grisly details of the killing and cannibalism. This was not done as part of any police investigation. Instead, it was standard practice governed by the Merchant Shipping Act of 1854, whereby crew gave accounts of ships' founderings so that increases in sea safety could be implemented. As part of Captain Dudley's deposition, the killing wasn't glossed over: "On the twentieth day the lad Richard Parker was very weak through drinking salt water. Deponent, with the assistance of Mate Stephens, killed him to sustain the existence of those remaining, they being all agreed the act was absolutely necessary."

A policeman, Sergeant Laverty, overheard the deposition and asked to speak to the men. Dudley, with nothing to hide, again told in great detail how it was that he had dispatched Parker, even producing the penknife he had used to stab Parker in the neck. Dudley's candid assertions may seem foolish in hindsight, but he had every reason to think he would come to no trouble. He had nothing to hide; killing and cannibalism at sea were accepted, albeit squeamishly. Besides, despite the presence of Sergeant Laverty, Dudley wasn't giving a confession; instead, he was merely conforming to the requirements dictated by the Merchant Shipping Act. Then, he believed, he'd be free to go home to his wife and children, the harrowing ordeal behind him.

Public sentiment was also on the side of the survivors. Captain Dudley's last letter home to his wife was made public and engendered even more compassion. It read in part: "I am sorry, dear, I ever started on such a trip, but I was doing it for our best . . . If this note ever reaches your hands, you know the last of your Tom and loving husband. I am sorry things have gone against us thus far, but I hope to meet you and all the dear children in heaven." An editorial in the *Lake's Falmouth Packet and Cornwall Advertiser* argued that no one could reasonably conceive of the horrors of starvation, thirst, and anguish at the prospect of excruciating death "without the mind becoming in a measure at least deranged; and without thus [the men] becoming to the fullest extent irresponsible for their actions." When Dudley was reunited with his wife, the two made their way home by train; in the ornate lobby of Victoria Station, men doffed their caps in deference to the captain. When Brooks returned home, a crowd of people was there to greet him as a hero. Even Richard Parker's older brother met the men and offered his hand to them.

Despite this, there began a groundswell in favor of at least seeing the men on trial. After all, they had admitted to murder, and seeing them get off without at least a question as to the appropriateness and reasonability of their actions would have been doing Parker a disservice. And here the question of drawing lots plays great importance. Had the men done so, it would have removed the taint of unfairness; without it, one could imagine the stronger men preying on the weakest. The story of the *Essex* was well known in England and the fact that those men had drawn lots made it a lamentable story, but not one tinged with injustice. Without lots, it was simple barbarism. Indeed, in all of the many cases of survival cannibalism at sea, the men of the *Mignonette* were the first (and according to one expert on maritime law, the only) men ever tried on the charge of murder in such a situation.

While none of the men in his official deposition mentioned the drawing of lots, some twenty years after the event, Brooks claimed in a conversation with a relative of Parker's that the men had indeed drawn lots, but had rigged the procedure to land on Parker. This discrepancy might be explained by the apparent confusion of the last days before Parker's death—or, in fact, some embarrassment over the way the lot drawing had been conducted. According to Dudley's deposition, he raised the prospect of drawing lots soon after the turtle had been consumed. The others in the boat disregarded it, either refusing to participate or claiming that it was premature. After another few days, Dudley proposed the idea again, saying, "We shall die." The others again said no to drawing lots. Dudley replied, "So let it be, but it is hard for four to die, when perhaps one might save the rest." Brooks replied, "So let us all die together." This statement would loom large later, as the men were being prepped for trial. But as the days on the boat continued to pass without relief, and Parker became more ill, some sort of tacit agreement was made to draw lots eventually. The moment, it seemed, would present itself, and all would have no choice but to agree. But as Parker slipped in and out of consciousness, the decision to cast lots seemed superfluous. What if one of the other three should receive it, when the cabin boy would be dead very soon regardless? So, according to Brooks, they drew lots, but it was a sham. Dudley whittled four slivers of wood, one smaller than the rest, and laid them in his palm. He closed his hand around them, the lots still in the same place, so that each of the conscious men could see where the short stick was. Parker's lot would have to be drawn for him, of course. Brooks and Stephens drew their lots; Dudley was about to do the same when he grew disgusted at the farce and threw the remaining sticks into the sea.

So in the absence of the great equalizer, the men were regarded, at least in the eyes of the law, as murderers. However, even as the idea of a trial gained momentum, there was still little call for actually punishing the men. Instead, it would serve everyone's interests if there could merely be a case to settle the question of necessity.

The prosecution needed a witness and of course this was limited to Dudley, Stephens, and Brooks. Because all agreed that it had been Stephens and Dudley who had first agreed to killing Parker and it was Dudley who did the deed as Stephens held Parker's legs, Brooks was deemed innocent. The prosecution, William Danckwerts, stated, "I have come to the conclusion that [Brooks] was in no way an actor or participator in the crime of his two companions." Brooks was now free to go; he eventually made money off his ordeal, employed by freak shows as "The Cannibal of the High Seas." He prowled in a cage, unshaven and in tattered clothing, while chewing on raw meat to the delight of horrified onlookers.

So that left two on trial: Dudley and Stephens. But Danckwerts went to great lengths to also state understanding for the men. The *Lake's Falmouth Packet and Cornwall Advertiser* editorialized: "Counsel displayed sincere sympathy with the accused: and intimated as plainly as he could, without saying it as much in so many words, that the clemency of the Crown would be extended to them in the event of a conviction." During the initial hearing, both Dudley and Stephens struggled. Stephens "exhibited a good deal of emotion," and Dudley, while remaining composed throughout, finally burst into tears at the conclusion.

But the trial proceeded. The case of the *Mignonette* could easily become a "Leading Case," important in determining common law and setting precedent. Indeed, *Regina v. Dudley and Stephens,* as the case would be formally known, is still studied today by students of American and English law. The essential question in this case is the determination of the line when one is so desperate that he may kill another to sustain his own life, or the lives of others.

The judge to initially receive the case was one Baron Huddleston. Because it would be a leading case, putting Huddleston's indelible stamp on the proceedings would assure a certain legal immortality. But Huddleston's personal interest in the case might have sprung from another source as well. According to A. W. Brian Simpson, in his exhaustive legal account of the *Mignonette* case, *Cannibalism and the Common Law* (University of Chicago Press, 1984), "Men who have risen socially in life, as Huddleston had done, sometimes fall into a tendency to reject the world out of which they have risen, and Huddleston was a snob. It is perhaps not too fanciful to suppose that when Huddleston was confronted . . . with the ugly reality of the sailor's world which he had learned many years earlier from his father, his reaction was less than sympathetic."

Huddleston would eventually rule that killing was acceptable only in cases of self-defense. Through an unconventional procedure, the jury was disallowed rendering a verdict. Instead, Huddleston made his pronouncement on the case, and then punted it to a five-judge panel to make the final decision. Huddleston's position was clear; the men were guilty. He reasoned that in the case of the prostrate and dying Parker, the men certainly had no fear for their lives. "What really imperiled their lives," he wrote, "Was not the presence of Parker, but the absence of food and drink." Later, addressing the jury, Huddleston would add, "All they required was something to eat; but the necessity of something to eat does not create the necessity of taking and excuse the taking of the boy. That is the question—was there any necessity of taking the boy *rather than drawing lots*. I should think you would consider no [emphasis mine]." The jury concurred, and Huddleston had reached a guilty verdict without having the jury actually vote.

Initial sympathy for the men began to turn in some quarters. *The Times* of London congratulated Huddleston on his logic, writing, "The English law as laid down by Baron Huddleston is averse from entertaining the notion that peril from starvation is an excuse for homicide. It would be dangerous to affirm the contrary, and tell seafaring men that they may freely eat others in extreme circumstances, and that the cabin boy may be consumed if provisions run out."

Lord Chief Justice Coleridge, reading the final decision, asked, "By what measure is the comparative value of lives to be measured? Is it to be strength, or intellect, or what?" Clearly, the judges, too, were troubled by the actions of the *Mignonette* survivors. However, they weren't immune from the still strong general sympathy extended the men for all they had been through.

Coleridge read the sentence: "You have been convicted of the crime of willful murder, though you have been recommended by the jury most earnestly to the mercy of the Crown; a recommendation . . . in which we all unanimously concur. It is my duty, however . . . to pronounce . . . you be taken to the prison where you came, and that, on a day appointed for the purpose of your execution, you be there hanged by the neck until you be dead." It was the first time in almost 140 years that a death sentence had been handed down in the Court of Queen's Bench.

The sentence was harsh but still regarded as something of a formality. Extreme mercy was expected, and the sentence had to be read in accordance with process. In the end, the men got the expected mercy, receiving sentences of six months without hard labor. But the sentence had the intended effect, as *The Spectator* editorialized, "The conviction that such murders are justified by the law on self-defence, and are not, therefore, illegal, is so general amongst seafaring men, and has so infected naval literature, that a solemn judgment to the contrary . . . become indispensable." It was felt important, furthermore, that the two men couldn't be let go unscathed, to be returned home as heroes when they had committed an act worthy of censure.

While the men didn't get death, their sentence was, however, light-years from what they expected when they arrived in England, survivors of a terrible and ghastly experience. Dudley would remain at least somewhat haunted by the ordeal. "It makes my blood run cold to think about it now," he wrote. "I wished I had died rather than to have pain cast on those who are dear to me or had let the poor lad died." It was also claimed that Brooks spent his last years drunk and shouting "I didn't do it" during lonely night walks.

An eerie historical footnote accompanies the case of the *Mignonette*. Edgar Allan Poe, best known for his short stories, published one novel, *The Narrative of Arthur Gordon Pym*. In it, three survivors of a shipwreck take to the open sea, catch a turtle and eat it, and then propose drawing lots. The loser is killed and eaten. The victim's name is Richard Parker.

Incredibly, Poe's novel was published in 1837, almost fifty years before the *Mignonette's* crew replayed the scene almost exactly—with poor Parker stealing the scene once again.

CONFLICTING ACCOUNTS

When we have shipwreck survivors who were literate, we often get great stories. But the impulse to write down their stories rarely sprang from a sailor's desire to simply give the world a great yarn. Often, the incentive was financial. According to Edward E. Leslie, author of *Desperate Journeys, Abandoned Souls* (Mariner Books, 1998), "Sailors did not earn high wages to begin with, and they were not paid at all if the cargo was not delivered to its destination. Thus, seamen whose vessels went down might struggle through months or even years of terrible hardship as castaways or maroons and then, having finally been rescued, arrive home with nothing to show for what they endured . . . No wonder such survivors were so quick to sell their stories or to display themselves before whoever would pay."

When the number of literate seamen was at a minimum, there were often only one or two printed accounts, so the opportunities for variation were limited. When there do exist several versions of the same wreck, it's not surprising that the narratives might contain some inconsistencies or stretches of truth. Considering the extraordinary circumstances usually attending such a catastrophic event, it's too much to expect strict adherence to actual events. And of course, we can't dismiss the impulse for many of the people writing the narratives to cast themselves in the most favorable, and heroic, light. Often, doing so was a simple matter of self-preservation. If he ever wanted to work again, a captain of a sunken ship had every incentive to craft a narrative that made him out to be a gallant and beneficent figure, often amidst incompetence, confusion, and distress. Indeed, without his steady hand, the tragedy of a lost ship would have surely been much worse.

What often happens, however, when several accounts survive, is that we begin to see some striking variation. Differing minor details are easily accounted for. One only needs to consider the physical position of a seaman at the time of the wreck: was he asleep belowdecks, was he astern, did he call the alert? But there are some shipwreck accounts that give such startlingly differing versions that piecing together "the truth" is often impossible. In spite of that—or perhaps because of that—these tales are sometimes the most fascinating. Accounts often betray particular agendas and biases, telling us more about the real humans who endured the wrecks than a simple recitation of facts could ever accomplish.

Nottingham Galley (1710–11)

The *Nottingham Galley's* commander was John Dean, a man who, unbeknownst to him when he left port, would become embroiled in one of the great maritime controversies of his day. When the ordeal of the *Nottingham Galley* was over, Dean would have to endure the wrath of his brother Jasper, who, though publicly defending John, also owned the ship and didn't take its loss well; fend off insistent accusations of intentionally wrecking the ship; and eventually take a job in the Russian naval service just to remove himself from scrutiny back home in England. However, by his death in 1761, his version of events survived as the most trustworthy, in part because at eighty-three years of age, he had outlived all others who told a different tale. He also eventually ended up British consul at Ostend, evidence that he didn't suffer any irreparable damage to his reputation. And in 1956, the novel *Boon Island,* by the acclaimed American author Kenneth Roberts, further strengthened the view of Dean as hero of the extraordinary events that took place on and near the foundering *Nottingham Galley.*

Dean's story: After a sail from London to Killybags, Ireland, to load up with butter and cheese, the *Nottingham Galley* began its journey across the Atlantic on September 25, 1710. By the beginning of December, the crew of fourteen men had made it across the ocean and sighted land east of Piscataqua, heading south toward Massachusetts Bay. Enduring a vicious New England winter storm complete with driving, slanted rain and wind-whipped hail and snow, the crew sailed on for another ten days without sighting land again.

On the evening of the eleventh, Dean came on deck to take watch. Horrified to see breakers ahead in the opaque darkness, he called for the crew to pull the helm hard to starboard. But it was too late.

The *Nottingham Galley* slammed into Boon Island.

As the ship sat impaled upon the rocks of Boon Island, the storm continued to swirl, to such a degree that none of the men aboard could even see the island they were now adhered to.

Dean, unfailingly devout, ordered the crew belowdecks to pray for deliverance. To his mind, it was as reasonable an action as could be undertaken in the circumstances. However, Dean was also a man of action and a steadfast leader. Prayers complete, he ordered everyone up to cut the masts, hoping the loss of weight would free the foundering ship. Some of the men complied; others remained below and continued their supplications, sure they were about to meet their end and resolving to confess for all their sins before they met judgment. In either case, it made no difference; the storm and waves had done the job of slicing the masts. Unfortunately for the men, it didn't have the desired effect. After going back down below to retrieve "some money and papers that might be of use, also Ammunition, Brandy, &c," Dean saw that this too was a hopeless enterprise. "The Ship bulging, her decks opening, her back broke, and beams giving way, so that the Stern sunk almost under water, I was oblig'd to hasten forward to prevent immediate perishing." There was nothing left to do but abandon ship.

But this was no easy task. It required leaping from the dying vessel onto an unknown and unseen landscape. According to Dean, "I cast myself with all the strength I had toward the Rock, and it being dead low water and the Rock exceeding slippery I cou'd get no Hold, but tore my Fingers, Hands and Arms in a most lamentable manner." Every time Dean and the men got purchase, the sea would conspire to throw them off again. They continued to battle in this way until each, miraculously, made it ashore alive.

Unable to find any shelter from the snow and rain on the leeward side of the island (Dean consistently referred to it as "the Rock," a more apt description for Boon Island, which is roughly one hundred by fifty yards), the men huddled together. They passed a fitful night and by first light went to the spot of the wreck hoping to recover pieces of the *Nottingham Galley* that might be of use. They did find some planks and timber, as well as old sails and canvas. Unfortunately, all that the ship gave up in food were some small pieces of cheese, bobbing in the water and entwined in seaweed. In all, the meager cache totaled roughly "three small Cheeses," nowhere near enough for the fourteen already hungry men. They also retrieved some small beef bones.

Worse, because everything was thoroughly drenched, the men—even in possession of a flint—could not get a fire going. They passed another excruciating evening, a large piece of canvas their only protection from the bitter cold. The Massachusetts Bay Colony (Boon Island is now part of present-day Maine) could actually be sighted from where the men stood, tantalizingly close and forever holding out hope of rescue. But conditions were so unbearable that waiting around to be saved was out of the question; instead, they took the spare pieces of wood that had washed ashore and began to build a small boat. Only some of the men could help; three others were "seized with frost." Adding to these disabled men was the cook, who had complained from the moment they arrived on Boon Island that he was exceedingly ill and almost starved. By noon he was dead.

They placed his body in the sea, giving it a little push toward land in the hopes his washing ashore there would alert someone to the terrors going on at the horizon. Dean sets the stage for what's to come; of the cook's body, he writes: "None mentioning eating of him, tho' several with my self afterwards acknowledged, had Tho'ts of it."

Popular accounts of cannibalism inevitably and uniformly present the actual consumption of fellow humans and shipmates as a terrible but unavoidable and desperate last resort. It comes only after a period of time which strains the bounds of credulity because one wonders how anyone could be alive after such a period of extreme deprivation. In contrast, the men of the *Nottingham Galley* had "Tho'ts of it" after only one and a half days. The men hadn't suffered a loss of rations on board prior to the accident either.

They continued in various states of distress for another two days, and still the weather was unrelenting. If it wasn't raining or snowing, the cold was intense and unremitting. Their limbs were rendered virtually useless with numbing. The men feared "mortifications," or severe frostbite. "We pulled off our shoes, and cut off our boots, but in getting off our stockings, many whose legs were blister'd, pull'd off Skin and all, and some the nails of their toes." The resulting odor quickly became almost unbearable. Dean says he "daily dress'd their Ulcers, and Washing them in Urine, or Salt-Water, bound them up in clean Rags."

By this point, only three of the men, Dean being one of them, were able to work outside of their canvas tent, trying to put together a small craft and having to return to the tent every few hours to escape naked exposure to the weather. Conditions inside the tent were hardly better. The men still had no means of making a fire and only their shared body warmth kept them alive. Of course, it also kept them in perpetual contact with one another's open, festering sores.

Still without a constructed boat and suffering on the island a week, the men exhausted their store of cheese and beef bones, having beaten them to pieces before consuming the remnants. Then they spotted three boats about five leagues away. As best they were able, the men crawled out of their tent and shouted toward the boats. They waved their arms and screamed, desperate to make themselves noticed. But the boats continued on their steady way, all members on deck completely unaware of the castaways. The loss of salvation, and the expended energy, both physical and psychic, in attempting to bring the boats to them, was deflating. The men crawled back into the tent, not speaking to one another and slowly acknowledging that hope was lost.

But John Dean did what good captains are supposed to do; he rallied his troops by pointing out that a ship sighting now meant there were fishermen out there, and it would only be a matter of time before another would be along. And surely one of them would find the stranded men. In the meanwhile, there was still the matter of constructing their own boat. They would not simply sit and wait for death. In better news still, and for Dean another sign of divine protection, the carpenter's ax washed onto a rock and the men were then able to complete the boat. The weather also complied. The winds died down, the rain and snow ceased, and the water smoothed itself to a degree none of the men had seen since landing on Boon Island.

Seven men, including Dean, his first mate, and his brother Jasper, took the boat to the water. With the surf as it was, pounding against the rock, the men had to wade out chest deep into the freezing water just to get it afloat. Dean and one other just managed to haul themselves into the boat at the precise moment a sea swell overtook their small craft, flipping it on top of them. Nearly drowned, they managed to escape and get on shore, just in time to watch the sea smash their boat to pieces against the rock. For reasons not altogether clear, the men had kept their ax and hammer in the boat, and so these valuable tools were lost as well. It looked as though they had reached the end of their limits. Dean described their general condition this way:

> How dismal such a circumstance must be, is impossible to express; the pinching cold and hunger, extremity of weakness and pain, racks and horror of conscience (to many) and foresight of certain and painful (but lingering) death, without any (even the most remote) views of deliverance. How heighten'd! How aggravated is such Misery! and yet alas such was our deplorable Case: insomuch that the greater part of our company were ready to die with horror and despair, without the least hopes of escaping.

One of the men, described as a stout and brave Swede who had lost both his feet to frostbite, begged the captain to assemble a raft out of the remaining wood and let him go toward land. The labor involved in assembling the raft was extraordinary considering their weakened state and the uselessness of their frozen limbs. But the men managed it. They were ready to make the attempt. But to their great joy, they spotted another sail coming out of the Piscataqua River, some seven leagues westward. Again, the men summoned all their strength and tried desperately to attract the ship's attention. But the ship passed without ever changing course. Looking at their feeble raft, lashed together by deadened fingers, the men realized it was their only hope. The Swede and one other man got on the raft and headed toward the mainland. Within seconds, the sea overset them just as it had done the earlier boat. The Swede swam to shore, while the other flailed and sputtered, finally making it back to the island very nearly drowned. That was it for him; he crawled back into the tent, mortified and utterly spent. But the Swede, living up to his reputation, persuaded Dean to let him have another go at. One of the other men volunteered to take the place of the first, and together the two set off. Their parting words were, "Pray Sir oblige all the People to join in Prayers for us as long as you can see us." This time, the operation looked to be a success. Dean watched as the two men made their way toward land. As the sun set, they looked to be halfway there, and Dean judged that they would make landfall by two that morning.

The rest of the men on Boon Island awaited their rescue and were thoroughly encouraged by the sight of smoke arising from the shore two days later; this had been the agreed upon signal of safe landing. Days passed, the smoke continued, but no ship arrived to rescue them. In the meanwhile, the men subsisted on seaweed and a few mussels that Dean was able to fish out of the freezing water, endangering his fingers. By then, the men of the *Nottingham Galley* had been on Boon Island two and half weeks. This proved too much for the carpenter, "a fat Man, and naturally of a dull, heavy, Phlegmatick Constitution and Disposition, aged about forty-seven." Too weary to dispose of the dead carpenter's body, the crew let him lie among them inside the tent throughout the night. One can only imagine what effect this must have had upon the weary men—sharing space with the newly deceased, his withered body (surely no longer fat) a harbinger of what they would soon become. Of course, he also represented temporary salvation, and it can't be denied that any of the men considered otherwise, not if they were already thinking cannibalism on day two of their ordeal.

In the morning, Dean went out for his daily watch for food and passing sails, and instructed the men to dispose of the body. When he returned about noon, the body lay exactly where he had left it. The men complained that they were still too exhausted to remove it. Dean tied a rope around himself and managed to drag the body out of the tent, where he then collapsed from the exertion. The other men whispered it at first, then began to raise their voices in collective pleas: let us eat the body, sir! Please! As for Dean, "This of all I had met with, was the most grievous and shocking to me, to see my self and my Company, who came thither laded with provisions but three weeks before, now reduc'd to such a deplorable circumstance, as to have two of us absolutely starv'd to death, the other two we knew not what was become of [the two on the raft, gone now a week], and the rest of us at last Extremity and (tho' still living, yet) requiring to eat the Dead for support."

Dean agonized over the decision, weighing in his view sinfulness and lawlessness on one hand with judgment and conscience on the other. First, he refused the idea out of hand, and remained obstinate on this point throughout their supplications: "For nothing that ever befel him [Dean ,writing in the third person] from the Day of his Birth, no not the Dread and Distress of his soul upon quitting the Wreck, when he did not expect to live a Minute, was so amazingly Shocking as this unexpected proposal."

Finally, he decided in favor of necessity, giving in to the men's pleas. Dean ordered the carpenter's skin, head, hands, feet, and bowels buried in the sea. The rest of the body was to be quartered, "for Conveniency of drying and carriage." Of course, ridding the island of the man's bowels and extremities also allowed the men to strip its human features so that they would not have to suffer constant reminders of what it was they were actually doing.

Dean spent the entire day in this "very nauseous and difficult Task" cutting the remaining body into slices and washing it with saltwater, also collecting more seaweed to eat with the flesh. Four of the men, including Dean, refused to partake, finding it all too odious to even consider. After all, the men still hadn't any means of a fire, and so were obliged to eat the carcass raw. But they were starving. By morning even the final holdouts succumbed to basic needs and "earnestly desir'd to partake with the rest." (Dean concedes in a later version of his published narrative that he had, just a day or two prior to the death of the carpenter, looked with longing at the tips of his own fingers and had even eaten some of his own excrement.)

Dean watched at they devoured the flesh with unabashed rapaciousness. He took the remains and placed them far outside the tent, where the enfeebled men could not access them. He conjectured that had he not kept a close eye on the carpenter's remains and rationed it, the men certainly would have devoured it all and then been "forc'd to feed upon the living." Dean recognized the ravenous, animal looks on their faces, and he knew that fights, even murder, could easily come of squabbles over the remaining meat. His assumptions about their behavior proved correct, as their "very natural dispositions chang'd, and that affectionate, peacable temper that had all along hitherto discover'd totally lost; their eyes staring and looking wild, their Countenances fierce and barbarous . . . nothing now being to be heard but brutish quarrels, with horrid Oaths and Imprecations, instead of that quiet submissive spirit of Prayer and supplication we had before enjoy'd."

The new year 1711 arrived, its first day passing in continued despair. Then, on the morning of January 2, Dean crept out of the tent and espied a shallop, a small boat used for rowing in shallow waters, halfway from shore, heading right toward them. "How great our Joys and Satisfaction were, at the prospect of so speedy and unexpected deliverance, no tongue is able to express, nor thoughts to conceive." The boat came as close as possible without running risk of also getting smashed upon the island. Dean shouted across the surf a catalog of the horrors he and his men had endured. He made no mention of the dead carpenter; however, knowing that any would-be savior might reconsider coming ashore if he thought there was any chance he might end up marooned there and suffering the same conditions.

One man alone (something he would soon regret) rowed to Boon Island in a canoe. He came on shore and stood dumbfounded. Dean asked him for fire. Still, the man stood silent, no doubt shocked into dumbness by coming face-to-face with a living skeleton. He eventually managed to say a few words and follow Dean to the tent, where, no doubt, seeing and smelling the condition of the men within stood an even greater shock than upon first landing. The seaman wasn't long among the living dead, starting a fire, and making quickly for his canoe. Dean went with him, but just as had happened twice before, the sea upset their boat and Dean barely managed to survive getting back to Boon Island. The seaman got into his canoe and made for the shallop, promising to send a rescue party, fully provisioned, the next morning. Dean and the others watched in sad resignation as the ship made back for land. They would later learn, however, that a storm had sunk the shallop, and the men on board barely escaped with their lives. Had Dean and the remaining men of the *Nottingham Galley* been on board, there is little chance any of them would have been able, in their conditions, to have survived.

The men stoked the fire in the tent, and soon fell out ill and coughing, having forgotten to cut a hole for ventilation. This remedied, Dean increased the ration of the carpenter's flesh, and the men, still awaiting their rescue, devoured their portions. Next morning, the promised ship arrived and managed to ferry all the survivors to land. As for the two men who had left Boon Island on their raft, they died. Ironically, their sole purpose—alerting people on shore to the plight of the others on Boon Island—was successful. When the raft washed ashore, and the Swede's companion was found nearby, dead with a paddle lashed to his wrist, mainlanders figured it out. The Swede's body was never found.

The survivors' appearance on land, of course, excited alarm; Dean recounts how at first sight of him, the woman and children of the house in which he was offered shelter ran off in fear. Almost all of the men had lost fingers and or toes, but only one lost "a great part of one foot." Otherwise, their eventual recovery was nothing short of phenomenal.

It should have been a happy ending. However, a competing, and damning, version of events was soon to follow.

Three crewmen, mate Christopher Langman, boatswain Nicholas Mellon, and seaman George White, published *A true Account of the voyage of the Nottingham Galley of London John Dean Commander from the River Thames to New England, Near which Place she was castaway on Boon-Island, 11 December 1710 by the Captain's obstinacy, who endeavoured to betray her to the French, or run her ashore; with an Account of the Falsehoods in the Captain's Narrative.* This was only about half of the full title, but even in an abridged version it makes no bones about its intent. In the preface, the men give their reasons for publishing their account: "To lay before the World, and before those Gentlemen and others who have lost their Estates and Relations in this unhappy Voyage, the true Causes of our own and their Misfortunes, and how they might, humanely speaking, have been easily avoided, had Captain Dean been either an honest or an able Commander."

The main charge leveled within was that Dean and his brother Jasper (in cahoots with merchant Charles Whitworth, owner of the *Nottingham Galley*'s cargo) had overinsured the ship and wanted to collect the insurance money. Their first attempt at doing so, according to Langman, Mellon, and White, occurred when the *Nottingham Galley* encountered a pirate ship in the Atlantic and Dean attempted to surrender to it. The men on board prevented it. This allegedly occurred early in the journey. As the crew neared North America, Dean again attempted to turn over his ship off the coast of Newfoundland, but was disappointed to learn that what he saw wasn't pirates, but the "friendly" English galley, the *Pompey*. Seeing his chances at the insurance money slip away, Dean steered the *Nottingham Galley* straight for Boon Island, intending to wreck her. Langman tried to prevent it, but Dean struck him with a wooden block so violently that he knocked Langman out cold. According to the dissenting account, Dean "came behind the Mate, and struck him three Blows on the Head, upon which he fell down and lay as dead for several Minutes, all in Blood." So now they were wrecked upon a desolate island and were forced to suffer horrible privations.

Dean's account has been accepted as the most believable by people familiar with the conflicting versions. There are several reasons for this. First, Langman and the others claimed that the first time Dean tried to give the ship to pirates took place between London and Killybags. While there is some dispute about specific dates, all accounts have the *Nottingham Galley* docked in Killybags for a solid month before it set sail for Boston. Surely this was plenty of time for any of the three men (or any other on board) to inform someone in port what their barbarous captain intended to do. The three dissenters even claim that two of their best sailors had been so disabled by Dean's beatings that they couldn't help in loading the ship in Killybags.

As for the wreck, the men claimed that Dean was told in no uncertain terms by the mate that had they steered their intended course, they would have made landfall ten days earlier than the date upon which they slammed into Boon Island. But after keeping the ship at sea and then wrecking it, Dean allegedly let out a triumphant yelp, satisfied now that he would soon recover his insurance money. In fact, according to this account, Dean muttered, "We must now all prepare for Death, there being no Probability to escape it." Of course, if true, it would take someone bordering on absolute insanity to intentionally wreck his ship in the middle of a New England winter with scarce provisions, endangering not only the lives of the crew, but also his own and his brother's, and then declare they all prepare for death, which would, of course, prevent him from collecting anything.

Not surprisingly, the version of events concerning the eating of the carpenter differed as well. According to the three men, it was Dean who first had the idea to eat the carpenter, telling the men, "It was no Sin, since God was pleas'd to take him out of the World, and that we had not laid violent Hands on him." Then, they claimed, "There was no man eat more of the Corps than himself [Dean]." Neither did the men ever turn into barbarous brutes, as the captain suggested. Indeed, the only swearing to be heard was between "the Captain, his Brother, and Mr. Whitworth [the three signers of Dean's published version], who often quarrel'd about their Lying and Eating." It doesn't end there. When the men got safely on land, Dean conducted himself in the same officious manner. Allegedly, he told the children in his lodging that he was going to cook them and eat them. He then collected the provisions intended for all the men and distributed them between himself and his brother, in turn getting the rest of the men turned out of their lodgings before they could sufficiently heal (despite the fact that they did heal, by their own accounts).

The allegations against Dean lingered at least long enough for him to feel compelled to write a second version of events some fifteen years after his *Narrative of the Sufferings, Preservation, and Deliverance of Capt. John Dean and Company* was rushed to print by his brother Jasper in August 1711 in anticipation of Langman, Mellon, and White's version, which appeared later that year. In the interim, Dean felt his reputation sufficiently damaged that he eagerly accepted a post far from home with the Russian navy.

Dean's revised version and subsequent republications, plus the fact that he outlived all detractors, meant that his version of events came to be accepted as the one that most adhered to the truth. It is indeed striking that in his revised version of 1726, Dean makes no mention of the varying accounts of Langman, Mellon, and White. Either their version had faded from public view or had taken on the sheen of ridiculousness. Either way, the competing versions remain as a stark reminder of the impassioned views and inflamed recollections of such an extraordinary event as that which took place on Boon Island in the winter of 1710–11.

Francis Mary (1826)

Born in Liverpool in 1802, Ann Saunders lost her father when she was very young. Saunders's penniless mother, unable to take care of five children, scattered them to various, better-off families. At the age of eighteen, Ann Saunders met James Frier, and she fell in love. Saunders's aunt, with whom she had been living, was a friend of Mrs. James Kendall, wife of ship captain John

The Melancholy Ship Wreck of the Francis Mary (1827), J. Kendall Master

From the London Illustrated News, September 20, 1884

Kendall. Both Frier and Mrs. Kendall would be aboard ship for a passage from the west coast of England for New Brunswick. Kendall and Frier implored Saunders to accompany them. She would act as the captain's mistress and enjoy the close company of her intended. Saunders agreed; the *Francis Mary*, with its crew of twenty-one (nineteen men plus Mrs. Kendall and Ann Saunders), left Liverpool on November 10, 1825.

Despite smooth sailing, Saunders, unused to the sea, spent the first three days of the voyage confined to her cabin belowdecks, seasick and miserable. However, when she recovered, she joined the crew and they all enjoyed continued smooth sailing until they reached Saint John, New Brunswick, on January 18, 1826.

In New Brunswick, the *Francis Mary* loaded up with timber and made preparations for the return trip to England. For two weeks, the crew once again enjoyed easy and good sail. But this would be the last of their trouble-free passage. On February 1, a severe gale ripped off some of the *Francis Mary*'s spars and yards. Worse, the wind took one of the spare boats over the side and into the ocean. Should the crew have to jump ship, one of their escape vessels was now gone. All the violence on deck also severely injured several sailors.

The crew spent the next four days recovering; the two women on board dressed the wounds of the injured and did all they could to ease their suffering.

The able-bodied employed themselves in clearing the decks of debris and trying to reestablish useful sails.

On the fifth, an even worse gale blew in, rendering the *Francis Mary* a speck in the valleys of mountainous waves. The crew worked frantically to pull down the sails and batten down all loose articles on deck. It was to little avail. The sea swept away most objects, tied down or not, and eventually the whole stern was stove in by relentless and crushing waves. During the tumult, one of the seamen was swept overboard but was saved. Had he known what was coming, he might have wished for the end in the ocean.

The gale, already fierce, seemed to redouble as dawn approached. All hopes of saving the ship and keeping her on course were gone. Now all efforts were directed toward simply maintaining lives. To this end, the crew stove in the bow port and saved fifty pounds of bread and a few pounds of cheese, strapping these provisions in the main top. Below, the cabins were full with water.

The day progressed thus, with the women on deck supplicating the heavens, and the men trying their hardest to keep everyone alive and out of the murky deep. Despite the efforts, daybreak revealed the death of one of the seaman, the crew's first fatality. He was discovered hanged by some rigging. The crew lowered him into the ocean. Saunders was understandably horrified: "As this was the first instance of entombing a human body in the ocean that I had ever witnessed, the melancholy scene made a deep impression on my mind, as I expected such eventually would be my own life."

By next morning, things began to brighten a bit; rescue seemed inevitable. An American ship appeared on the horizon and the crew of the *Francis Mary* was able to flag down the vessel and ask for aid. The American ship sailed in company through the next day but had to abandon the *Francis Mary* when the rough sea forced the ship's captain to sail off; it was clear to him that any assistance he would have liked to have given would be made a series of futile attempts by the violence of the sea. The disappearance of the American vessel was understandably a blow to the crew of the *Francis Mary*; their desertion now felt like a death sentence. Saunders noted, "It would be impossible for me to attempt to describe the feelings of all on board at this moment, on seeing so unexpectedly vanish the pleasing hope of being rescued by this vessel from our perilous situation."

They were, for now, on their own. The crew set up a tent from spare canvas on the forecastle; this was to be shelter for the surviving twenty people. Each member on board was rationed a meager quarter of a biscuit a day. The crew passed the days huddled together in the makeshift tent, the poor ship buffeted on all sides by the unrelenting gales. Only its cargo of timber prevented the *Francis Mary* from sinking. (In fact, the *Francis Mary* remained something of a macabre floating museum for several months after eventual rescue, until an English crew towed her to Jamaica, where she was repaired and sent back into service.)

Just when all seemed lost, a sail was spied along the horizon just two days later. Captain Kendall's hail for aid was spotted and the ship came toward the beleaguered *Francis Mary*. But in a repeat of the previous time the crew met with a passing ship, this one too remained for a day but was prevented from giving any aid by the rough sea and the continuing gale. By morning, the ship was gone. The *Francis Mary* was alone again.

Three days later, the crew saw another ship in the distance, but this time they were unable to flag it down and it sailed on. According to Saunders, "We had now arrived at an awful crisis. Our provisions were all consumed and hunger and thirst began to select their victims." The next day, seaman James Clarke died. He was followed ten days later by seaman John Wilson. Clarke was committed to the sea, as had the *Francis Mary's* first victim. But all remaining survivors now rested on the brink of starvation, and no one was too quick to lower Wilson to the ocean for the sharks. By this time, the crew had not eaten in ten days, and before that they had spent a week subsisting only on a biscuit and a half a day. Saunders's reaction to what was proposed was shock:

> As the calls of hunger had now become too importunate to be resisted, it is a fact, although shocking to relate, that we were reduced to the awful extremity to attempt to support our feeble bodies a while longer by subsisting on the dead body of the deceased. It was cut into slices, then washed in salt water and, after being exposed to and dried in the sun, was apportioned to each of the miserable survivors, who partook of it as a sweet morsel. From this revolting food I abstained for twenty-four hours, when I too was compelled by hunger to follow their example. We eyed each other with mournful and melancholy looks, as may be supposed of people perishing with hunger and thirst.

This new form of sustenance, however, wasn't enough for J. Moore, who died the next day. Perhaps because the crew already had human flesh in its possession, the full treatment that Wilson's body received didn't extend to Moore's. The crew also committed Moore to the deep, but not before removing the heart and liver for future use. These items, too, did little for much of the rest of the crew. Over the next twelve days, seven more men died.

Such quick and repetitive death would have been hard to endure in any circumstances. But the manner in which the men expired made the entire spectacle all the more gruesome. Most of them died stark raving mad. Saunders described their last throes as punctuated by "heart-piercing lamentations." At least two of the men spoke at great length to family members who weren't there, at turns pleading for sustenance and then hurling dreadful recriminations against those present, and those not, for withholding food and water. Survivors watched in horror, and when the mad died, they were immediately set upon. Once the last breath had been drawn, the newly dead's throat was cut and the blood eagerly sucked.

Among these seven deceased was James Frier, Saunders's intended. "Judge then, my female readers (for it is you that can best judge)," she wrote, "what must have been my feelings, to see a youth for whom I had formed an indissoluble attachment—him with whom I expected so soon to be joined in wedlock and to spend the remainder of my days—expiring before my eyes." Worse, she went on, "to be driven to the horrid alternative to preserve my own life to plead my claim to the greater portion of his precious blood as it oozed half congealed from the wound inflicted upon his lifeless body!" To be driven to such bestiality, Saunders reasoned, was God's way of "weaning me forever from all the vain enjoyments of this frail world."

Perhaps it was because the women hadn't initially exerted themselves in the gales. Perhaps it was due to a complex psychological makeup. Or perhaps it was simple biology: extra layers of fat (and thus energy reserves) endowed by nature upon women for the sake of child rearing. Whatever it was, Saunders and Mrs. Kendall enjoyed health and strength relative to the remaining men. In fact, the grim job of cutting up bodies as they fell and parceling out the fleshy cargo fell to Saunders, as she was the strongest. Though she makes no mention of it in her narrative, this means that she also had to push off the grisly remains of the bodies into the ocean.

There is some evidence of Mrs. Kendall succumbing to mental fatigue and stress. Saunders related that after Mrs. Kendall ate the brains of a dead seaman, she declared, quite openly, that the meal was delectable. Captain Kendall, while lauding his sturdy wife for bearing the entire horror, concurred on this point, writing, "She ate the brains of one of the apprentices, saying it was the most delicious thing she ever tasted!"

A counterintuitive effect of starvation is eventual cessation of the pangs of hunger, to be replaced by unquenchable thirst and dehydration. This happened to the crew, so much so that they took to washing their lips with salt water just to keep them from adhering to one another.

Yet another ship appeared on the horizon, and then sailed off, seemingly without taking notice of the *Francis Mary* and its enfeebled crew, now totaling less than one-third its original number. Finally, on March 7, the HMS *Blonde* made its determined way to the *Francis Mary* after picking up distress signals on the far horizon. The *Blonde*'s captain, Lord Byron, hove to and made rescue of the six remaining survivors. Saunders described the grisly scene this way: "When relieved, but a small part of the body of the last person deceased remained, and this I had cut as usual into slices and spread on the quarter deck; which being noticed by the Lieutenant of the *Blonde* . . . before we had time to state to him what extremities we had been driven, he observed 'you have got, I perceive, fresh meat!' but his horror can be better conceived than described when he was told that what he saw, were the remains of the dead body of one of our unfortunate companions."

Byron delivered the survivors to a vessel bound for Europe, and the crew landed at Portsmouth, England, on March 20. The six survivors had lived at sea for twenty-two days.

Ann Saunders wasn't a sailor, of course, and her financial future wasn't dependent upon the successful delivery of the *Francis Mary*'s cargo in England (though, of course, the opposite is true for her fiancé James Frier, and thus, to some degree, Ann Saunders herself). But she certainly had a ripping yarn to tell, and an audience hungry for such lurid tales of the sea. In short, Saunders had a platform. And she used it to further her religious convictions. Her book, *Narrative of the Shipwreck and Sufferings of Miss Ann Saunders,* was published in 1827 by Z. S. Crossmon of Providence, Rhode Island.

The slim volume ran just thirty-eight pages, with Miss Saunders's text beginning on page 8. In essence, the story of the *Francis Mary* ends on page 20. For another eighteen pages of her narrative (over half in all), Saunders lays out a series of arguments designed to give her readers reasons for eternal faith in God and Jesus Christ. She includes an exhortation to young people not to turn away from their faith in him, and to know that faith alone in his divine workings will be what saves them from calamity. Further, all humans should spend much time in the contemplation of their end, which will come inevitably. In her view, the only logical preparation for that "exchange of worlds" is to worship God and his mysterious ways and live the present life on earth in goodly preparation for meeting his son in

Heaven. In her view, "Religion not only purifies, but also fortifies the heart; so that the devout man is neither lifted up by success nor enervated by sensibility; he meets the changes in his lot without unmanly dejection."

By any accounts, Ann Saunders's story, and the story of the entire crew of the *Francis Mary*, is horrible, and her deep religiosity gave her reason to write the memoir. But hers wasn't the only version of events. And the other, Captain John Kendall's, was in some crucial aspects so vastly different from Saunders's, it's hard to believe that the truth sits even somewhere between the competing versions. Instead, it's probable that one of them was outright lying, despite some convergence of events in both of their accounts.

All that befell the crew, and when, is consistent between the two versions, though Kendall's writing style is very wooden in comparison to the rhetorical flourishes employed by Saunders. For example, while Saunders relates the first death, the accidental hanging, with horror and pity, calling it a "melancholy scene" and vowing that the image would remain with her forever, Kendall relates it this way: "At daylight, found Patrick Cooney hanging by his legs to the cat-harpins, dead from fatigue; committed his body to the deep." He spends no more time ruminating on the fatality of one of his crew. His accounts of cannibalism are also without flourish or even emotion: "Feb. 22. John Wilson, seaman, died at 10 a.m.; preserved the body of the deceased, cut him up in quarters, washed them overboard, and hung them up on pins."

Kendall does also confirm Saunders's accounts of several of the men going crazy before they died: "From want of water, those who perished drank their own urine and salt water. They became foolish, and crawled upon their hands round the deck when they could, and died, generally, raving mad!"

Where things diverge is in the way Saunders reacted to the deeds she had to perform by virtue of her remaining strength—cutting up the bodies and parceling out the flesh. Kendall pays tribute to Saunders; he describes her as possessing more strength "in her calamity than most of the men." However, according to Kendall, she used this strength to satisfy her literally bloodthirsty desires.

After lauding her authority in the face of such horror, Kendall suggests that in some perverse way, Miss Ann Saunders made love to the gruesome task at hand. He writes, "She performed the duty of cutting up and cleaning the dead bodies, keeping two knives for the purpose in her monkey jacket; and when the breath was announced to have flown, she would sharpen her knives, bleed the deceased in the neck, drink his blood, and cut him up as usual."

The scene described thus shows a woman of cool calculation, one who waited with breathless anticipation of the necessary deeds—quite a contrast to a woman drawing upon great reserves of strength (especially in a day and age when women were expected to give in to bouts of hysteria) to simply do what needed to be done.

While Saunders ruminates for some time on the terror and dismay of watching her beloved die and then having to drink his blood to survive, Kendall paints a picture of a woman who was almost mad with desire for it: "James Frier was working his passage home, under a promise of marriage to Ann Saunders, the female passenger, who attended on the master's wife, and who, when she heard of Frier's death, shrieked a loud yell, then snatching a cup from the Clerk, the mate, cut her late intended husband's throat and drank his blood! insisting that she had the greatest right to it. A scuffle ensued, but the heroine got the better of her adversary, and then allowed him to drink one cup to her two."

Contrast this with Saunders, who writes, " 'Think, mortal,' says the poet, 'what it is to die'—but I would add, think how distressing it must be to see those we tenderly love, die before our eyes, die agonized with pain, after languishing with lingering disease, and without being able to contribute to their ease, or add one moment to their existence."

Why did Kendall bring out such a libelous version? No one could say for sure (though it was Saunders's version that was widely believed). But the financial strains put upon shipwreck survivors perhaps give a clue. As captain, Kendall was responsible for ship, crew, and cargo. He lost both ship and cargo and fifteen of the twenty-one people on board and fifteen of the nineteen crewmembers. He would have been ruined.

Plus, one can only imagine the mental strain the man must have felt as he sat by on deck, utterly helpless and watching his men die off one by one, and seeing his beloved wife reduced to eating the brains of one of them. When Saunders's book hit the public, the picture of John Kendall as a ship captain wasn't a terribly flattering one. While painting Ann Saunders as a bloodthirsty maniac wouldn't do much to restore Kendall's image or reputation, it might, at least, deflect some of the negative views of his skills at guardianship.

There isn't much evidence to suggest it worked. Saunders remained a figure worthy of compassion while Kendall slipped into oblivion, mentioned now only as a somewhat absurd and cynical counterpoint to the more sympathetic Saunders.

Stirling Castle (1836)

On October 22, 1835, the double-masted 350-ton brig *Stirling Castle* left London, intending to reach Hobart, Van Diemen's Land (modern-day Tasmania) and then the bustling port of Sydney. The captain of the *Stirling*

Eliza Fraser. Sketch by unknown artist.
Courtesy of the State Library of Queensland

Castle was a Scotsman named James Fraser. Fraser's wife, Eliza, accompanied him, leaving the couple's three children in the care of a minister.

Initially, the *Stirling Castle* had a relatively good time of it. Her crew reached Hobart after five months; though Captain Fraser had fallen ill during the voyage, Eliza nursed him to health. After taking on a few fresh crewmen in Hobart, the ship sailed into Sydney Harbor, best known then as a penal colony. It was into this wild frontier that most on board the *Stirling Castle* decided to get off and stay. Some did so simply to avoid another transoceanic journey with Fraser and his wife, whom they disliked immensely. She was a bossy and opinionated sort, but because she was the captain's wife, they had no choice but to tolerate her. Now that they had reached a city with some 77,000 people (albeit a third of these convicts), they had a choice—and they exercised it. The *Stirling Castle* had to take on a new crew. At least one of the replacements, Harry Youlden, also despised Eliza Fraser, calling her "a very vixen."

The *Stirling Castle* lifted anchor at Sydney on May 13, 1836, bound for Singapore to load cargo intended for London. As it would turn out, the men who decided to stay in Sydney made the right choice.

Fraser steered his ship north along the east coast of Australia. Four hundred miles north of Sydney sat the penal colony at Moreton Bay (today's Brisbane), a place so remote, it was established precisely to house the commonwealth's most intractable criminals. At Moreton Bay, men who managed to escape routinely came back, ready to face increased penalties in lieu of having to survive a day longer in the unforgiving bush. Fraser kept on past Moreton Bay and squeezed his way along the coast past Bribie Island and onto Great Sandy Island, the largest sand island in the world. In the glittering twilight of May 22, the officer on watch was just able to make out a roiling line in the shape of a horseshoe. He barely had time to call out before the *Stirling Castle* was sucked into a powerful crosscurrent that laid her up against the barely concealed coral of Swain's Reef. And there she stuck, her side smashed in and a powerful current pouring its way right through her. The carpenter on board axed the mast, but it made little difference. The *Stirling Castle* was taking on more water and breaking up.

Everyone set about freeing the boats but neglected to throw many barrels of meat and water overboard to collect later. With only scant provisions, the crew did manage to get safely stored on the *Stirling Castle's* two boats, a twenty-foot longboat and an eighteen-foot pinnace. However, the longboat took a severe pounding against the reef; it was barely seaworthy, taking on vast amounts of water. Men on board bailed furiously but became so exhausted that the boat started to sink with its extra water weight. During the confused taking on of water, Eliza Fraser, now in the final trimester of pregnancy, delivered a baby boy who immediately drowned. One of the crewmen ripped his shirt and wrapped the child, consigning him to a dignified watery grave. Mrs. Fraser, almost unbelievably, later claimed that she hadn't even been aware of what happened. It wouldn't be the last unbelievable thing she would later recall.

The longboat was still afloat, but in poor shape. After five days of open water floating on the Coral Sea, the two boats reached an island. The crew decided to stop and get at repairs. They had been subsisting on meager rations of cask ale and pork and biscuit. Once on land, Eliza Fraser scrambled up a cliff and found a pothole full of water. She dipped in her sleeve and then climbed back down, where she wrung her clothing into a cup for her ailing husband. Crewman Harry Youlden grabbed it from her, angrily condemning her and declaring that he would drink it himself. Fraser, assuming control from her husband, snatched it back, denouncing him in front of everyone. "Damn you, you she-captain," Youlden replied. "If you say much more, I'll drown you!"

It could have been a serious breach, but they were five hundred miles from the nearest settlement at Moreton Bay. Their only real worry was simple survival. They had no choice but to put back in their boats and make for Moreton Bay. They followed the coast, searching for suitable places to temporarily land and scout for food and water. Trouble was, the entire coast seemed protected by razor sharp coral and a multitude of stinging, biting, and poisonous marine life. But these marine hazards were preferable to what presumably awaited on land: cannibalistic savages.

Afraid of landing, the crew floated for a month, surviving on fish and rainwater. Eventually, the team decided to take advantage of a good landing spot and head to shore, though it was a difficult decision. Youlden would later write: "To remain longer at sea was to perish slowly from starvation; while feeble and unarmed, ashore we might reasonably expect to be massacred by savages. Any change seemed desirable, and we determined to throw ourselves upon the mercy of our fellow-men, savage though they were."

Once on shore, the crew agreed to let the boatswain, a fellow named Stone, take the pinnace and search for more promising land. He set off with John Allan, John Fraser (the captain's nephew), Robert Hodge, James Major, Jacob Schofield, and John Wilson. Those left behind, numbering twelve including the captain and his wife, waited two long days before they speculated that they had been abandoned. The remaining crew set to sea again, and spent the next seven days making their way along the coast, now out of food and water and growing increasingly despondent. Captain Fraser raved, and the rest of the crew openly talked about drawing lots.

But the captain, momentarily restored to sanity, successfully managed to hold them off this idea. He could not, however, stop them from insisting that he take the boat back to shore, where they would take their chances of being found by missionaries while walking along the shoreline. Fraser was loath to do it; he was obsessed with aboriginal cannibals, who he insisted lived along the coast. He was only partly right; there were in fact hostile aborigines (whether they were cannibals is highly doubtful), but the crew were not, in fact, on the coast of mainland Australia. They were instead only on the edge of Great Sandy Island. Following the shoreline of Great Sandy would merely bring them to the channel separating the island from the mainland. This spanned three miles and made "walking" to Moreton Bay an impossibility. But they couldn't stay in the boat. Strong winds blowing toward shore prevented them from making any real progress.

Aborigines in the area of Great Sandy belonged to the Kabi tribes; among these were the Badtjala people. The Kabi are among the oldest civilizations on the planet, a group that in 1835 functioned in essence in the Stone Age. To

European castaways, they presented a frightful sight: facial features, skin color, and a propensity toward nudity that the Europeans simply never saw at home.

The first sign of aboriginal activity came toward the castaways in a particularly chilling manner: a long "*coooo-eee*," which was a typical Badtjala greeting—or warning, depending on the precise intonation. The castaways, looking up to a bluff, saw the silhouette of five tribesmen, spears in hand, looking down on them. Soon, the aborigines approached, stopping short of the castaways. They threw something on the sand and gestured for the party to come and retrieve it. Captain Fraser was ready with his pistol, but crewman Robert Darge convinced him to drop it, relying instead on his abilities to peacefully bridge the massive cultural divide. To that end, Darge retrieved the object, which turned out to be a piece of rancid kangaroo meat. The aborigines considered this acceptance as an invitation to trade. They rushed the Europeans and began stripping their clothes; to the castaways' view, this was no fair trade at all.

Captain Fraser ordered his crew to stay put, ignoring repeated attempts by the aborigines to get the white people to follow them into the woods. The crew spent four miserable days subsisting on diarrhea-inducing fruits and the rancid kangaroo. When the natives returned, this time several of the crewmembers demanded to go with them, hostile or not. Fraser, rallying three crewmen to his side, insisted on staying where they were. They still had their boat, and they could try to relaunch if the winds allowed it.

Despite his orders, six crewmen wrestled Fraser's gun from him and walked down the beach. The abandoned party had little choice but to reluctantly follow, petrified of future encounters with the natives they understood so little. But cultural misunderstandings would prove to be the very foundation of this burgeoning relationship.

According to Eliza Fraser, things took a terrible turn when the original party of *Stirling Castle* survivors left. Her story: Soon, the aborigines began making outrageous exchanges: small bits of rotten fish, say, for a trunk of clothing. Though the remaining five found the situation increasingly intolerable, they were still at the mercy of the winds, which would still not allow them to try the voyage in their rickety boat. So in the darkness of night, they decided to walk.

The next day, they were spotted by the natives, who seemed to take offense at their attempted flight. They ripped the clothes from their backs; Captain Fraser even came within centimeters of meeting death or terrible injury when one of the natives thrust his spear into Fraser's face, cutting his cheek. Then the aborigines left them alone. The two *Stirling Castle* groups managed to reunite on the beach only briefly before a large band of natives returned, carrying away all the men into the bush and leaving Eliza Fraser by herself.

The next time Eliza Fraser saw people, they were all aboriginal females, ranging in age from little girls to old wrinkled women. They laughed at Fraser and poked her. Then, all at once, they picked up globs of wet sand and plastered her naked body. This proved agonizing, as her skin was badly sunburned. The women then trundled Fraser off to a clearing in the woods. There, a sickly and pitiful woman held an infant. Seeing Fraser's swollen breasts—still engorged from her recently terminated pregnancy—the woman pushed the child onto Fraser's breast. The child latched on and began suckling. The spectacle was a horror to Fraser, who regarded the child as "one of the most deformed and ugly-looking brats my eyes ever beheld." More indignities were soon to follow: the women held Fraser down and smeared her with a foul concoction of charcoal and reptile effluent, turning her skin black. When it came time to eat, the women threw her barely edible scraps: fish heads, ant larvae, and a fiery root that left her mouth scalded.

Fraser endured five lonely weeks in debased servitude, doing all manner of menial chores. One day she was accidentally reunited with her husband in a forest clearing. He was collecting wood, and having a hard time of it. He was terribly ill and complained to Eliza of frequent beatings. During this conversation, one of the ruthless natives threw a spear at Captain Fraser; it entered his back and protruded from his chest. Eliza Fraser tells the rest of the story: "I saw no blood, and I pulled the spear from his body. He turned his face to me and said, 'Eliza, I am gone forever!' and from his mouth an immense quantity of blood spouted, and he at once died."

The newly widowed Eliza continued in servitude; she was forced to wade into knee-deep bay water and retrieve marine delicacies while insects and crabs tormented her. Unless she filled a bag with mussels and crabs, she couldn't go back to the village without receiving blows. On the trek back, she had to endure stifling humidity and all manner of jungle insects bombarding her mostly naked body.

One day, Fraser was paraded to a *corroboree,* which was a gathering of tribes where important communal events, such as manhood initiation rites, took place. For this *corroboree,* Fraser was the main exhibit, placed on a raised platform for all to see as the crowd danced and sang atonal songs. During the ceremony, a powerful and elderly chief approached and declared that Fraser should become his wife, or "mate," as she called it. The man was, in Fraser's estimation, "One of the most ugly and frightful-looking Indians that my eyes ever beheld or that the whole island probably contained." Fraser explained, "I was now indeed placed in a situation more horrid than I had ever previous conception of! yea, even so much as to be compelled to decide, and that too, immediately, whether to become the willing companion and associate of a wild barbarous savage, or voluntarily suffer myself to become the defenceless victim of brutal outrage!"

A younger man, the brother of Fraser's aboriginal mistress, interposed after her hysterical pleading; Fraser asked him to "do me the kindness either to stab me in the heart, or to knock me on the head with his tomahawk, as death, even in that savage manner, would be preferable to that of yielding to the desires of him who professed to have power to do as he pleased with me!" The younger man did in fact intercede on her behalf, but lost his life for the effort. All hope seemed lost. But little did Eliza Fraser know that her salvation would come in the form of a convict named John Graham.

At least that's the story that has been handed down over the generations.

Graham had been serving seven years in Moreton Bay for larceny when he escaped, living with the aboriginal natives for six years, all the while learning their customs and language. He had even taken an aborigine wife and been accepted into a Kabi tribe. He also became quite adept at successfully negotiating the difficult terrain of the coast. When he voluntarily returned to Moreton to surrender, he believed that because seven years had elapsed, he would be free to go. That would have been true years earlier, but in his absence that rule was changed and his self-imposed exile didn't count toward his sentence.

While Graham served his remaining years, a lieutenant named Charles Otter, on leave from Moreton Bay, while relaxing in the vicinity of Bribie Island, was approached by three ragged survivors of the *Stirling Castle;* among them was Joseph Corralis, a black-skinned South American who was treated relatively considerably by his aboriginal captors. Otter contacted the commander of the penal settlement, Captain Foster Fyans, who assembled a rescue team; Graham, with his experience, was the logical choice to lead. And for the convict, a chance to redeem himself just might be his ticket out of bondage.

On August 11, the party set out with rations for several weeks and barter goods to make their approach with the aborigines easier. Graham splintered from the rescue party, rightly believing that one man who spoke the language would be met with far less hostility than an entire party of white men. When he did make contact with the natives on August 15, however, they did treat Graham with wary antagonism. However, he managed to ameliorate them with his fluency of their language. He asked after the white woman. The natives admitted that they knew of the woman, but that she was no longer being held in the vicinity, taken instead to the *corroboree* on the mainland. They did, however, produce a man near death: *Stirling Castle* survivor John Baxter. Graham described their meeting this way: "I ever must remember the emaciated form of this man, while leading through the crowd, a Skeleton of an arm extended to me, with those feeble words scarcely articulate: 'What ship, mate, do you belong?'"

Graham persuaded the natives to take Baxter the sixteen miles down the beach to Fyans's waiting boats, promising them that they would receive many trade goods in exchange. Meanwhile, he set off to find Eliza Fraser. When he came upon the camp where Fraser was being held, he announced himself as Moilow in the native language; he was here to claim the ghost of his dead aboriginal wife, Mamba (Eliza Fraser). Everything in Graham's claim gelled with aboriginal custom and belief. However, there was immediate and angry opposition to his claim. After all, he could simply be a liar, and he wasn't recognizable to many there—it had been nine years since he had lived in the bush with the natives. But three tribesmen, stepsons of Graham's—Murrow-Dooling and Caravanty—as well as his father-in-law, Mootemu, rushed to his defense. This defused the situation, and Graham was allowed possession of the woman. A ragged and hardened convict, his account of the first meeting with Fraser aroused understandable pity: "Fortitude was what I now called from Heaven to assist me in seeing a woman survive in the most distress'd state that can be painted, and one but a few months since rolled in the affluence of plenty, doomed to subsist on the husks of the Earth, and forced to bear the wood on them sun burnt shoulders where the tender skin hung in places, ordered to hop on lacerated feet to fetch them water." Graham escorted her out of camp; a difficult trip back to the rescue ships awaited, but the following day, the deliverance of Eliza Fraser was complete.

Many differences in the account of the wreck and its aftermath exist; some of these are relatively minor in detail (not to be unexpected), while others figure enormously. As for the matter of why the crew hadn't procured any water when the *Stirling Castle* went down, Youlden, for one, claimed that the water casks had been stove in. But both Baxter and Eliza Fraser claimed that the crew simply refused to go belowdecks to retrieve them. Another example of divergent records comes in the immediate aftermath of the wreck. Baxter asseverated there was a chaotic free-for-all, a situation that added to the poor state of repair efforts. Youlden, however, claimed that the crew worked together professionally, but to relatively little effect. A third divergence of events comes in the confrontation on the beach. Baxter claimed that the group that split off, determined to walk to Moreton Bay, forcibly took weapons from Fraser. But Youlden asseverated that a lack of weapons was the primary reason why the crew didn't attempt landing earlier than they did. Youlden also wrote in his journal that the captain had starved to death, a wild divergence from Eliza's assertion of a spear through the chest. There's another problem concerning the accounts of Captain Fraser's death. Eliza's version given to her eventual biographer has her husband dying immediately after uttering his farewell to his wife. But months earlier, in an account given to Foster Fyans in Sydney, she again repeated the claim about the spear, but this time she claimed that "[Captain Fraser] gradually pined away until his death which took place some eight or nine days later."

A larger and more mysterious divergence in the long-established story of Eliza Fraser is that it might not have been John Graham who rescued Fraser at all. It might have been someone named David Bracewell. Not surprisingly, Graham, based upon his purported actions in rescuing Eliza Fraser, asked for a pardon from his sentence. That could be granted only by the governor in Sydney and it was long in coming. When Graham wrote a second appeal, he made specific mention of rumors about a second man who had assisted in the rescue, vehemently denying this and repeating the claim that he had acted alone and at great risk to himself.

But Bracewell, an escaped convict from Moreton, had been living in the area for years, and had assimilated so fully into Kabi culture that when two white British men looking for timber and grazing land years after the Fraser affair met with Bracewell, they hardly recognized him as European. One of the men, Andrew Petrie, wrote: "He had the same appearance as the wild blacks . . . When I spoke to him he could not answer me for some time; his heart was full, and tears flowed, and the language did not come readily to him."

Bracewell told the men that in fact it was he who had saved Eliza Fraser, scurrying her away in the dead of night while the natives were preoccupied with their *corroboree* festivities. Henry Stuart Russell, in his 1888 book *Genesis of Queensland,* takes a dim view of Eliza Fraser and her machinations and turns his sympathy to poor Bracewell, who Russell conjectures deserves the credit for Fraser's rescue. Russell writes of their escape: "The will of the one helpless creature being nerved by her tremendous desolation: of the other by prospect of large reward, and that which under the despairing cry of the woman had become 'father to his hope'—viz, the recovery of liberty by pardon, in return for this risky service to an Englishwoman." Russell's contempt for Fraser is obvious: "It is hard to accept the belief that under the reaction of supreme joy upon deliverance from such an agony of life as this woman's must have been, it could have been possible that any human soul should be possessed by any other power but that of unspeakable priceless gratitude to the worker of such a restoration to kin and country."

But according to this version, Fraser turned on her benefactor. As she reached her saviors, she allegedly told to Bracewell that she would speak ill of him. Russell, the *Genesis* author, spent weeks with Bracewell and looked hard for contradictions or signs of lying. He found none and believed every word Bracewell said, that he fled back into the bush upon sight of Otter and his rescue crew, believing that he would be made to go back to Moreton Bay to serve out his sentence. Certainly without Fraser's testimonial of his service, that would have been true.

But if Bracewell's story is true, it still begs the question of why Fraser would do this—what would she have to gain by denying her rescuer his due? According to Barry Dwyer and Neil Buchana, authors of *The Rescue of Eliza Fraser* (Noosa Graphica, 1986), "There can only be one explanation of this, as some historians have seen. On the night that Bracewell and Mrs. Fraser spent between Coothbara and Tin Can Bay, he had taken advantage of his female companion. Weak and tired, she had been unable to resist him. It is on record that when Mrs. Fraser reached Moreton Bay she was placed in the care of the settlement's doctor. His official report records that she made a rapid recovery but that she was beset with a worry that she might be pregnant."

Whether this conjecture is true or not can never be solved. However, it is worth noting that Bracewell's version of events, not Graham's, has always been the version accepted by the aborigines. Word of the rescue, first disseminated at Moreton, then at Sydney, and then on to London, all spoke of an escaped convict who helped with the rescue. But Graham's name was never mentioned, apart from reports given by officers at Moreton Bay. In fact, survivors of the wreck only spoke of "a convict who had been some years in the bush among the savages." If this means that the convict was *currently* living in the bush, it certainly doesn't describe Graham. But it does Bracewell. In Foster Fyans's report, he offers something that, taken in the context of the Bracewell story, takes on real importance. Fyans wrote of Fraser's initial meeting with Graham: "Graham saw Mrs. Fraser, endeavoured to speak with her, which she avoided, saying that the white men she had met were worse than the blacks." "White men" can only mean escaped convicts, of whom Bracewell was one. Further, when Fraser was later giving depositions in England about her capture, she complained bitterly of "another white man," but never named this person. Subsequent versions of her story dropped this reference altogether.

It's quite possible that Bracewell and Graham had worked together to save Fraser, but each had his reasons for later claiming that he acted alone. In any case, Fraser's own veracity about her captivity and her general honesty would be questioned repeatedly in the coming months.

Plans were put into place to return Fraser to Europe. A ship, the brig *Mediterranean Packet*, was made ready at Sydney. There, one of the original crew of the *Stirling Castle* had already landed and told of the terrible wreck; this was Robert Hodge. His story, though impossible to corroborate, related the mystery of the missing pinnace. According to Hodge, the crew of the pinnace didn't intentionally abandon the others, but had simply lost its way. They decided to try and sail for Moreton Bay, where they could summon help. Instead, they were wrecked. The men thereafter began to die one by one: by accident, starvation, drowning, sheer exhaustion. Hodge reported that one of the men, James Major, was eaten by aboriginal cannibals. But rumors persisted in Sydney that any cannibalism was the sole work of the Europeans, subsisting on one another until there was only one left: Hodge, who, for obvious reasons, wouldn't admit to this when he was rescued and brought to Sydney. When Hodge's rescue was later reported, it included some grisly details about James Major's death, apparently a cannibalized victim of the aborigines: "It appeared, from small fragments of bones which lay near his disfigured trunk, that the natives had placed his head on a fire, which consumed the thorax and descended obliquely to a part of the left side of the abdomen, when it appeared to have satiated its vengeance, or perhaps its flame was extinguished by the gushing of the heart's blood of the victim! . . . But the work of the destruction did not end here—it was quite apparent that the kangaroo dogs had made a hearty meal on the most fleshy part of the thighs and legs of the poor fellow, so that what remained of him was a horrid spectacle to behold" (John Curtis, *The Shipwreck of the Stirling Castle*, 1837). Of course, it defies logic for cannibalistic aborigines, in want of food, to leave huge portions of the body for "kangaroo dogs."

Upon Eliza Fraser's arrival in Sydney, she became the toast of the town; her extraordinary story was required listening for the city's elite. She garnered so much sympathy over her increasingly bloodcurdling story that a subscription was taken in her name and she eventually received four hundred pounds. Harry Youlden couldn't help himself as he burned with indignation: he told of never seeing the money that was supposed to be parceled out to him and the other survivors, noting, "Where the rest of the money went I will not say; but if it will help his conscience at all who has it, I freely make over to him my share of it."

Despite the hard feelings, there can be no denying that it had been a harrowing experience for all involved; it was, finally, time to start heading home—but not before some further twists and turns in this story.

The brig *Mediterranean Packet,* the ship that would take Fraser back to Europe, was captained by a man named Alexander John Greene. He visited Fraser in Sydney and apparently made quite an impression. The two were married on February 23, though the witnesses were few; Fraser wished to keep it a secret. After all, her husband had been dead barely eight months and tradition dictated a bereavement period of at least a year. But there may have been other reasons for secrecy.

When the *Mediterranean Packet* arrived in Liverpool in mid-July, Fraser made a call to a Mr. Dowling, the commissioner of police; she repeated her tale of suffering and asked for assistance in getting to London, where she could begin to make her journey back home to the Orkney Islands. However, by the time the commissioner finished an investigation, he found out that Fraser was married and that she often appeared in public wearing clothes well out of the reach of the destitute woman she purported to be. Worse, when Dowling interviewed her himself on the particulars of the "savages" with whom she had lived, she gave out some ridiculous stories: namely, that the aborigines sported tufts of blue hair on their shoulders and a long stream of the same that sprouted up from the middle of their heads. "Mr. Dowling's confidence in her veracity immediately underwent a considerable diminution," read the official report. Angry, the commissioner sent her out of town without a penny. But the Greenes were undeterred.

In London, Fraser performed the same charade; this time it was initially successful, aided in large part by John Curtis. Curtis was a court reporter in London and covered the Lord Mayor's Inquiry into the capture of Eliza Fraser. In 1837, Curtis published *The Shipwreck of the Stirling Castle* through George Virtue of London. The book was a sensation and presented Fraser once again as a very sympathetic creature. The Lord Mayor, initially distraught over this woman's poor treatment, eventually got wind of her less than honest nature from Liverpool; the money collected in her name then went to a fund for her children. Perhaps the Lord Mayor should have taken his wife's view, when she uttered upon seeing Mrs. Fraser (Greene) for the first time: "I was not a little surprised at the healthy and placid appearance of a woman who had been doomed to a companionship compared with which an intercourse with the beasts of the wilderness would have been a refuge and consolation."

When word of all this reached Sydney, where local residents were furious that they were being portrayed as stingy in their offerings to Fraser when she recovered there, the *Sydney Gazette* printed an article on February 1 that determined to set the record straight. The article began: "The statements made by Mrs. Fraser and others regarding the loss of the '*Stirling Castle*' on her voyage from Sydney to Singapore differ so materially in detail from the statements made by the same parties here that we have been induced . . . to publish them." In other words, the jig was up; Fraser, if she had any credibility left, was exposed.

Despite its qualms with the author of the outrageous stories, the article's writers furthered the already horrendous reputation the natives had to live with. Details of the story had, by this time, become exaggerated to the point of absurdity; for example, the death of Captain Fraser was reported this way: after Fraser was speared, "Mrs. Fraser ran to her husband, cried out, 'Jesus of Nazareth, I can endure this no longer,' and pulled the spear out of the body, but the breath was gone forever!" When James Major was killed, according to this same article, "A couple of savages set to work, and by means of sharpened shells severed the head from the body with frightful lacerations. Then they ate parts of the body and preserved the head with certain gums of extraordinary efficiency and fixed it as a figure bust to one of their canoes."

There is nothing in the recorded history of the aborigines to support such a claim. But even Eliza Fraser can't be blamed for this ridiculous story. In fact, it should be noted that when she gave her accounts, Fraser may very well have been laboring with mental instability after her terrifying ordeal. This possibility, coupled with the probability of her new husband's financial machinations, may make her a bit more innocent than it appears. However, this sympathy has to be tempered with another, terrible reality: her story gave every impetus to white settlers to treat aborigines in the most brutal manner.

Slavery wasn't something that existed in aboriginal cultures; however, the Europeans' claiming that they were taken as slaves is understandable. Europeans in the 1830s were certainly aware of slavery and its dehumanizing effects. Forced into difficult labor with little sustenance surely felt like slavery to these white people.

However, what they could not have known was that white people—a real rarity in that place at that time—were considered by the aborigines to be the ghosts of dead ancestors because of the peculiar appearance of dead bodies preserved in traditional aborigine ways—the cutis vera, or "true skin" is white in all humans, and was revealed after aborigines scorched the corpse and the cuticle was then peeled off.

In their belief system, the aborigines were required to take in the ghosts. And here, suddenly, were a dozen ghosts; their presence would put a serious strain on already taxed supplies of food and resources. Divvying up the group so that they can be more easily absorbed by different clans makes sense; however, simply having them around and tending to their needs was impossible. No, these ghosts would have to contribute by working, just like all the others in the tribe. If this meant breastfeeding a child, collecting firewood, or catching sea crabs, each ghost had to do his or her share to earn keep.

Set in this context, the treatment of Eliza Fraser takes on a more benign patina. No doubt having sand thrown on sunburned skin, as Eliza Fraser related, is extremely painful. Likewise, having your skin then smeared and covered in odoriferous grease is unpleasant as well. But it must be remembered that the crew of the *Stirling Castle* landed on Great Sandy in winter; a traditional aboriginal method of protecting against the wet and cold of night was to rub the body with animal fats, and sand on the skin was used as a protection from the sun—what Fraser saw as an ultimate indignity may very well have been an attempt to shield her from harm. True, Fraser was belittled and tormented when performing her chores; however, by her own admission, she performed these tasks with incredible ineptitude. Plus, she made her feelings about the chores—that she considered them demeaning and debasing—quite well known.

Another example of pure, if not unfortunate, misunderstanding can be seen in the case of Charles Brown, one of the survivors of the *Stirling Castle*. John Baxter, who was with Brown before his death, later told an inquiry that Brown had remarked that the aborigines had been unusually nice to him before his death. However, Brown soon fell seriously ill. According to Fraser, "For some days, [Brown] had been unable to walk as the flesh had fallen from his feet and the bones of his knees protruded through his skin." Baxter went on to relate that after he and Brown were separated, Fraser told him that Brown had been "inhumanly tied to a stake and, a slow fire being placed under him, his body, after the most excruciating sufferings, reduced to ashes."

Contrast this to an aboriginal method of dealing with infection, offered by Gerry Langevad in *Some Original Views Around Kilcoy: Book 1. The Aboriginal Perspective* (Brisbane, 1982): open wounds were cleaned, filled with hot charcoal, and then covered with white clay. Fire was then applied to the clay as a means of killing bacteria. The process, though effective, was extremely painful and the recipient generally had to be restrained during the procedure. Surely, such a cure would have seemed like pure torture to any European.

There was an early assumption among the *Stirling Castle* crew that the natives practiced ritualized cannibalism. After Curtis's sympathetic portrait of Eliza Fraser's sufferings, that belief was reinforced. The problem with that conception is that it wasn't true; ritualized or ceremonial cannibalism simply wasn't part of Kabi culture. One of the survivors, Robert Darge, was asked specifically about this. His response: "I do not believe that any of the tribes I was amongst ate human flesh. I never saw anything of the kind." Darge gave this information as part of an interview with the Lord Mayor of London, where he hoped to gain some of the subscription money raised for Eliza Fraser; he would have had every motivation to lie to inflate the real hardships and terrors he had suffered in Australia.

Dwyer and Buchana make the point that for all the alleged horrors thrown at the Europeans by their "savage" captors, in the end, "of the twelve survivors landing on the island, two drowned, three were killed, and the other seven were left alive." Also, the punishments the survivors received for perceived shirking of work, for example, "is much less than they would have received from European overseers had they been transported convicts and not working to the best of their ability."

Despite the fact that there were great exaggerations and misunderstandings, it is true that the crew of the *Stirling Castle* did suffer hardships, and several did meet death at the hands of the tribesmen. But tribal laws, thousands of years old, were strict and intractable. It is very possible that the killed crewmen unwittingly committed some breach or taboo that was punishable by death, such as removing the bones of a dead ancestor from a tree hollow. The horrified Europeans, not understanding, reported savagery.

Besides, the aborigines often had real reason to hate all white men, as the testimony of Robert Darge shows; when asked by the Lord Mayor of London whether he believed that the natives had designs on killing him, Darge answered: "I don't think they would have killed me. But there were some who could not bear the sight of a white man at all. I believe the reason they had such hatred of me was that the [white] soldiers wounded them. I observed in particular that a man who had lost his leg had a desperate hatred of me."

It is difficult to take a fair or objective view of Eliza Fraser. Curtis, for one, was terribly sympathetic: "It appeared evident that the poor woman had evinced symptoms of aberration of the mind," he wrote, "And if it be so, who can wonder." Even the editors of the *Sydney Gazette* softened somewhat toward the unfortunate woman. They never did lose sight of the fact that she had suffered—well and true.

In the end, what remains so important about the story of Eliza Fraser is that it formed the basis of ethnographic studies of aboriginal cultures in and around Fraser Island; starting from a point of accepted barbarism on the part of the native "savages," one couldn't begin to suppose subsequent generations of Europeans would assume any differently. As a result, Fraser's story was used to justify brutal treatment by colonials against the Aborigines. Fraser's story was also used as justification for setting up missionary posts on the island, so that the "savage brutality of the tribes on the coast" could be "subjected to the humanizing influences of Christian civilization" (John Dunmore Lang, an Australian Presbyterian clergyman, in a letter to London). This "humanizing" was deemed necessary for 130 years; aborigines in Australia were officially classified as "fauna" until 1967.

Not surprisingly, the very name Eliza Fraser conjures real and deserved resentment from Badtjala people, even today. Shirley Foley, contributor to Shawn Foley's book, *The Badtjala People* (Hervey Bay, Queensland, 1994), wrote: "For too long people have abused our culture, and they have used it to their best advantage." Ian McNiven, in his essay, "Shipwreck Saga as Archaeological Text: Reconstructing Fraser Island's Aboriginal Past," writes: "The Badtjala captured Eliza Fraser for less than two months, but she ended up capturing Badtjala history for eternity."

INCOMPETENCE, DISORDER, AND EVIL

Cannibalism was an unfortunate result of absolutely distressed circumstances. Such a decision was never entered into lightly, but good and able seamen understood the necessary evil in it. But sometimes circumstances came to such desperate states because of a simple lack of competence. And often, when disaster did strike, the needed response of discipline, teamwork, and selflessness was immediately thrown off for more base natures. Sometimes, the new disaster provided an opportunity for men's darker sides to prevail: self-preservation at all costs, mayhem, even murder.

Human beings are not born good or bad. There is scarcely such a thing as "human nature." Instead, we are just the ensemble of our acts and whether we are heroes or goats depends entirely upon the decisions we make in the face of difficulties. Shipwrecks presented people with the opportunity to engage in heroism or bravery, or to move in the opposite direction. The bottom line is that in the frothy swell of a seething sea, pushing its way into cracked holds, a decision must be made. Which direction that turns is this chapter's point of inquiry.

Here we have three stories, all differing in timing and degree of bad or wicked decisions. In the first case, only the wreck prevented a planned mutiny. But with the ship's leaders gone and mutiny no longer attainable, there emerged a vacuum of power that was filled with rape and indiscriminate murder. Next we see terrible judgment precipitating a wreck, and continuing afterward, condemning hundreds to the most excruciating deaths imaginable. Last is the case of an accomplished polar explorer taking enough shortcuts and displaying enough impatience that his decisions consigned many members of his expedition to a demise in the frozen wastelands of the Arctic.

Batavia (1628–29)

The *Batavia* was a Dutch trading vessel in the service of the Verenidge Oost-indische Compagnie, (VOC), the United East India Company, at the time the wealthiest and most powerful private company on the planet. The skipper was in charge of navigation; in the case of the *Batavia,* this was an experienced seaman named Ariaen Jacobsz. He was, in rank, subordinate to the ship's upper merchant, or supercargo, as he was known. His name was Francisco Pelsaert, the equivalent of the ship's captain. Jacobsz and Pelsaert were hostile to each other, Jacobsz holding a grudge against the man who was his superior in rank, but who he felt was inferior in every other regard. To make matters worse, Jacobsz developed an infatuation with Lucretia Jans, a cultured female passenger who was, by all accounts, exceedingly beautiful. The fact that she preferred the platonic company of Pelsaert was another reason for Jacobsz to despise his superior. Thus, before the journey through two oceans had even begun, the seeds of discontent had already been sown.

The *Batavia* left home on October 27, 1628, bound for present-day Indonesia, then a Dutch trading colony. Only two days' sail out of Holland, the *Batavia* ran aground during a squall on the Walcheren sandbanks; it was an inauspicious start, but no damage was done to the ship. But during the subsequent, incidentless voyage, a larger storm was brewing: Two men began plotting to overthrow Pelsaert. There was a lot of treasure on board, and the two men would be rich if they could pull off the mutiny. They would then simply steer the boat to a Dutch competitor (the English and the Portuguese had easy-to-reach harbors) who would welcome them.

As the ship passed through the Indian Ocean, squeezing between Amsterdam Island and Saint Paul Island, it made its interminable way toward its destination. A computation by Jacobsz put the *Batavia* some six hundred miles from land. However, in the middle of the night, the lookout noticed white water ahead. He alerted Jacobsz, who declared it nothing more than the reflection of the moon on the water. Minutes later, the *Batavia* smacked into the obscure reef of the Houtman Abrolhos, a series of coral islands about sixty kilometers off the western coast of present-day Australia. Pelsaert's journals record the incident this way: "June 4th; on the 2nd day of Whitsuntide. I was lying in my bunk feeling ill when felt suddenly with a terrible rough motion the bumping of the ship's rudder. And immediately after that I felt the ship held up in her course against the rocks so that I fell out of my bunk. Whereupon I ran up and discovered that we lay right in the middle of thick spray."

The initial hope was that an incoming high tide would carry her off the reef and set her back afloat; however, it turned out that it was already high tide when the *Batavia* struck. So the crew began to lighten the ship by tipping the heavy cannons overboard. The skipper gave the order to cut the mast, hoping to relieve pressure and weight and allow the crew to get the *Batavia* off the reef. But instead of falling over the side of the ship, where the men could then set to work dumping the mast into the sea, it instead fell straight down onto the deck, tearing through equipment and imperiling the ship even more.

In the morning light, a small crew launched one of the *Batavia*'s yawls and scouted the coral islands. They determined that the ship would remain above the tide line, but it was stuck fast to the coral below. Plans were discussed to begin evacuation. But within a few hours the hull burst and seawater came roiling into the lower decks. Mass panic ensued. The strongest people on board forced their way into the *Batavia*'s two small boats. Others leapt into the surf, hoping to swim to shore. All those who did drowned almost instantly. Seeing this, many stayed behind on the stressed *Batavia*.

The two boats began making repeated trips between the ship and the closest island, a windswept and desolate speck of land not even two hundred yards across and composed entirely of sharp coral. By midday, some 180 people huddled onto this godforsaken patch of land. Another 120 or so remained aboard the *Batavia*.

With the senior VOC officers off the boat, many of the ordinary seamen took the opportunity to head belowdecks and break into the stores of alcohol, finery, and jewels. They drank themselves almost into oblivion, parading around the ship in drunken stupors, wearing the captain's clothes, and fingering jewels and coins. Of course, the riches meant nothing to them, as death seemed inevitable. Instead, the drunken men began tossing the coins at one another in inebriated merriment.

On the island, ferries began taking large numbers of survivors to another, larger island in the distance. After repeated trips back to the *Batavia* as well, another fifty people left the ship, battered but still upright. Pelsaert and seven other VOC loyalists rowed toward the larger island, with its new concentration of survivors. The men aboard the yawl watched as Pelsaert began to head for shore. They looked at one another, and by unspoken decree, hauled him back into the boat and told him they wouldn't allow him to go to land. They reasoned that if he did, he would be held there by the desperate mob, now without provisions. The experienced seamen told Pelsaert, as cruel as it might seem, that the only way to salvation would be for them to abandon everyone and attempt a voyage to Java, some eighteen hundred miles away, and summon

Sketch 1647, artist unknown.

Reprinted from the book The Voyage of the Batavia, *Australian Maritime Series, published by Hordern House.*

help. Perhaps there would be no survivors by the time they got back. But if they didn't leave now, the chances of anyone surviving were virtually nil.

Pelsaert was persuaded to leave, but reluctantly: "It was better and more honest to die with them if we could not find water than to stay alive with deep grief of heart." Despite his misgivings, Pelsaert was among the forty-eight people who left, in the darkness of night, to sail for Indonesia, leaving approximately two hundred maroons on the islands and another seventy on the *Batavia*.

Along with Pelsaert was Jacobsz; the chances of something explosive taking place were great. Pelsaert wouldn't learn this until later, but Jacobsz had actually been a main actor in the plot to kill Pelsaert, start a mutiny, and make off with the *Batavia* to friendly ports.

The principal concocter of the mutiny plot was a Haarlem apothecary named Jeronimus Cornelisz. Despite being a very charismatic and well-educated man, Cornelisz had suffered a string of disappointments. He had recently buried an infant son, and his business was close to bankruptcy. He was also most probably wanted by Dutch authorities as a heretic. Only such a state of affairs would drive an upper-class man to take a place upon a Dutch trading vessel. Often its arrival in the Indies spelled quick death for upward of two-thirds who made the trip; the pestilent climate was something almost impossible for northern Europeans to endure. Plus, the passage itself was almost intolerable. The fifteen-thousand-mile journey to Java often took as long as eight months, and conditions were deplorable. On the *Batavia,* there were only four bathrooms for more than three hundred people. Mike Dash, in his book, *Batavia's Graveyard* (Three Rivers Press, 2003), describes the latrines as "Nothing more than holes in the deck under the bowsprit. These heads were open to the elements and in full view of all those waiting in line. The only additional amenity was a long, dung-smeared rope that snaked through the hole in the latrine. The frayed end of the rope dangled in the sea and could be hauled up and used to wipe oneself clean." When the latrines couldn't be used because of particularly foul weather, Dash writes, "Soldiers and sailors relieved themselves in corners or crouched over the ladders down to the hold, and if the weather was bad enough for the pumps to be called into action, the urine and feces that had been deposited below made an unwelcome reappearance."

Before the wreck, Cornelisz and Jacobsz had struck up a friendship, partly on the strength of their mutual attraction to Lucretia (Creesje) Jans. Indeed, her beauty hardly escaped the notice of any man on board, Pelsaert included. She was attended by another woman, Zwaantie Hendricx. Even though both were married Jacobsz had pursued Creesje with no success. He silently fumed as he watched Pelsaert treat the fair Creesje with great ceremony. One day, Jacobsz confided his hatred of Pelsaert to Cornelisz; while the apothecary could have turned him in as a potential mutineer, a crime punishable by death, instead he encouraged Jacobsz's line of thought, eventually turning it toward full-fledged entertainment of sedition.

Soon enough, the machinations of the two became clear to Pelsaert, though it's unlikely he considered that they were plotting a mutiny full-on. He did recognize, however, the corrosive effect of the captivating Cornelisz on Jacobsz: "Jeronimus was the tongue of the skipper and served as pedagogue to insinuate into him what he should answer if I wanted to speak to or admonish him." Despite Pelsaert's wariness, he didn't act. In the meanwhile, Cornelisz and Jacobsz quietly went about recruiting men for a mutiny, enticing a rough lot of sailors with promised riches. The two men, driven by Cornelisz's charm, managed also to persuade several senior officers and experienced seamen. In all, they could easily control the ship once Pelsaert and others were dispatched.

But plans were set on hold as spring approached. Pelsaert became very ill, so near death that his recovery appeared unlikely. Had he died, the control of the ship would have gone to Cornelisz and Jacobsz anyway, as they represented the most senior officers on board. But miraculously, after almost a month, Pelsaert recovered. The plan to mutiny was back on.

Its inception began oddly. Cornelisz and Jacobsz came up with the idea to attack Creesje Jans. Late at night, several men grabbed her and dragged her to a dark corner on deck. One man reached under her skirt while others smeared a black, tarry substance over her face. When it was done and the men retreated back into the shadows, Creesje lay stunned, covered in excrement. Pelsaert was enraged. The two conspirators assumed his reaction would be so severe and punitive that the men on board would feel completely justified in throwing him over. But Pelsaert ruined this plan; yes, he was furious, but his punishment wasn't nearly as harsh as hoped. In fact, he did nothing. So the men would have to simply break into his cabin in the wee hours of the morning and throw him over board. They decided to do so as the *Batavia* approached Australia.

But the grounding of the ship on the coral reefs spoiled the plan. Now survivors of the wreck sat scattered on two islands, and Pelsaert and Jacobsz were together in a small boat headed for Java.

The survivors would have traded their places on that godforsaken set of coral islands for a coveted spot on the boat. Where the bulk of the survivors were now marooned they called Batavia's Graveyard, not even fifteen hundred yards square. With roughly one hundred eighty people stuck on this patch of island, the food and water they managed to salvage from the wreck was gone within a day. After a few days, ten people died; the others resorted to drinking their own urine.

There were still about seventy people on board the *Batavia,* and while they enjoyed food and water, the reason they had stayed behind was simply because they could not swim. Now, after nine days of battering by the sea, the *Batavia* began to break apart. The men on board were forced into the sea, where they made mad, flailing attempts toward land. Of these, only twenty-five made it. The last to arrive on land, half drowned, was Cornelisz.

The disintegration of the ship did provide one fortunate result. Hundreds of barrels, full of water and wine, along with copious amounts of driftwood, floated to Batavia's Graveyard. Carpenters on shore began making small skiffs and erecting shelters. For now, at least, the inhabitants of Batavia's Graveyard were saved. But some order had to be maintained if the survivors hoped to formulate a plan. Cornelisz, now the most senior VOC official left, took the reins of power. His charisma and eloquence made him a logical leader in any case. There was a problem, however: he had been sowing the seeds of a mutiny before the *Batavia* went down. If word of this got out, when the inevitable rescue ship appeared on the horizon, Cornelisz would be tortured and killed.

Cornelisz began to surround himself with sycophants, attracted to his silver tongue and promise of riches. Hugh Edwards, who in 1963 led an expedition team to recover the remains of the *Batavia,* wrote of Cornelisz, "He was emperor over two acres of sand." Among his minions were ruthless enforcers who kept others in line with intimidation. They collected and controlled all the weapons on the island. But they were desperately outnumbered, so before there was an uprising, Cornelisz began devising plans to drastically reduce the number of people on Batavia's Graveyard. This he did rather easily.

Two nearby islands, Seals' Island and Traitors' Island (so named for Pelsaert and the others who set off from there), were said to contain food and water (lies concocted by Cornelisz and his followers). As a result, about forty people were ferried to Seals' and left there. Another fifteen were left at Traitors'. About a mile away to the west sat two more previously unexplored islands, today's East and West Wallabi. When another twenty men proposed searching these for freshwater, Cornelisz was happy to see them go, believing they would find nothing and die after Cornelisz left them there without rafts or skiffs. Among these men was a sailor named Wiebbe Hayes. On Wiebbe Hayes' Island (West Wallabi), he managed to keep his twenty men alive with water from rain puddles and the meat from slaughtered island animals. For three weeks he did this, keeping up unsuccessful searches for fresh springs and waiting for return rafts from Batavia's Graveyard. Of course, they never came.

Back on Batavia's Graveyard, the opportunity to begin thinning the ranks of survivors presented itself in early July when a soldier named Abraham Hendricx was caught helping himself to one of the barrels. Cornelisz, now presiding over the council, or *raad,* announced a guilty verdict on not only Hendricx, but also a gunner named Ariaen Ariaensz, who had apparently partaken of the wine that Hendricx stole. Cornelisz charged both with death, though the council upheld it only for the thief, Hendricx.

Cornelisz promptly dissolved the council, which was in his rights, and replaced them with loyal followers, who swiftly put Hendricx to death and found two carpenters guilty of spurious charges of having borrowed a boat without permission. The verdict was death and the executions were carried out immediately and in front of all. It was now clear to everyone that resistance was a dangerous—probably fatal—proposition. Most chilling for the other survivors on the island—now cowed into silence and submission—was the apparent glee the killers took toward their charge. Ship journals record one of the victim's deaths this way: "Daniel [the executioner] has pierced the foresaid Warnar with a sword; of which he boasted later, saying it went through him as easily as butter."

Events on Batavia's Graveyard had taken a dramatic turn.

Still, Cornelisz had to be pragmatic. A mass killing spree could prompt an uprising. And while Cornelisz and his followers enjoyed possession of the weaponry, they could probably still be overrun by a determined revolt. Cornelisz set about sending small parties to Wiebbe Hayes' Island, ostensibly as reinforcements and to aid in the search for water. Over the next few days, two separate groups of four men were rowed by coconspirators toward Wiebbe Hayes' Island. Once they were out of sight of Batavia's Graveyard, the unsuspecting victims were bound and tipped into the ocean. In both cases, one of the four men successfully pleaded for his life. They were allowed to return to Batavia's Graveyard, but the condition for salvation was sworn allegiance to Cornelisz.

Killings on Batavia's Graveyard continued unabated until there was a sudden and unexpected set of smoke signals from Wiebbe Hayes' Island. The men there, still ignorant of the horrors back on the main island, were, amazingly, still alive. Further, the smoke signals indicated that they had found water. So not only wasn't the group starving and dehydrated, they apparently were doing okay. And so long as they remained in that state, they remained a threat to Cornelisz. The smoke signals set off a mass exodus from Traitors' Island, where the survivors intended to join their old shipmates on Wiebbe Hayes' Island. Cornelisz ordered a band of his men to set out and attack, intercepting those from Traitors' Island and initiating another mass killing. Had there been any lingering doubt about Cornelisz's intentions, no one on Batavia's Graveyard now harbored any illusions. Gijsbert Bastiaensz, the ship's *predikant* (clergyman), lamented: "We all of us together expected to be murdered at any moment, and we besought God continuously for merciful relief . . . O cruelty! O atrocity of atrocities!"

Life on Batavia's Graveyard became, in essence, a wait for death. Falling ill, for example, became an immediate death sentence, as someone incapacitated with sickness became merely another mouth to feed. Women survived in a disproportionate percentage, but the reason was sinister: they would be used by the mutineers for "common service."

Cornelisz sent more of his men to Seals' Island, where they initiated a series of ruthless slaughters. The official after-report recorded the horror:

> Andries Jonas has been ordered by Jeronimus [Cornelisz] to go, together with Davidt Zeevanck and others . . . to kill there the

remaining 4 women and about 15 boys who had not been killed in the previous murder on 15 July. Therefore Zeevanck has asked whether he had a knife; Andries Jonas answered that he had a knife but it was not very sharp. Whereupon Zeevanck handed him his own knife saying 'Cut the throats of the women.' So Andries has gone to Mayken Soers who was pregnant, has taken her by the hand and led her a little to one side and said to her, 'Mayken love, you must die,' and thrown her underfoot and cut her throat. That being done he saw that Jan Pelgrom was trying to kill Janneken Gist, therefore he went to help . . . and stabbed Janneken to death with his knife.

Events were progressing on Batavia's Graveyard to Cornelisz's satisfaction. When a baby was killed in the third week of July, its incessant crying an annoyance to Cornelisz, it constituted the 105th murder, leaving fewer than sixty on the island. A slaughter of another eleven people occurred soon after. But an intended twelfth victim, Aris Jansz, managed to escape when his attackers landed blows across his head and shoulders but were unable to cause any severe damage because of the bluntness of their swords. By the end of August, some of Cornelisz's enforcers had grown almost mad with restlessness simply because there was virtually no one left to kill; all those spared were artisans useful for Cornelisz, or people who had signed oaths of allegiance. Jan Pelgrom, a servant to Cornelisz, ran around and screamed: "Who wants to be stabbed to death? I can do that very beautifully."

On Hayes' Island, the men managed a pretty luxurious existence compared with those on the other islands, including Batavia's Graveyard. The waters around Hayes' Islands proved a productive fishing ground, and the islands themselves were populated by tammars, an easy-to-catch relative of the kangaroo. At roughly thirty inches in height, they made a satisfying and delicious meal. There were enough food and water even to satisfy a contingent of almost thirty men who had somehow managed to escape the slaughters and killings on Seals' Island and Batavia's Graveyard, including Aris Jansz, who had fled into the night and eluded discovery until his attackers gave up, leaving him for dead. Jansz made his way to the other side of the island, where he stealthily untethered a yawl and rowed to Wiebbe Hayes' Island. By this point, Hayes was well aware of what was going on. Now reinforced, he steeled himself for battle, knowing that Cornelisz and his men would probably be launching an attack any day. Without proper weapons, Hayes and his band fashioned what they could: rocks, sharp boards, and an armory of stones to throw upon invading

The Remains of Hayes Fort

groups of Cornelisz's men. Hayes, a soldier and natural-born leader, ran daily training exercises, and put the men to work making defensive battlements and fashioning crude weapons from driftwood and anything else they could get their hands on.

When the attacks came, they did so in a cloak of ineptitude. Smallish bands of Cornelisz's men were easily spotted and repelled by Hayes's army, called the Defenders. Cornelisz, still believing in the powers of his own charisma, decided to try diplomacy. He came to Hayes' Island himself, accompanied by five bodyguards. Cornelisz's plan was simple, but in hindsight absurd: he would talk directly to Hayes while his bodyguards would move about the Defenders and lure them to their side by offering money and jewels. But none of the Defenders was swayed. They killed Cornelisz's men and took their leader prisoner. It was all so easy and so quick. After months of a reign of absolute terror, Cornelisz had simply—albeit unwittingly—delivered himself directly into the hands of his nemeses.

But things weren't over so quickly. There were still men loyal to Cornelisz back on Batavia's Graveyard. They launched several attacks to rescue their leader. In fact, the mutineers were slowly winning the battle. It appeared that Cornelisz might even be rescued and reinstated.

It was during just such an attack on the Defenders that Francisco Pelsaert, steering a rescue ship, appeared on the horizon and bore down upon the scene.

On July 3, Pelsaert and his crew had made land at Java. Everyone on board had survived, despite severe water rationing and miserable conditions. VOC executives at Java didn't take the news of the *Batavia*'s misfortune well. They were quick to send Pelsaert back with a rescue ship, less out of concern for the probable mass deaths from drowning and starvation than in hopes of recovering the great fortune that had been on board. (Indeed, when the rescue ship would eventually return and a reckoning of the ship's fortunes could be made, the official report noted the recovery of a large amount of treasure, and concluded, despite hundreds dead: "Thanks be to the Almighty for this, we would not have expected it to come out so well.")

It would be another two and a half months before Pelsaert and his crew managed to find the elusive Abrolhos—they spotted Hayes' Island on September 16. They surely never expected to see any survivors, but they were greeted by the sight of boatloads of men making their way toward his ship, the *Sardam*. Hayes's men got there first, but only had time to warn Pelsaert of the coming mutiny. When the mutineers arrived, they told tale of a different mutiny by Hayes's men. But those spinning this tall tale sat in their boats laden with weapons and wearing flamboyant uniforms. Pelsaert quickly realized that Hayes was telling the truth; he barely had enough time to pull the ladders up on deck and warn his crew. The mutineers, finally sensing defeat, threw their weapons into the sea and came on board, where they were immediately bound and held. Pelsaert questioned the men, and "Learned from their own confessions, and the testimony of all the living persons, that they have drowned, murdered and brought to death with all manner of cruelties, more than 120 persons."

But Cornelisz gave up nothing. According to the *Batavia* reports, "He tried to talk himself clean, with his glib tongue telling the most palpable lies, making out that nowhere had he had a hand in it." Dutch law stipulated that a man couldn't be convicted of a crime without his confession. However, all manner of wretched torture could be used to extract that "confession." Cornelisz wasn't spared. He was tortured, then confessed, then retracted his confession, and the process would begin anew, some five times in all. Finally, Cornelisz confessed to the satisfaction of Pelsaert. He read the punishment: "Cornelisz . . . shall be taken to a place prepared to execute justice, and there first cut off both his hands, and after that punish him on a gallows with a cord until death shall follow."

When it came time for Cornelisz to be hanged, he and his accomplices all began to turn on each other, blaming each in turn until they were all led to the gallows. The *predikant*, Bastianesz, whose wife and six of his seven children had been murdered in the chaos, recorded the end: "If ever there has been a Godless Man in his utmost need, it was [Cornelisz]; he had done nothing wrong, according to his statement. Yes, saying even at the end, as he mounted the gallows: 'Revenge! Revenge!'"

Those words, apparently, were the last Cornelisz ever said.

Of the original crew of 330 people on the *Batavia,* 70 came back alive with Pelsaert, including 16 detainees of Cornelisz's band. Two of these, Wouter Loos and Jan Pelgrom, were abandoned (as a way of commuting their death sentences) on an empty Australian beach. Pelsaert declared: "They shall be put ashore as scoundrels and death-deserving delinquents, in order to know once, for certain, what happens in this Land." Nothing is known of their fate once they were marooned, but their abandonment most probably makes them Australia's first white "settlers."

In all, two-thirds of the passengers on board the *Batavia* when it left Holland were killed. Only four or five of the people who survived on Batavia's Graveyard did so without signing oaths of allegiance to Cornelisz.

Simon Leys, author of *The Wreck of the Batavia* (Basic Books, 2005), sums up the bizarre and ghastly episode, still the bloodiest in Australian history, this way: "A civilized society is not one in which the percentage of criminals and perverts is lower (the proportion must be about the same in all human communities); it is simply one that gives them less opportunity to indulge their inclinations. Without Cornelisz, his two dozen henchmen would probably never have shown—or even discovered—their true natures. There is no doubt that it was the personality of the former apothecary and the inspiration he imparted to his followers that made it possible to set up and sustain over a period of time of three months a weird and gruesome kingdom of murder amongst a population of two hundred and fifty decent individuals."

Medusa (1816)

Less than a year after Napoleon fell at Waterloo, the colony of Senegal, once a French possession, had fallen into the hands of the rival British. But as part of the terms of a new peace agreement, the colony would revert to the French once again. It wasn't much of a concession on the part of the British. Senegal colony, still largely unexplored, had to this point yielded little return and had actually claimed the lives of many administrators. It was a hot, dusty, sickly place, ill suited for the constitutions of urban Europeans.

But the French, fresh from defeat, were eager to take back their old possession. Four ships sped toward the African coast to establish the settlement. The convoy consisted of the brigantine *Argus,* the corvette *Echo,* the transport *Loire,* and the flagship frigate *Medusa,* laden with four hundred passengers and crew.

The captain of the *Medusa* and leader of the entire expedition was a man named Hugues Duroy de Chaumareys. Not everyone liked Chaumareys. The captain of the *Loire,* for example, found him largely insufferable: "He seemed to find it natural that I would be his obedient servant. First, I made him understand that I was myself as true a gentleman as he was, and that I did not think that I had done wrong in serving my country during the time he had chosen to go into exile. Then he changed his attitude towards me. This was quite characteristic of him. Was it just a gentlemanly reflex or did it show a basic lack of character? The latter, I think, for it seems that in spite of his 'show-off' manner Chaumareys was easily manipulated, like all cocksure fellows."

Though the French had relatively detailed maps of the African coast, there was one major obstacle, and its precise location was still something of a mystery: the Arguin Bank, a sandbank that jutted several miles into the ocean from present-day southern Mauritania, just north of the Senegalese border. The bank had claimed countless ships in the past, and because its extent was unknown, the best advisable course was to simply head out into the ocean, many miles off the coast, giving as wide a berth as possible before swinging back to the coast in time to reach the port of St. Louis in Senegal.

The captain of the *Loire* warned Chaumareys about the bank and offered to take the lead in plying a route around it. But his description of Chaumareys as being "easily manipulated" was on the nose. The new governor of Senegal, Julien-Désiré Schmaltz, on board the *Medusa,* pushed for the convoy to hug the coast, as this was the quickest route and also kept them free of the dangers of the open ocean in the coming storm season. Chaumareys acquiesced,

The Raft of the Medusa (1819), Théodore Géricault

Courtesy of the Louvré Museum, Paris

announcing that the four ships would take the quicker—and infinitely more dangerous—route. The three other ship captains were under orders, and were loyal, but they were not stupid. One by one, they followed the *Medusa* and then peeled off either out of sight or under cover of the darkness. Each headed to open water, and the *Medusa* was left on her own.

Chaumareys's unwise decisions continued. Instead of seeking advice from his second-in-command, an able seaman named Joseph Pierre André Reynaud, he turned to a braggart named M. Richefort, who held no official position on the vessel but was a blowhard fresh from prison who claimed extensive knowledge of the western coast of Africa. Chaumareys, perhaps recognizing a personality much like his own, and one in whom he could expect fealty, declared that Richefort would make navigational calls right up to the Arguin Bank. Alienation of the crew and officers had already begun; now it was irreversible. Richefort only made matters worse, ordering the ship to make dangerous ports of call in untenable conditions. When Richefort was ignored, Chaumareys raged. All that could be done by those with some competence was carry out Richefort's orders with extreme caution. In the words of two officers on board, "We are ignorant of the reasons which induced the commander of the frigate to give his confidence to a man who did not belong to the staff. He was an ex-officer of the marine, who had just left an English prison, where he had been for ten years; he certainly had not acquired there knowledge superior to that of the officers on board, whom this mark of deference could not but offend." All the while, Schmaltz, eager to get on to St. Louis, pressed the captain and Chaumareys for ever more speed, even in cases when caution was proper.

One day, while much of the crew and passengers of the ship crowded on deck to watch a school of leaping dolphins, one of the sailors leaned too far out and fell over. This was the first casualty of the *Medusa*. It wouldn't be her last.

As the *Medusa* neared the presumed location of the Arguin Bank, most of the officers on board pleaded, then angrily demanded, that they steer west. Richefort assured them he knew what he was doing, and Chaumareys was undeterred; in fact, the more that people on board complained and predicted disaster, the more he seemed to enjoy their "ignorance." He had full confidence in Richefort and all the insistent yelling in the world only made him more intractable.

On July 2, 1816, a sounding made early in the morning showed the ocean floor at only 530 feet. Another sounding a few hours later revealed the depth at close to four hundred. The next sounding showed the floor under a hundred feet. Then just six fathoms, or thirty-six feet. Then twenty feet. Then, a few minutes later, a shudder as the *Medusa*'s keel quivered once, twice, a third time. She was stuck.

Panicked crew and passengers swarmed over the decks, some of them setting on Richefort and threatening to throw him to the sharks. But soon everyone realized that the *Medusa* was only stuck; she wasn't sinking. If everyone calmed down and worked in concert, they could get the ship off the bank and afloat once more, this time toward the open sea where they should have been in the first place. They would have to move quickly, however. The *Medusa* was stuck at high tide, and because of the time of year, the high tide would be gradually lower each day for the next few months. If they weren't able to get her off now, their chances would diminish daily.

The crew got at the task. But once again, Chaumareys acted with extreme foolhardiness. Instead of exerting every effort toward freeing the *Medusa*, he ordered only half measures, seeking, no doubt, to minimize any damage to the ship or loss of its valuable cargo. Alexander McKee, author of *Death Raft*

(Scribner's, 1975), speculates that Chaumareys so ordered because taking drastic actions would have "proven his incompetence." Displaying a charade of calm and maintaining that loosing the *Medusa* would be relatively easy would give the appearance that everyone else was overreacting and he could indeed be trusted to keep a cool head amidst all the hysteria. Richefort, however, ceased giving orders and retreated into the shadows. Chaumareys tempered his loyalty to Richefort, but not to his king. When crewmen suggested dumping the *Medusa*'s cannons, weighing close to fifty tons total, Chaumareys wouldn't hear of it; these were property of the state. Dumping them would have probably freed the ship. One officer would later remark of the whole business: "More care should have been used, and all the difficulties would have been conquered; only half measures were adopted, and in all the manoeuvres great want of decision prevailed."

After several days with no movement, a plan was hatched to abandon the ship. Four hundred passengers would have to be ferried to the coast on the *Medusa*'s four boats, plus a massive raft that would be constructed from the ship's timbers. Then the entire group would march to St. Louis. Because of their large number, they could successfully avoid bandit attacks from the natives.

Lists were drawn up by the commanding officers, delineating who would go aboard what vessel. Considering the appalling incompetence to this point, it is not surprising that rumors began to circulate that the higher-ups were simply planning to save themselves and abandon everyone else. Sailors grabbed guns and guarded exit points, waiting for evidence of a quick or surreptitious escape. By the evening of the third day stuck on the reef, many of the sailors had broken into the stores of brandy. One of the passengers would later recall: "The tumult of the inebriated made us forget the roaring of the sea which threatened to engulf us."

By the break of dawn, the *Medusa* was being abandoned—and not in the orderly fashion promised by those in charge.

The best boat available was filled only halfway to capacity, but included Governor Schmaltz, his family, and their luggage. Chaumareys's barge was filled with the fittest sailors available. There was also a pinnace and a dangerously overloaded longboat, which carried almost ninety people, even though it was hardly any bigger than Schmaltz's boat, which carried less than half that number. That left roughly two hundred people for the raft. Anyone who could see soon realized the folly in this; no sooner had fifty people climbed on the raft than it sank to knee depth. After 150 crammed aboard, the water was up to the passengers' waists. Another eighty people were still on board the *Medusa;* naturally, they waited for one of the boats to come get them. It soon became clear this wasn't going to happen. It was, evidently, every man, woman, and child for him or herself. One of the commanding officers claimed he would soon be on the raft to lead, but then disappeared to one of the other boats. One of the passengers left on the raft later posed the rhetorical but exasperated query: "How is it possible that a French sea officer should be guilty of such bad faith to his unhappy countrymen, who placed all their confidence in him?" Even those who were "lucky" enough to take passage in the longboat were shocked by the behavior of those in charge; one passenger remarked: "As this disaster was unfolding, His Excellency the Governor of Senegal, whose sole preoccupation was to save his own skin, was seated in his armchair and carefully transferred to his large life-boat that was already well-stocked with large trunks, all kind of food supplies, his precious friends, his wife and his daughter."

The commander of the longboat, Lieutenant Jean Espiaux, was the first to act admirably. He rowed back to the *Medusa* and loaded up with more people, despite the fact that his boat was terribly overloaded. After he managed to get approximately another sixty people aboard, it was obvious that not one more would fit. Almost twenty people were left behind, either to watch in horror as the pathetic convoy made its way to shore or, more likely, sit belowdecks, too drunk to move. Despite the awkward movements of the heavily laden longboat, Espiaux managed to bring it to the other boats to help offload some passengers. They were refused.

This was coldhearted and unnecessary. However, the passengers in both the governor's barge and the pinnace could at least claim, truthfully, that the raft they were towing was already acting like deadweight, and they could barely make any progress in the water. The solution to this problem, as they saw it, was simple. Members of the pinnace's crew slipped the rope into the water; the governor's barge was left to tow it alone. Realizing this, Governor Schmaltz was quick to act. "Let go of the rope," he commanded.

The frayed coil of their lifeline was tossed into the choppy sea in front of the stunned passengers on the raft.

Joseph Reynaud, the man who Chaumareys had passed over for advice in favor of Richefort, was the one to throw the rope—though, he later declared, under orders from Schmaltz. Worse than this ignominy, to which Reynaud could at least claim that he was simply following orders, was the fact that when pressed for a solution by Chaumareys, he was overheard saying, "We abandon them."

A midshipman on the barge turned to take in the spectacle of the loosed raft and its pathetic cargo. Apparently, there was no protest. According to the midshipman, "We could not see the least movement on board the raft, not even a cry was uttered. They seemed reduced to nothing."

The raft was roughly sixty by twenty feet and carried 150 astonished people.

Initially, the members of the raft assumed a better plan was being hatched and that soon enough one or more of the boats would be back for them. Perhaps they were off in the distance, juggling their passengers to lighten a boat enough to resume the tow. Or maybe they would head to the coast, off-load, and then come back. Surely they hadn't just been left to die on a barely seaworthy raft without mast or sail.

But more and more time passed with nothing. Suddenly, this mass of humanity, crammed on an ill-provisioned raft with nary an inch to move and submerged to their midsections in water, realized their desperate situation. They had only a few casks of wine, water, and flour paste.

The best account of the horrors was given by J. B. Henry Savigny and Alexander Corréard, two officers who survived the raft and subsequently published *Narrative of a Voyage to Senegal in 1816*. According to Corréard and Savigny, "After the disappearance of the boats, the consternation was extreme: all the terrors of thirst and famine arose before our imaginations, and we had besides to contend with a perfidious element, which already covered the half of our bodies." It would only get worse—much worse.

The evening was pitch black. Wind whipped the waves to a great height. The effect was such that each person on the raft, wiped out from a day without food or drink, had to constantly battle the waves that sometimes ran over their heads. Many people were simply swept away and never seen again. Others fell under the waterline in their exhausted state, and failed to get up. Some got their feet trapped in the gaps of the raft and were unable to pull themselves to safety. Because of the darkness and the necessity of each person concentrating wholly upon his own predicament, no one could help anyone else. It was a great paradox: this flailing mass of humanity, all jammed together in such a crowded space, but each member fighting his own isolated battle. By morning, it was estimated that twenty people had perished during the evening.

When dawn greeted them, the survivors didn't cheer for salvation; instead, the grisly prospect of loosing those who had become stuck beneath their feet made their despair even more acute. It was too much for some: "Two young lads, and a baker, did not fear to seek death, by throwing themselves into the sea, after having taken leave of their companions in misfortune. Already the faculties of our men were singularly impaired; some fancied they saw the land; others, vessels which were coming to save us; all announced to us by their cries these fallacious visions." It would get even worse.

The officers managed to build a little mast during the day, which helped somewhat. But the next evening made the previous seem tame. In Corréard and Savigny's words:

> From the violence of the sea, the men passed rapidly from the back to the front of the raft, we were obliged to keep in the centre, the most solid part of the raft; those who could not get there, almost all perished. Before and behind the waves dashed with fury, and carried off the men in spite of all their resistance. At the centre, the crowd was such that some poor men were stifled by the weight of their comrades, who fell upon them every moment; the officers kept themselves at the foot of the little mast, obliged, every instant, to avoid the waves, to call to those who surrounded them to go on the one or the other side, for the waves which came upon us, nearly athwart, gave our raft a position almost perpendicular, so that, in order to counterbalance it, we were obliged to run to that side which was raised up by the sea.

All night they kept this up.

Meanwhile, those on the boats that had fled the raft and the *Medusa* were by no means enjoying a pleasure cruise. Despite the fact that several of the boats weren't crowded (only the longboat was packed), all still had a difficult and dangerous open-sea voyage along the coast toward St. Louis. When land was sighted, debates broke out as to whether they should continue in the water and make for the colony, or whether they should land and walk. Both options had their dangers: the sea could swamp them at any moment, and the marauding bandits ashore could press them into slavery. Soon, the prospect of spending one more moment in the boat became too much to bear. Days saw them scorched by unrelenting sun, and evenings saw them clasping to one another as storms savaged their boat. Charlotte Picard was just eighteen when she sailed on the *Medusa* with her family. She wrote a book eight years later: *The African cottage, or the story of a French family thrown on the western coast of Africa after the frigate Medusa was wrecked.* A portion of the text appeared in Archibald Duncan's *Mariner's Chronicle,* under the name Madame Dard (Picard's married name) and the title, "Shipwreck of the *Medusa*." She wrote of the last evening on the boat: "[My sister] Laura, aged six years, lay dying at the feet of her mother. Her mournful cries so moved the soul of my unfortunate father, that he was on the eve of opening a vein to quench the thirst which consumed his child; but a wise person opposed his design, observing that all the blood in his body would not prolong the life of his infant child one moment." Two-thirds of the members of the longboat decided to go ashore, among them Charlotte Picard and her family, little Laura still alive.

There, they would trade the ravages of the sea for the ravages of the desert— and the possibility of unfriendly Moors. There was a certain irony to this arrival on the coast of a group of French nationals. As Gaspard-Théodore Mollien, one of this group, would write in his book *Découverte des Sources du Sénégal et de la Gambie en 1818* (Discovery of the Sources of the Senegal and the Gambia in 1818): "What pitiful a shape we were upon landing on African soil where we were expected to take over as Masters."

During their long march toward St. Louis, the survivors did in fact meet with large bands of natives, who offered them not servitude, but food and water, though often selling these items at what was described as an "exorbitant cost." There were treaties with the Moors that stipulated that if they should deliver shipwrecked Europeans to the fort at St. Louis, large rewards would await them. The group managed to make it to the colony in under a week.

It was almost impossible to conceive, but the third night on the raft was even worse than the previous two. This time, the raft was beaten by a fierce gale; mountainous waves swamped them and driving rain lashed the pitiful crew. Only the middle of the raft, where the mast and the crowded officers stood, had any semblance of solidity. There was a general and unrelenting crush toward this part of the raft, and those unlucky enough to be on the outside or edges of the raft were picked off one by one by the waves, like tentacles rising out of the sea to drag them to their doom. It was all too much; a group of soldiers, crazed by the circumstances, broke into the wine casks still on board, and drank themselves into oblivion. Soon, the effect of frayed nerves and drink caused a singular change in the men:

> The fumes of the wine soon disordered their brains, already affected by the presence of danger and want of food. Thus inflamed, these men, become deaf to the voice of reason, desired to implicate, in one common destruction, their companions in misfortune; they

openly expressed their intention to rid themselves of the officers, who they said, wished to oppose their design, and then to destroy the raft by cutting the ropes which united the different parts that composed it. A moment after, they were proceeding to put this plan in execution. One of them advanced to the edge of the raft with a boarding-axe, and began to strike the cords: this was the signal for revolt: we advanced in order to stop these madmen: he who was armed with the axe, with which he even threatened an officer, was the first victim: a blow with a sabre put an end to his existence.

Not only did the passengers have to fight the sea, their own dehydration, sleep deprivation, and storms, they now had to fight one another. The officers, armed with sabers, slashed at the wriggling, mutinous mass of drunken sailors. It was a bloodbath, and those who were vanquished were pushed into the sea. And then, suddenly, the fighting stopped. The sailors retreated to the back of the raft and sat down quietly. But it wasn't over. As if some silent signal had been given, the sailors attacked again:

> Thinking that order was restored, we had returned to our post at the center of the raft, only we took the precaution to retain our arms. It was nearly midnight: after an hour's apparent tranquillity, the soldiers rose again: their senses were entirely deranged; they rushed upon us like madmen, with their knives or sabres in their hands. As they were in full possession of their bodily strength, and were also armed, we were forced again to put ourselves on our defence. Their revolt was the more dangerous, as in their delirium they were entirely deaf to the cries of reason. They attacked us; we charged them in our turn, and soon the raft was covered with their dead bodies. Those among our adversaries who had no arms, attempted to tear us with their teeth; several of us were cruelly bitten; Mr. Savigny was himself bitten in the legs and the shoulder; he received also a wound with a knife in his right arm which deprived him, for a long time, of the use of the fourth and little fingers of that hand; many others were wounded; our clothes were pierced in many places by knives and sabres.

By morning, those left on the raft numbered about sixty; half of the crew had been lost.

Not all of them were in the ocean, however. And this fact—while horrifying on the first morning—now presented the survivors with opportunity, as repugnant as they may have found it. One of the midshipman on board, Jean Daniel Coudein, later reported: "Among the unfortunate people spared by death, the most starved ones rushed onto the remnants of one of their brothers, tore flesh off the corpse and fed themselves with this horrible meal." Savigny and Corréard wrote: "But an extreme resource was necessary to preserve our wretched existence. We tremble with horror at being obliged to mention that which we made use of! We feel our pen drop from our hand; a deathlike chill pervades all our limbs; our hair stands erect on our heads!"

By the next morning, a further dozen people died. To this point, many of the officers had refrained from eating their brethren. But when a shoal of flying fish swam through and over the raft, the men on board managed to catch some and mixing fish with human flesh made the ghoulish scavenging more palatable. Now, everyone ate, even the last holdouts.

During this time, of the four boats that had left the *Medusa* and its raft, only two were still afloat: Schmaltz's and Chaumareys's. The other two had broken up and deposited their survivors on shore. More than one hundred people were now on their way toward Senegal, miles through as unforgiving a landscape as one can find on earth.

Back on the raft, another mutiny was afoot, this time spearheaded by the large number of sailors of African descent. Their bodies were responding much better to the elements than their European counterparts. They declared that if they threw off the officers and could make it to the shore, there they would find league and succor with the African natives. Another melee ensued. When it was over, another twenty people had died, leaving only thirty alive. Of these, ten couldn't stand upright, their bodies so ravaged by saltwater that all they could do was sit and crane their necks when waves passed over the raft. The men were now seeing the coming of the fifth day.

Schmaltz's boat had by this time arrived in Senegal. From there, he sent a rescue ship back to retrieve those left on the *Medusa,* and to recover as much of her cargo as possible. Those on the raft had been assumed long dead. Other rescue ships were sent by the British, still technically in charge because an official handover had yet to take place. The English rescue ship recovered the large tattered crew heading along the coast. When they arrived in Senegal, Charlotte Picard noticed that in the large contingent of well-wishers, two figures—Schmaltz and Chaumareys—were absent.

Back on the raft, the survivors were so tormented by schools of jellyfish that they tore off planks from the end of the raft and built a platform in the middle. Unbelievably, another week passed. And still people were alive on the raft. They were at the end of their wine ration; the human flesh was almost gone and unspeakably repellent in any case, as it had been broiled by the sun. On the thirteenth day, the last of the wine was distributed, and the men gave themselves up to death.

Then one of them saw a sail. Shouting, he began to tear off the cask hoops and wave them. Everyone else somehow summoned an impossible reserve of strength and lifted him in the air so he could be spotted. They all shouted and waved. But to no avail. Savigny and Corréard reported: "The brig disappeared. From the delirium of joy, we fell into profound despondency and grief; we envied the fate of those whom we had seen perish at our side." They crawled into a makeshift tent and lay down, waiting for death's relieving grasp. Then it happened: "After we had passed two hours, absorbed in the most cruel reflections, the master gunner of the frigate wishing to go to the front of the raft, went out of our tent; scarcely had he put his head out, when he turned towards us, uttering a loud cry; joy was painted on his countenance, his hands were stretched towards the sea, he scarcely breathed: all that he could say was, 'Saved! See the brig close upon us.'"

The brig *Argus* was sailing for them. When it arrived, the crew must have recoiled from what they saw: fifteen emaciated men (out of the original 150), skin completely gone from their legs, riotous matted beards, feral eyes.

Like a series of sick jokes, their ordeal wasn't over. A fire broke out that night aboard the *Argus* where the survivors were sleeping, and the men barely escaped with their lives. It was all too much for several of the officers, who raved about decks and had to be physically restrained from throwing themselves overboard. Sadly, five of the fifteen survivors died at St. Louis, their bodies incapable of healing. The other ten were afflicted with psychological scars that stayed with them the rest of their lives.

Savigny and Corréard were too wasted, and relieved, to give voice to their indignation when they arrived at St. Louis: "We were received in the most brilliant manner; the governor, several officers, both English and French, came to meet us, and one of the officers in this numerous train, held out to us a hand, which a fortnight before, had, as it were, plunged us in the depth of despair by loosening the tow-rope which made our raft fast to the boat."

Five days later, fifty-eight members of the longboat who had voluntarily cast themselves upon the shore arrived in St. Louis; their march had lasted three weeks and covered 250 miles. Amazingly, only five of the original number had died along the way.

Almost two months later, a ship returned to the wreck of the *Medusa*, after two earlier failed attempts. It couldn't be rightly called a rescue ship, in that its primary purpose was to "rescue" the gold that had been aboard. But to the captain's amazement, he found three men, crazed and barely alive. The other fourteen had died, most of them after leaving the ship. They either drowned attempting to make shore, or they were taken off as slaves after making landfall. The fact that the three men had survived so long attested to a startling fact, taken here from Alexander McKee's *Death Raft* (2000):

> Three men had survived for 52 days aboard the *Medusa* after she had been abandoned as in danger of breaking up. And . . . great prizes in the way of stores and supplies were being taken from her intact hull two months afterwards. Without a doubt, there had been time enough for Schmaltz and De Chaumareys to have everyone aboard ferried ashore in relays by the boats . . . an able and resolute commander would have never abandoned the ship at all, but dispatched the two best boats to St. Louis for help. The raft need never have been used, let alone filled up with men and then cast adrift. There was not the shadow of an excuse for the loss of a single life.

Schmaltz wasn't done with the survivors. He was aware that Savigny had penned a narrative of the horrors, and Schmaltz acted quickly to publicly claim that not only was Savigny libelous, he was the principal figure responsible for the terrors on the raft. The charge of Reynaud exclaiming, "We abandon them," was false. And Savigny was a downright ingrate; after all, it had been the *Argus*, on order of Schmaltz, that had saved his life.

Schmaltz and Reynaud then worked together, collecting signed statements from crazed raft survivors that indeed it was Savigny who was primarily responsible for the melees on the raft, and that the rope connecting the raft to the boat had been severed by waves and currents. Corréard's was one of the few signatures not on Schmaltz's accusatory document. When he recovered from the ordeal, months later, he told of the undue pressures put on those who did sign. Some of them, he alleged, scarcely knew what they were signing. In his words, "Some yielded to the fear of displeasing His Excellency the Governor; others conceived hopes of obtaining his protection which, in the colonies, is no trifling advantage."

When the case went to court in France in 1816–17, Chaumareys was found guilty of five offenses: he failed to positively identify Cape Blanc; the *Medusa* and the *Echo* had split up, which was against regulations; he had altered course against good advice; the raft had been deliberately abandoned; and Captain de Chaumareys was not the last to leave the ship. When the sentence was handed down, Chaumareys's name was struck from the Navy List, he had to return all his orders and decorations, and he received three years in prison.

Many thought the sentence lenient (including one member of the court, who voted for the death penalty). Considering his incompetence, Chaumareys got off rather well; by contrast, the innocent Savigny and Corréard were brought to the brink of ruin by the well-connected machinations of Schmaltz, whose reach extended into the upper echelons of Paris. In Senegal, Corréard was warned by the English Governor, Major Peddie, who told him: "I know mankind, and without pretending exactly to guess how your Minister of Marine will act towards you, nevertheless, I think myself justified in presuming that you will obtain no relief from him; for, remember that a minister, who has committed a fault, never will suffer it to be mentioned to him, nor the persons or things presented to him, that might remind him of his want of ability; therefore, believe me my friend; instead of taking the road to Paris, take that to London." But was a Frenchman, and love of country prevented him from heeding this wise advice.

Corréard and Savigny did the only thing left them: they penned their book and while never explicitly naming their chief malefactor, laid out the case in such a way that there could be no mistaking him. The book was an instant and widespread sensation in France. By 1818, Schmaltz had been recalled to Paris, stripped of his governorship.

Senegal, however, would remain in French hands for another 142 years.

Karluk (1913–14)

One thing the 1913 expedition didn't lack was ambition: if successful, it would constitute the largest scientific mission ever undertaken to the Arctic. One of the goals was to discover a continent that expedition leader Vilhjálmur Stefánsson believed lay beneath the polar ice cap. As Stefánsson wrote, "[It] will close forever the chapter of geographical discovery." For such an expedition, its leader should have taken all pains to provide it a ship that would meet the rigors ahead; instead, Stefánsson bought the *Karluk*, almost thirty years old and retired for a decade. She had originally been a fishing barque, then converted to a whaler. She was ill suited for Arctic exploration; for one thing, she was not fitted with steel plates to break ice. Her main attraction for Stefánsson was that she was, in a word, cheap.

When Stefánsson's first choice of captain, C. Theodore Pederson, got a good look at the *Karluk,* and became acquainted with Stefánsson's slipshod manner of organization, he resigned the post. Stefánsson then tapped Robert Bartlett, a distinguished and decorated ice captain who had been with Robert Peary on his trip to the North Pole. Bartlett arrived at the Esquimalt naval yard in Victoria, British Columbia, looked over the *Karluk,* and dashed off a letter to the deputy minister of the Canadian naval service, claiming that the *Karluk* was "absolutely unsuitable to remain in winter ice." Still, Bartlett was an explorer, to his very bones. He simply couldn't pass up the opportunity. Besides, if anyone was capable of keeping the *Karluk* in open water and out of the ice, it was he. So he reluctantly signed on.

Stefánsson had made a good choice in Bartlett. His expedition's scientific team was also top-notch, an assemblage of the some of world's most respected men of science. But of the large staff, only two of them had any Arctic experience. Worse was the state of the crew, hired more for expediency than experience. Jennifer Niven, author of *The Ice Master,* wrote of the crew: "One . . . only had a pair of canvas trousers to his name before signing on, two of the sailors were traveling under aliases, two men smuggled liquor aboard even though it was forbidden, and the cook . . . was a confirmed drug addict." They were on board mostly because they wanted adventure and the pay that came with it. They were completely unaware of and unsuited for the ravages that lay ahead. None of them had any Arctic experience whatsoever and Stefánsson never offered any training. According to one Canadian government official, the crew had been "picked up along the coast."

Stefánsson's overall attitude was summed up by his own words, from a dispatch sent to the press before the expedition began: "The attainment of the purposes of the expedition is more important than the bringing-back safe of the ship in which it sails. This means that while every reasonable precaution will be taken to safeguard the lives of the party, it is realised both by the backers of the expedition and the members of it, that even the lives of the party are secondary to the accomplishment of the work!" Perhaps, but no one had polled the "members of the expedition" to see if they concurred.

Regardless, the *Karluk* set sail on June 17, 1913. From the first, there were harbingers of disaster. For one thing, the party was leaving later in the season than was very safe. When they left, it was already a week later than originally planned. Considering where they were going, almost as far north as possible, and that summer would be ending in barely two months, that meant thick and impassable ice. The *Karluk* left behind another ship, the *Alaska,* which would

Vihjalmur Stefánsson.

Courtesy of the Bain News Service

form the second half of the expedition's party. Stefánsson also purchased a schooner, the *Mary Sachs,* to ferry supplies. It was an impressive convoy— or at least it would have been had the parties ever reached Herschel Island together, as was originally planned. It was there they would divvy up supplies needed on each ship. In the haste to get going, this wasn't done before the ships set sail from Esquimalt. The eventual result is fairly obvious: equipment needed by the *Karluk*'s men was on another ship. This mix-up wasn't limited to equipment, either. Five of the men aboard the *Karluk* should have been on the *Alaska.* When some of the men aboard the *Karluk* called a meeting to ask about these problems, Stefánsson became indignant. Magnetician William McKinlay's diary of July 10 reads, in part, "Stefánsson seemed to resent our attitude in endeavouring to obtain details as to provisions for food, clothing, facilities for work, etc."

Stefánsson was no fool, however. He was an extremely accomplished Arctic explorer, and he had every reason to feel confident. During his very first Arctic expedition, the ship on which he was sailing sank; he lived for months with the local indigenous people, until he could hunt, fish, and speak just like them. Later, he spent four years in the Arctic, where he discovered a previously unknown tribe of Inuit, the so-called Blond Eskimos, named for their light hair and blue or gray eyes. During this same expedition, he charted previously unexplored land. As a result of his exploits, Stefánsson received numerous geographic medals and honorary degrees from scores of prestigious universities.

But it was precisely this past success that made Stefánsson such a bad expedition leader. The entire enterprise was predicated upon Stefánsson's belief that the Arctic was a "friendly" place, where a man possessing a gun, a sledge, and his wits could survive indefinitely. The *Karluk* disaster would provide a fierce counterpoint to that argument.

Despite the *Karluk*'s obvious deficiencies, Stefánsson's faith was never shaken. By his own admission, the *Karluk* was dangerously overloaded to begin with: "She would never have been allowed to sail had there been at the port of Nome rigid inspectors unwilling to except an exploring vessel from the rules that are supposed to promote the safety of ships at sea." One week into the trip, she had broken down twice.

But spirits on board were still high. After all, the crew had just spent weeks being the toast of Victoria, where government officials and upper-class citizens threw honors and laurels at the men. However, these high spirits masked a real problem on board; the crew and the scientific team were like oil and water, never mixing and not bothering to hide their blatant antagonism toward each other. On the easiest of sea voyages, the cooperation of all onboard is essential. On the *Karluk*, however, there wasn't even any pretense of pulling together as a team. There were even splinters within each group of men. One of the scientists, Bjarne Mamen, at twenty-two the youngest, found many of his colleagues insufferable: "It is disgusting to see such ignorant persons who can do only what they have been trained to do . . . It is maddening to see people who always must have other people do everything for them." Mamen, along with geologist George Malloch and magnetician William McKinlay, occasionally helped do some of the ship's chores, but as a general rule, the crew and the scientists didn't mingle, sleeping, eating, and socializing on opposite ends of the ship.

Five weeks out, the ship crossed the Arctic Circle. It wasn't long before she came up against sea ice thick enough that she couldn't get through. Bartlett turned her south and into waters farther from land, hoping to find sea lanes on the way deeper into the Arctic; Stefánsson tried to persuade Bartlett to head toward shore and take on the thick sea ice. By August 2, she was stuck. The crew had little choice but to wait it out, hoping she would soon be free and able to sail once again. But by the end of the month, it was clear that the *Karluk* was stuck fast and wouldn't be going anywhere that winter. By the third week of September, Stefánsson's impatience overtook him. He assembled the captain and several of the scientists and told them he would be leaving for ten days. He would take food, supplies, the best dogs, his personal secretary, a photographer, one of the scientists, and the Inuit who had signed on to the expedition. Stefánsson's stated destination was an island where they would hunt caribou to refresh the meat supply. It would be the last anyone on the *Karluk* would see of their expedition leader.

Whether Stefánsson ever intended to come back for his ship and crew isn't entirely clear. And in any case, it wouldn't have made much difference; just two days after he left, a blizzard struck with winds so fierce that the pack ice—with the *Karluk* stuck within—drifted dozens of miles into the Arctic. According to Bartlett, "We were stuck so hard and fast in that ice forty feet thick that all the motor trucks in Canada couldn't have pulled us out." But Bartlett suspected that Stefánsson wouldn't be making any attempt for them anyway. The men he chose to bring with him made up a pretty suspect hunting party, especially considering that he left behind expert hunters and marksmen. (Stefánsson would also later acknowledge that he knew that caribou were virtually absent from the location where he'd set off to allegedly hunt them.)

Fireman Fred Maurer wrote, "The ice around us gave no sign of opening up, and there day after day and night after night we lay in helpless imprisonment." But soon enough, this imprisonment, however maddening, would feel benign compared to the violence soon to come. When the ice began breaking up— shifting and moving, breaking and then refreezing—it caused such a change in landscape that the men couldn't help but feel awed, and terrified, by it. McKinlay wrote, "Huge ice-blocks larger than houses were being tossed about like pebbles . . . As we watched this terrifying work of Nature, we noticed that the area of contention was creeping slowly but surely towards us, & we fell to wondering, with a shudder, what would be our lot."

October turned to November and still the men were stuck fast. The buckling ice terrified them. Should it shift in just the right direction, the ship could be crushed. Then, without their home, they faced the prospect of starving or freezing on the ice during the long and brutal Arctic winter. Even during this first week of November, daylight barely extended beyond noon. By the middle of the month, the sun disappeared altogether. The men would have complete darkness for the next seventy-one days. This proved to be a big blow. Ernest Chafe, the assistant steward, wrote, "So long as the sun was with us to measure the night and day, it was not so bad. But when the orb disappeared, a sort of sickening sensation of loneliness came over us." What made it worse, no doubt, was the lack of real and deep friendship among the men.

To prepare for the worst, Bartlett ordered the men to put supplies on the ice next to the ship. Still, the prospect of the ice cracking made things almost intolerable. Bjarne Mamen summed up the general mood when he wrote in his diary, "I have gone to bed lately with a kind of feeling that I shall never wake up again, and when the morning comes and everything is all right, I feel highly surprised to be among the living." Of course, Mamen couldn't conceive of what was to come, for it would get much, much worse.

Stefánsson eventually reached the southern party (the *Mary Sachs* and the *Alaska*), and he told them he had no idea what happened to the *Karluk*—for all he knew, she could be sunk, or simply drifting in the pack ice somewhere. He made sure to mention that the disaster had been Bartlett's fault, for it was the captain who steered her into the open water in the first place.

There were some presumed sightings of the *Karluk*. Informed of this, Stefánsson gave instructions that no relief ships be sent because "the search for a ship placed like the *Karluk* has

The Karluk in the Ice Pack. (1913)
Courtesy of The Frederick A. Cook Society Museum, Baltimore, Maryland

only infinitesimal chances of success and a vessel so sent out would be likely no better situated herself." Publicly, Stefánsson was telling media outlets that he suspected that the *Karluk* and its men were fine, held by floating ice somewhere in the Arctic Ocean. When the loss of the *Karluk* was subsequently reported in newspapers, some editors took shots at Stefánsson, a proper target considering he was the expedition's leader. Stefánsson's response was typical: "Editors presumably . . . were asserting that all the knowledge ever gained in the Arctic was not worth the sacrifice of one young Canadian."

A rare happy time came for the men when Christmas arrived. The day was full of feasting and activities. Bartlett wrote, "Now that they were in the neighborhood of the place where Santa Claus came from they seemed determined to observe the day in a manner worthy of the jolly old saint." They held an Olympiad on the ice and spent the evening drinking, smoking, and singing. It was a rare moment when the men truly enjoyed each other's company. Alas, by the next morning, the ice outside the ship started cracking like cannon booms and the men feared that the crushing of the *Karluk* was imminent. It held, however, throughout the next week. But by the new year, the ship started to give way. However, a fortunate occurrence happened at this time as well: the men spotted land. They conjectured it was Wrangel Island. If they could make it there, they would no longer have to worry about drowning. Still, no matter how close they were, getting to the island wouldn't be easy considering the massive ridges and rafters of broken and shifting ice.

The dissolution of the *Karluk* was finally realized on January 10; when the men heard a loud snap, Bartlett and chief engineer John Munro rushed belowdecks to find that water was pouring in. The port side of the ship had been crushed by ice. Bartlett gave the order to abandon ship. In the bitter cold and total darkness, the men hurried, off-loading everything they could grab from the ship that hadn't already been set out on the ice. But this was no simple task. McKinlay wrote, "In the impenetrable darkness and the blinding snowdrift it was difficult to see where we were putting our feet—in the ocean, on a stable ice-cake, or on a small piece of ice which would tilt and up-end." By four in the morning, all men save Bartlett were off the ship and trying to get some rest, all of them unsure if they would ever see the ship again. Still on board, Bartlett pulled his Victrola phonograph onto the deck and played his beloved records, throwing each onto the fire on the stove when he was done. He sipped tea and ate. For the next ten hours, Bartlett continued to play his records, occasionally strolling the decks as the ship slowly sank beneath him. When it was clear that the *Karluk*'s life could be measured in minutes, Bartlett put on Frederic Chopin's "Funeral March" and climbed the rails, water sloshing now onto the decks. When the rails reached ice level, Bartlett walked off and watched with the other men, all crowded around now in silent contemplation, as the *Karluk* slipped under. McKinlay observed, "A slight puff of steam marked the mounting of the water over the galley fire." Chafe summed up the mood: "As we watched her settle and sink beneath the sea, a feeling of intense loneliness came over us." Bartlett recorded the event this way: "It was at 4 p.m. on January 11, 1914, with the blue Canadian Government ensign at her main-topmast-head, blowing out straight and cutting the water as it disappeared, and the Victrola in the galley sending out the strains of Chopin's "Funeral March," that the *Karluk* sank, going down by the head in thirty-eight fathoms of water. As she took the final plunge, I bared my head and said, '*Adios, Karluk!*' "

It took only until the following morning for the lead into which the *Karluk* had sunk to freeze over. She was completely gone. Despite having been wholly unsuited to her task, the *Karluk* had been home. Bartlett wrote that it was "not unlike losing some good and faithful friend."

The men's homes now consisted of an igloo, a box house, and a tent. And while these structures were well constructed, they were on ice, subject to bone-chilling winds and frequent blizzards, and of course the potential of the ice splitting open right beneath them.

By the end of January, Bartlett decided they couldn't just sit and do nothing at "Shipwreck Camp." He sent a scouting party, led by Bjarne Mamen, to Wrangel Island to set up a camp there. In breaking the trail, the men would lay supplies and form a sort of ferry system, with caches spread along the way until they all could make it to Wrangel. If things went well there, they could begin plotting a course to Siberia—and help. It was a great relief simply to be engaged in something. Even better, the sun returned on the twenty-fifth; true, it was barely a blip on the horizon, but each day it would grow. But it was also during this period that three of the *Karluk*'s scientific crew, already openly critical of Bartlett, decided they would strike out for Wrangel on their own. These were Alistair Mackay, surgeon; Henri Beuchat, anthropologist; and George Malloch, geologist. Edward Leslie, in his introduction to Robert Bartlett's *The Karluk's Last Voyage* (reissued by Cooper Square in 2001), sums up the scientists' attitudes this way: "[They were] sophisticated Europeans who had been with Sir Ernest Shackleton in the Antarctic, did not trust Bartlett because he did not look or act like a leader: he wore a sloppy sweater and baggy pants instead of a uniform and had an affable, deceptively casual manner; to them he seemed nothing more than a Newfoundland fisherman." Most surprising was the choice made by sailor Stanley Morris to join them. Despite the fact that the company had been fractured in spirit, they at least were, to this point, still whole in body. Now, four of them were striking off on their own. Worse, Bjarne Mamen hadn't returned from Wrangel, and he was overdue.

Mamen, in fact, hadn't made it to Wrangel. The landmass the men had seen wasn't Wrangel at all, but Herald Island, a desolate, windswept waste that could never sustain human life. When Mamen headed back to Shipwreck Camp to report the bad news, he left four others in the party—first officer Sandy Anderson, second mate Charles Barker, and sailors John Brady and Ned Golightly—to make their way to Herald to set up camp, awaiting the rest of the men. Unfortunately, like most of the *Karluk*'s crew, this was the first Arctic ice experience any of these men had. It boded poorly.

When Mamen finally returned, reporting terrible conditions, he got some well-deserved rest while Ernest Chafe, assistant steward, and two Inuit, Kuraluk and Kataktovik, readied themselves to head to the island and meet the other party. Their trip was harrowing, and horrible.

Chafe and the two Inuit had to climb one ridge after another. Between the ridges, moving ice opened leads of water, and the men had to be on their guard

The _Karluk_.

Courtesy of Dartmouth College

for fear of falling through. At least once they made a mad scramble to save their petrified dogs from falling in. Their first night out, the men got caught on a small floe of ice, surrounded by open water. They could do nothing but build an igloo and wait for morning when the ice would freeze again and allow them passage. During the night, their floe crashed into another and was severed in half. All they could do was sit out the freezing night, vigilant and terrified. By morning the men realized they were two miles from Herald Island. Chafe took his field glasses and scanned desperately for any sign of the four men left there; he found nothing. It was unlikely they had even made it to Herald, considering the conditions. The best hope was that they proceeded on to Wrangel. Whatever the case, Chafe was not optimistic. "I believe the poor fellows met with the same experience as ourselves," he wrote. "And not being as fortunate as we were to escape, they must have perished in the sea." He and the two Inuit turned around, sure they could go no farther.

On the way back to Shipwreck Camp, Chafe and the others ran into Mackay, Malloch, and Morris, three of the men who had voluntarily split from the rest. They constituted a pitiful group. Morris had accidentally stabbed himself trying to open a tin of pemmican and was suffering from blood poisoning. A mile farther down the trail was Beuchat, suffering badly from hypothermia and frostbite. His blackened hands were swollen into fists and would no longer fit in his gloves. His feet were in a similar case. His face, too, was puffy, and he was semidelirious. Chafe, as he had done with the others, pleaded for Beuchat to return with him to Shipwreck Camp. But like the others, he refused; it was no use. He would be dead soon, he said.

Back at Shipwreck Camp, a new plan was put into effect. The group would break into teams. One team would make a push for Wrangel; another would head first to Herald to look for the missing men and then head on to Wrangel. It was late February when they finally abandoned Shipwreck Camp. The weather was calm and fine and the temperature of minus forty Fahrenheit was certainly bearable without the winds. But the first party, sent toward Wrangel, had met with an enormous ridge they deemed impassable. When the second party, led by Captain Bartlett, met them on the trail heading back toward Shipwreck Camp, he was furious. "Climb the ridge!" he shouted. They had no other choice; there was nothing left for them back at Shipwreck Camp.

But Bartlett softened when he came to the ridge. He had never seen its equal. It was, in fact, a series of ridges, all immense and stretching endlessly east and west, sometimes rising upward of seventy feet. McKinlay wrote, "To look at the ice, one would think it impossible ever to get through it." There was, seemingly, no way around or over it. Bartlett decided that they would build a road right through it. It took the men six days to complete the exhausting task; the distance they covered was three miles (or about the average distance a person can walk in an hour). But at last they were on their way. The rest of the trip certainly wasn't easy, but at last, on March 12, they reached land. The relief was indescribable; no more would they have to worry about plunging through the ice and drowning in the freezing water. Fred Maurer wrote, "We were almost wild with delight . . . No more open leads — no more midnight alarms." The party landed on Icy Spit, on Wrangel's northeast coast. They had managed to haul enough food to last until June. They would then have to rely on their hunting skills to get birds, seals, and maybe even polar bears.

Within the week, Bartlett, with Kataktovik, set out for Siberia to get help. As it was, their destination was over a hundred miles away. But they would add another hundred miles because they planned to scout the nearby islands to search for the missing men. The already fractured group now lost their indomitable leader; without him, the simmering schisms threatened to crack the group into squabbling parties—the last thing any survival situation needs. Bartlett asked McKinlay to do whatever he could to keep the peace in camp.

The camp at Icy Spit was plainly miserable. McKinlay wrote, "We could go out only when it was absolutely necessary, and to spend almost twenty-four hours of every day in cramped quarters, cold and wet and weak, was the ultimate in misery." Worse, several of the men came down with some mystery illness; it left them unable to move due to overwhelming fatigue, and their hands and legs extremely swollen. This illness would come and go, striking men indiscriminately and without easy explanation. Ultimately, too late, the cause would be determined: the mysterious illness had been protein poisoning from the pemmican. Pemmican, a mash of dried meat and fat, had been used as an Arctic staple for years, and to great effect by none other than Admiral Peary. But like almost all of the planning that went into the *Karluk* expedition, there had been no due care to examine beforehand the quality of the pemmican daily. McKinlay later excoriated Stefánsson for failing in this regard: "There is not the slightest hint . . . that he accepted responsibility, as leader, for the deficiency of the pemmican, which was our staple diet, and which led to so much suffering and loss of life."

As the months passed, the able men moved up and down the coast of Wrangel, trying to follow game and establish better hunting spots. They built camps along the southeast coast to their southernmost point at Rodgers Harbour, their best bet for spotting any rescue ships.

Even though Icy Spit was pure hell, the men at Rodgers Harbour fared little better. Bjarne Mamen was afflicted with the mystery illness; geologist George Malloch seemed to have lost his mind, often wandering out into the snow without shoes on, laughing all the while, and urinating on himself during the night; and cook Bob Templeman was quickly losing all his strength trying to care for the other two. Malloch was the first to die, and Mamen was at the end of his tether, tired of suffering any longer. He was buoyed a bit by a visit from McKinlay, who, having hiked more than sixty miles from the other end of Wrangel, almost died in the process. When McKinlay passed through the rafters, he could easily imagine what had happened to the party that abandoned Shipwreck Camp; they "must have been in the center of those immense ridges as the gale piled them higher and higher against the immovable miles of land-locked ice. That area would be like some nightmare storm at sea, in which waves rising to a hundred feet and more would be made of solid ice, crashing and tumbling down in pieces as big as houses."

Mamen wrote in his diary of McKinlay's arrival, "A great joy came to me last night. Mac came down to us . . . It was a great grief to me to tell him about Malloch's death. He was still lying inside and a frightful smell came from him." Mamen, not surprisingly, began to consider his own demise: "I don't know how this will end. Is it death for all of us?" The three men at Rodgers Harbour were in such bad shape now that they decided to rest for a day or two and then make it all the way back to their original camp to heal. But Mamen was too ill; McKinlay decided to make the trip himself, leaving Templeman to look after Mamen.

During the trip back, McKinlay became hopelessly lost and snow-blind. This trip would constitute the worst McKinlay experienced during the entire

Karluk ordeal. More than a half century later, it still affected him: "It was the only time in all my experience, on the ship, in the ice-pack, on the island, that I felt fear . . . Even now, sixty years later, I can recall the sensation exactly; it still makes me feel ill and desperately unhappy." But somehow, he made it through. When he arrived in camp, "The soles of my boots were worn into huge holes. Where the holes were the skin was gone, and my feet were raw and bleeding. No other trip I made compared with this one for sheer torture."

John Munro and Fred Maurer then set out for Rodgers Harbour. When they reached it, they called out for Mamen and Templeman, but only Templeman came, hysterical and with tears streaking his cheeks. Mamen was dead, and time was running out for all of them; it all depended on Bartlett and Kataktovik.

The trip they undertook was dreadful. Bartlett characterized it as a never-ending struggle to get across open lanes of water; often, he had to go one direction while Kataktovik went in another until they found a suitable crossing. This could mean miles of travel just to cover a few hundred yards. At times, they had to simply throw the dogs over a narrow lead, lay the sleds over, and hope they wouldn't plunge into the icy depths. Eventually, they landed on Siberia on April 4, after seventeen days marching through the forbidding terrain. Soon after, they met Siberian natives; Kataktovik hung back, terrified that these Siberians would be hostile to him, the Alaskan. He was convinced he would be killed. Bartlett tried to convince him otherwise. Fortunately, Bartlett was right. The two men received extreme hospitality—warm igloos, food, and drink. They even had their coats brushed free of ice and snow. Bartlett was touched: "Never have I been entertained in a finer spirit of true hospitality and never have I been more thankful for the cordiality of my welcome." After another three weeks, the men made it to East Cape, their destination. It had been a trial; as Bartlett wrote, "We had been thirty-seven days on the march and had actually traveled about seven hundred miles, all but the last part of the way on foot." Now, Bartlett needed to find a way to Alaska, where he could try to arrange for rescue ships. But it would have to wait a few days. Now that he finally allowed his body to rest, the trek caught up to him with a vengeance. He became incredibly ill—swelling and deep fatigue. He could hardly move a finger; by his own reckoning, he had lost between thirty and forty pounds.

By the time Bartlett got to Emma Harbor, his next destination, he had been gone from Shipwreck Camp two months, and he figured it would be two months more before there was any chance of a rescue ship making it to the men—any ship would have to wait until midsummer when the sea ice became passable.

Back on Wrangel Island, the infighting grew. Rumors of inequitable sharing of game, petty thievery, and general distrust increased to dangerous levels. Without Bartlett to lead them, McKinlay wrote, "On our own the misery and desperation of our situation multiplied every weakness, every quirk of personality, every flaw in character, a thousandfold." One day, while alone in the tent, McKinlay caught assistant steward Ernest Chafe and fireman George Breddy helping themselves to McKinlay's soup. They also stole one of the birds that made up McKinlay's tent store.

On the morning of June 25, McKinlay was awakened by the sound of a gun, followed by second engineer Robert Williamson shouting that Breddy had shot himself and was dead, the bullet having entered his right eye. The men took Breddy's body outside and went through his effects; there were several articles that had belonged to McKinlay. Williamson conjectured that Breddy had been cleaning the gun and accidentally shot himself. Of course, it could have been suicide; after all, it had been a full year since the men began this terrible journey. But there was one other possibility, forever unprovable: Williamson, the only other man in the tent with Breddy, had murdered him. Indeed, McKinlay suspected as much, confiding in his diary, "Our suspicions have been raised by Williamson's strange conduct & by other circumstances, that Breddy did not die by his own hand." If nothing else, McKinlay noted, "His right hand was not in such a formation as would hold a revolver." John Hadley, who with McKinlay had buried Breddy's body, wrote in his diary, "I think its nothing but Murder."

Meanwhile, life went on. It had to. June ended; July came and went; August also ended, and with it, any good prospects for rescue. Soon, the winter ice would return and any passage from a rescue ship would be impossible. That would probably spell the end for the surviving crew of the *Karluk*. If they had to pass one more winter, depleted of ammunition and during a season when game would be next to impossible to find anyway, they would probably starve or freeze to death.

Little did the men know, but rescue had already been close. On August 24, the rescue ship *Bear*, with Captain Bartlett aboard, sat just 130 miles offshore of Rodgers Harbour. But with the ship stuck in the thick ice, its engines had been stopped. Ship and crew sat for three days before the *Bear*'s captain declared that they would have to return to Nome for coal. "My feelings at this moment can be easily imagined," Bartlett wrote. "The days that followed were days to try a man's soul. In fact, until the final rescue of the men, I spent such a wretched time as I had never had in my life." But at least Bartlett had succeeded in getting the word out about the desperate situation of his men. The *Bear* wasn't the only rescue ship trying to make its way to them.

September 7 broke like all other days, the men trying to catch fish and lighting their fires. Then they spotted a sail on the horizon. At first, it looked like the little schooner would sail right past them. The men started yelling and firing off ammunition. McKinlay wrote, "Then we saw her lower her sail, and as we watched, hardly able to believe our eyes, a party of men disembarked on the ice and began walking towards the beach. We were saved! Captain Bartlett had got through!"

In fact, Captain Bartlett wasn't on this ship, the *King and Winge.* But the next day, as the *Karluk* survivors were finally heading home, their ship was spoke by the *Bear.* On deck was the familiar figure of Robert Bartlett. He had won through, all right. The reunion on board was bittersweet; informed of the deaths of Breddy, Malloch, and Mamen, all Bartlett could do was sit silently. "It was an especially sad and bitter blow," he remembered. "To learn that three of the men whom I had seen arrive at Wrangell [*sic*] Island had thus reached safety only to die." Of course, these weren't the only deaths. The two parties of men who had separated were also presumed dead. The final tally was grim: of the twenty-five people who had escaped the *Karluk,* eleven died, eight trying to make their way over the ice, two of malnutrition and disease, and one who was shot.

The *Bear* tried to make a sweep of Herald Island to find the four men who had been sent there, but it was no use. The ice wouldn't let them get close enough, and frantic scans with field glasses revealed nothing. Eventually, the ship returned to Esquimalt, where the *Karluk* had begun its journey more than sixteen months earlier. There, and in subsequent years—even during service in the First World War—William McKinlay had time to ruminate over the events. In the end, he summed it up as a "pitiful, tragic failure." He would go on to write:

> Not all the horrors of the Western Front, not the rubble of Arras, nor the hell of Ypres, nor all the mud of Flanders leading to Passchendale, could blot out the memories of that year in the Arctic. The loyalty, the comradeship, the esprit de corps of my fellow officers and of the men it was my privilege to command, enabled us to survive the horrors of the war, and I realized that this was what had been entirely missing up north; it was the lack of real

comradeship that had left all the scars, not the physical rigours and hazards of the ice pack, nor the deprivations on Wrangel Island.

Of the Herald Island party, McKinlay wrote, they were "Four young men with no grand ideas about exploring the Arctic, or finding new land . . . just four sailors trying to follow orders." Ten years later, the four men—Anderson, Barker, Brady, and Golightly—were finally found; Captain Louis Lane and his Arctic party discovered the ghostly remains of their camp. "The beach was strewn with driftwood and a large log lay right in the middle of the camp," Lane wrote. "On the side opposite to the sled we found the remains of the party's tents. The end had collapsed upon the bed, and those in it, for, as we scraped away the snow and carefully pulled the frozen canvas from what was beneath, we found parts of human skeletons; they lay as if the men had died in their sleep." It was probably monoxide poisoning, or perhaps simple exposure. But, amazingly, these men with no Arctic ice experience, had actually made it to Herald when it had been deemed virtually impossible. How sad then, that as they dutifully waited for the others, all their efforts were for naught.

Stefánsson did not return from the expedition; he had been gone almost five years and had been given up for dead. But he had indeed lived his claim of the friendly Arctic, doing just fine and discovering three new islands. When he returned, he was toasted by other famous Arctic explorers and awarded the Hubbard Medal by the National Geographic Society. But as McKinlay pointed out, "No mention was made of the *Karluk*. Not the slightest mention was made of the loss of the eleven men." It would be Bartlett, not Stefánsson, who would receive the most honorable award from the expedition: the Back Grant, from the Royal Geographic Society, awarded for his leadership of the survivors.

The deaths from the *Karluk* expedition had been debated in the newspapers of the day, but a decade after the fact, Stefánsson shot back in his book *The Friendly Arctic* (Macmillan, 1927): "I am one of those who think the fighting of the Great War worthwhile not so much for what was attained as to prevent what has been prevented. But I never could see how any one can extol the sacrifice of a million lives for political progress who condemns the sacrifice of a dozen lives for scientific progress." When William McKinlay read those words, he burned, noting: "We felt not so much like soldiers sacrificing ourselves to a great cause, as lambs left to the slaughter."

One note in Stefánsson's favor, however, is this fact: when he left the expedition, he did discover some of the planet's very last landmasses to be added to world maps. How many lives that was worth is up for conjecture.

In his 1927 biography, *My Life as an Explorer,* (Doubleday, Page & Co) the famed Norwegian Roald Amundsen, first to the South Pole, wrote, "Some adventurous spirits seeking a fresh thrill in the North may be misled by this talk about the 'friendliness' of the Arctic, and will actually attempt to take advantage of this 'friendliness,' and adventure into these regions, equipped only with a gun and some ammunition. If they do, death awaits them."

Despite the deaths of the *Karluk* expedition, Vilhjálmur Stefánsson never abandoned his faith in the idea of a "friendly Arctic." In 1921, he put a party of four white men and an Inuit woman in a camp on Wrangel Island. They were given six months' worth of food, and were expected to live on the island for two years, eventually living off the land, proving Stefánsson's theory that the Arctic provides. By the following year, all the men had died; only the native survived.

McKinlay certainly had little love for Stefánsson, who died in 1962, but he did give him his due: "He was a great Arctic traveler," McKinlay wrote. However, "He created a mythology of *The Friendly Arctic* and a lot of people died because of it." McKinlay's real praise was reserved, instead, for Bob Bartlett: "Honest, fearless, reliable, loyal, everything a man should be."

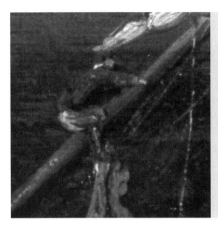

ON FOREIGN SHORES

One of the great fears of European and American sailors was the prospect of being taken alive on a hostile shore. Often, such accounts were dramatically exaggerated, informed more by preconceived notions of savages, beliefs that proved difficult to shake. Some of the more satisfying narratives of sailors in the hands of native "savages" are those in which the shocked seamen are saved and restored by those for whom they had previously reserved special contempt. The 1756 case of the English sloop *Betsy* is one such instance.

Wrecked off the coast of Dutch Guiana, the crew suffered badly until rescued by native Carib Indians. Upon first beholding the sailors, "tears flowed from the [Indians'] eyes." The Caribs dressed the sailors' wounds and cleaned them of vermin, gave them nourishing food, and generally sped their recovery. In Captain Philip Aubin's account of the experience, we can see all his paradoxical feelings at play: "I still recollect the moment when they disappeared from my sight, and the profound regret which filled my heart . . . I love them and will continue to love my dear Caribs as long as I live. I would shed my blood for the first of those benevolent savages that might stand in need of my assistance."

If we know the history of American conquest, aid delivered by friendly natives shouldn't surprise us. But during eras when colonial powers thirsted for justification of their occupations of foreign lands, accounts that related gruesome (if not exaggerated) tales of appalling hardships at the hands of uncivilized natives were, ironically, welcome. And sailors did have stories to tell; it wasn't terribly uncommon for Western seamen to get taken captive, endure extraordinary hardships for years on end, and then live to tell the tale.

The 1805 edition of Archibald Duncan's *Mariner's Chronicle* sums up the prevailing mood best: "Shipwreck is always, even in its mildest form, a calamity that fills the mind with horror; but what is instant death compared to the situation of those who had hunger, thirst and nakedness to contend with, who only escaped the fury of the waves to enter into conflicts with the savages of the forest, or the greater savages of the human race; who were cut off from all civilized society and felt the prolongation of life to be only the lengthened pains of death?"

Degrave (1701)

When *The Mariner's Chronicle* was first published in 1804, the story of the wreck of the East Indiaman *Degrave* was well known. The *Degrave* left England in February 1701 and landed safely at Fort St. George, in the East Indies. From there, an uneventful trip to Bengal followed. But upon the return voyage, the ship ran aground in the Ganges. The accident didn't prevent her from floating off, but it did render the ship a leaky one. For two months, men worked two chain pumps continuously to keep her afloat.

Captain Young (not to be confused with his father, who was captain during the journey from England but had died in India) steered the ship to the Dutch-controlled island of Mauritius. There, the crew rested and attempted—unsuccessfully—to make repairs to the ship. They also took on fifty lascars (as one seaman on the *Degrave* put it: "that is the name which our English seamen call these Moorish people") who could help in manning the pumps. Indeed, when they set off after a month on shore, the pump work proved very necessary. According to Duncan, "This resolution, thus rashly taken, of putting to sea before they had stopped or even discovered the leak proved fatal to them." Only a few days later, the water level rose so much that the pumps had to be kept going continuously just to keep the *Degrave* afloat. They were, at this point, still almost 2,000 miles from home.

The crew was sure they would never make it, and they persuaded the captain to make land at the next possible location. This meant Madagascar. There, they got as close as they could to shore and then threw weight overboard, cut the masts, and constructed vessels to take them the rest of the way. It was a difficult landing, but everyone made it. Behind them, the *Degrave* fell to pieces in the Indian Ocean. The youngest seaman on board was soon horrified by the prospect of the natives—friendly though they were—killing a bullock for the new arrivals to eat: "It was shocking and even terrible to me to see the negroes cut the beast, skin and flesh together, and sometimes the guts too, then toss it into the fire or

Madagascar

Courtesy of Scott McGrew

ashes, as it happened, and eat it half roasted. I did not know but they would devour us so, for they seemed to me like what I had heard related of cannibals. Everything before our eyes appeared horrid and frightful and excited most dismal thoughts and dreadful expectations."

Duncan continued the story from there: "The crew were quickly made prisoners by the king of that part of the island, who carried them fifty miles up into the country, where they found a Captain Drummond and a Captain Stewart [two Scottish captains caught years earlier], with a few of their ship's crew, in the same situation with themselves, and who soon let them into a perfect knowledge of their situation, by assuring them that the king intended to make them serve him in his wars and would never permit them to return to Europe; which intelligence, it may well be imagined, struck them with the utmost consternation."

The three captains, in consultation with their First Mates, decided on a bold plan: they would capture the king, Andriankirindra, and hold him for ransom; their reward would be their freedom. "It is not very easy to conceive a bolder enterprise than this," Duncan stated, "Where between 50 and 60 white people . . . carried off a black prince out of the midst of his capital, and in the sight of some of his subjects, better armed than themselves [the men managed to procure about thirty guns]; who were, notwithstanding, restrained from firing upon them by Captain Young's threatening to kill their king if they did." Incredibly, the plan worked rather easily. The white men not only ensnared the king, but his queen and his son the prince, as well, though the queen was subsequently set free "from a motive of compassion."

The plan was to carry the king and prince to the far end of the island, where passing European ships might be hailed. But the white men, unnerved by the prospect of traversing such a thick and strange land, and trailed also by 2,000 armed subjects of the king, agreed to give up the sovereign in exchange for six guns. The deal was struck, but this did not stop the king's pursuers. Worse, the march across the dusty landscape was terribly difficult. Without anything to drink, the men "to so great an extremity were . . . reduced that we crawled on the ground to lick the dew, and this was all the means we had to moisten our lips." The Europeans now gave up the prince as well, thinking this would stop the march; it did not. So they steeled themselves for a fight. But the natives made another proposition: if the Europeans surrendered their guns, they could have their freedom. It was agreed to do so the following morning. But the two Scottish captains who had been long on the island thought better of it. During the night, they stole away and made for the far shore. Eventually, they did find passage home after a period of two years in which they lived more or less freely. "The rest were cruelly murdered," according to Duncan. "Except for Robert Drury, a boy fifteen or sixteen years old, whom they preserved and made a slave."

In fact, there were five survivors; one of them, John Benbow, lived amongst the natives as a slave for years afterward, eventually escaping aboard a Dutch ship and arriving home in England. There, he wrote a manuscript entitled *A Description of the South Part of the Island of Madagascar*. The book kicked around his family and friends for a few years before it disappeared.

The most extraordinary aspect of Duncan's summary isn't the omission of the other survivors and Benbow's subsequent book; it's the scant attention he gives to the one he names, Robert Drury. As it turned out, Drury would pen a volume about his time on Madagascar that would confound critics for centuries.

Drury's account of the beginning of his servitude reflected the indignity the men felt not only at being treated the way they were, but by "heathens," no less: "it galled us to the quick, to think how we were forced up the country at the pleasure of heathenish negroes, like a flock of sheep, without power to make terms for ourselves like men."

After the events described by Duncan above, Drury was taken as a slave by the Tandroy, people who still inhabit the same part of Madagascar today. It didn't start out well: "We came that evening to a little town, which we no sooner entered, but the women and children came running about me, pinching and striking me with the back of their hands, and showing other signs of derision and contempt." However, things began to look up almost immediately. One of the king's daughters took an interest in the sixteen-year-old Drury. "She sat down over against me," Drury wrote. "And though I had no notion of love, yet I could not help observing a particular softness in her speaking to me; and when she asked . . . of our misfortunes, she showed a great deal of concern and pity, and looked at me with some uncommon pleasure, as people do at pictures which please them."

Despite having a sympathetic person nearby, Drury lived as a Tandroy slave for several years before fleeing toward the western part of the island. There, he was captured and enslaved by the Sakalava. Though still a slave, Drury's prospects improved.

Living with the Sakalava, Drury was made a cowherd. On one occasion, a few of the other cowherds ate one of his charges, a crime in the eyes of the king that was punishable by castration. But he managed to escape punishment on this occasion. On another, he was very lucky again; Drury had been ordered to go steal cattle. He resisted, fearing he would be caught and killed. His master did not take the refusal well: "He turned suddenly, and espying me going off, took up his gun and fired at me; the shot went through the straw cap I had on, and I was so near that the wadding hit my back."

Drury eventually enjoyed an odd place in Sakalava society. He was still forced to fight in clan wars. But in so doing he availed himself well enough to enjoy some of the spoils; he was made a royal butcher, which brought with it a level of leisure he hadn't known since first setting foot on the island, a decade earlier. Of his new job, he wrote: "I had an employment here which maintained me handsomely; and it seemed as if Providence had pleased to appoint it on purpose for my support in this time of scarcity."

He was often required to travel to new villages, where his presence never failed to cause a shock. There had been no precedent for a white slave in these villages. At one particular village, "The people . . . had never seen a white man before, so that I was a very surprising sight to them at first; but they were soon acquainted with me, and I became very serviceable, for whenever they had an ox to kill they were forced to go a great way for one of the royal family. This trouble I now saved them, and lived well myself by it. I was frequently sent for on these occasions, and had always my fee, which was four or five ribs to carry home with me, besides the leg roasted for my entertainment there."

As a representative of a powerful king, Drury himself sometimes had his feet licked when he ventured into towns; feet licking was a sign of high reverence. He even took a native wife, something he felt compelled to defend to his English audience: "Some of my readers will, perhaps, wonder how I could so passionately love a black woman; but let them consider I had been several years in the country, and they were become natural to me. Then she was very handsome, of a middle stature, straight, and exactly shaped, her features regular, and her skin soft, fine, and delicate, as any ladies in Europe."

Drury consistently spoke in terms of "we" when describing the battles in which his master's clans engaged. But despite his acceptance, there were reminders that he was an outsider. During a lead-up to one battle, "My skin appeared white, they thought it might be seen at a distance in the dark, and thereby discover us to our enemies' spies. They, therefore, made me daub myself all over with mud." However, when the battle was over, and Drury had fought well, he retired to a campfire, where he regaled the women with stories: "At night we sat very socially round the fire, while I entertained them with the story of the fight, and my own danger. I also roasted my meat and hung it up in trees out of the reach of wild dogs and foxes. When it was time to go to sleep I told them I had no bed, having forgot my mat in the hurry. They laughed at me for this, so we lay down very close together all night, but very innocently." And thus was Drury's strange and tenuous position: he was a slave, but so long as he worked well and contributed to the fighting, he enjoyed a relatively good life.

But thoughts of home were never too far away. Drury saw an opportunity to flee, but he could not persuade his wife to accompany him. "She was superstitious . . . and afraid I should be hurt . . . so I could not insist upon it any further. But to part with her . . . was a mortifying stroke to me, for I loved her sincerely." He decided to break for freedom anyway: "There was a necessity; my resolution was fixed, and I had no time to lose."

While he was not yet successful in making his way to England, he did receive the mercy of another powerful clansman some sixty miles from his previous home. Here, he enjoyed all the privileges of the upper crust, spending his time hunting and roaming freely. Apart from missing his wife, it was a bit better than the life he had been living. And he was now closer to the western shore, where he had hopes of hailing a Europe-bound ship.

But the hard life of a man without true freedom caught up to him. It wasn't long before he was plotting his escape—not necessarily to freedom, but to live amongst an even friendlier clan. It was well understood in Madagascar that a white man there would stay with whatever master treated him well; as it was explained to Drury, "White men have no home on this island; all places are alike to them, and they will stay with them longest who treat them best, and feed them well." He undertook a difficult journey to reach more western areas of the island and settle there, even closer to the shore. The prospect of a better life sustained him, as did his familiarity with the land. He sang tunes in the native language, as he had virtually forgotten his English. And he was able to hunt and shelter himself with little trouble.

He continued on, week after week, dodging foxes and alligators, and constantly on the lookout for pursuers from his old village. His plan was to fall in with a kind master; failing that, he resolved to live indefinitely in the forest. But on the twenty-sixth day of his journey, he came to a village where the inhabitants had heard of him; indeed, the novelty of a white slave on the island had by this time traveled far. The people in this village were sympathetic to Drury; they lived in similar circumstances. Caught between warring kings, they moved about the coast in a seminomadic existence, spending their time avoiding raiding kings and their machinations. Drury stayed with them only a night and carried on. It was clear that this band could be no help in getting him to a ship.

He soon gave himself up to some benevolent masters, asking for the opportunity to go on a European ship, should one arrive. It was granted, but in the meanwhile—which could be a very long while—the living wouldn't be easy. Internecine battles meant that as he kept his eye out for passing sails, his life would constantly be in danger. He noted, "In this fine country their quarreling with one another and frequent wars do often reduce them to the greatest necessity, in the midst of the greatest plenty almost at their doors; but they are confined sometimes by too powerful an enemy, that they durst not go out of their houses to fetch what the land produces naturally." Worse, he was once upbraided by his master for casually remarking that "If this war continues three or four years, a man will be glad to sell a child for a calabash of honey." The villagers considered that the white man possessed knowledge of future events and was letting slip that indeed they could expect that long period of war. Drury's master then assumed that his desire to catch a ship home was due to the dire circumstances the islanders would have to endure for years. All Drury could do was respectfully protest and apologize. It was also during this period that he was "beset with an ague" that rendered him virtually lifeless for three months. But on some perverse level, these instances increased Drury's standing in the eyes of his master, as Drury related: "I had so many escapes, that he did not think it would be my fate to die in their country, but that I might see England again (repeating his promise to send me thither)."

His master was eventually killed, crushing Drury's spirits, for he had developed a sincere and deep respect for him. Besides, the king's promise to deliver him to a ship died with him. "It was a mortifying stroke to me," Drury recalled. "And I remained inconsolable, not knowing what evil might attend me in this country." Despite the master's death, his men were victorious in battle; when they brought back slaves with them, one was given to Drury himself. He obtained the post of sentry guard, a relatively easy occupation and one that carried with it a level of respect. Drury also remarried. He then met another young British lad named Will Thornbury who had been accidentally left on the island nine years earlier. Drury then got word of a slave ship on the coast and asked if he, like Will, could be sold to the slaver and sent home. It was disallowed; Will had been left here, but Drury had been taken a slave in battle. There was a big difference; he wouldn't be going home just yet. Drury wept, and was "distracted with despair."

But one day, years later, Drury walked again to the seashore and what awaited him was a welcome shock: "Here were two ships, the *Drake* and the *Sarah*. I stared at them as if I had never seen a white man clothed before; and what added to the wildness of my appearance, I was naked except the lamber, my skin swarthy and full of freckles, my hair long and felted together, so that I really made a frightful appearance to them."

One of the Europeans, a Mr. Hill, cleaned him up and presented him with a letter:

"To Robert Drury on the Island of Madagascar," it read:

> "LOUGHBOROUGH, Feb. 27, 1715.
> SON ROBERT DRURY,
> I am informed by one Mr. Thornbury, that he left you in health on the island of Madagascar; which I was glad to hear. My very good friend Mr. Terry hath a friend, commander of a ship, the bearer hereof, that hath promised to do all he can to get you at liberty. I therefore desire you to do the captain all the service that you can in the country. And in so doing you will oblige our good friend Mr. Terry, and your ever loving father till death,
> JOHN DRURY."

After more than fifteen years—half his life—Robert Drury was going home.

In 1705, a London newspaper reported: "A boy lately arrived in a galley from the Indies gives account that the *Degrave*, an East Indian Ship of 800 tun, valued at 100,000, sprung a leak some time since on the coast of Madagascar, where the men landed, with their effects, and also carried their guns on shore, but could get no provisions of the inhabitants, who said 'twas not customary to supply strangers till they delivered up their arms; which they had no sooner done but those barbarous people killed them all but the boy now come over."

Of course, this wasn't entirely accurate. They weren't all killed; but after another decade passed, surely anyone in England would be forgiven for thinking there had been no survivors. But when Robert Drury showed up in London in September 1717, he had an incredible story to tell: clan wars, slavery, and life on a strange and exotic island.

Another decade passed before Drury wrote his story. The account, *Madagascar, or Robert Drury's Journal, during fifteen years' captivity on that Island,* was published in 1729, and it caused a sensation. Virtually nothing was known of the exotic world of Madagascar, and in an era preceding the big boom in British colonial expansion, there was no shortage of interest in foreign worlds. Adding to the titillating nature of the account, readers were invited to meet with the author himself, who virtually took up residence in a London coffeehouse and gladly told of his travails and adventures on the great island off the southeast coast of Africa.

Despite carrying prefatory notes from authorities claiming the legitimacy of the book, *Drury's Journal* would eventually meet with much skepticism. For one thing, Drury didn't possess the literacy skills needed to write the book; indeed, he had never even received a formal education. There is one intriguing explanation for this, however. Early editions of the book acknowledged authorial assistance that put the text "in a more agreeable method," though it didn't name the source. By the 1800s, some doubts were spread about the authenticity of *Drury's Journal.* Several scholars made the claim that Drury wasn't even a real person; his book was written by none other than Daniel Defoe.

Such a claim certainly wasn't far-fetched. After all, one of Defoe's most popular works was *Robinson Crusoe,* a highly fictionalized version of the story of Alexander Selkirk (see Part 5, Extraordinary Survival). And Defoe was the author of many other works that drew upon the real-life drama of the high seas and piracy but were embellished to resemble little of the original source story. The belief in Defoe's authorship grew over the decades. In fact, an 1890 edition of *Drury's Journal,* published by W. Meadows in London, actually lists Defoe as the author. And thus the book was widely considered Defoe's fictional account. By the middle of the 20th century, even historian John R. Moore, a trusted source on Defoe, repeated and asserted the claim with great conviction.

But in the mid-1990's, Mike Parker Pearson, an archaeologist at Sheffield University, turned to *Robert Drury's Journal* for some historical background for his research on burial customs in Madagascar. What he found there gives great credence to Drury's story. Place names, customs, and even locations of sacred villages were all there in his book, and this was information no other outsider knew. Only one other Westerner, the Frenchman Étienne de Flacourt, had previously written anything about Madagascar that had been disseminated. And while there was some similarity between the two texts, Drury's account contained information that didn't appear in Flacourt's. For example, Drury's book includes lexicographic terms for activities specific to southern Madagascar. Also, Drury recounts how he used to lick the feet of his master. While this is no longer practiced in Madagascar, there is a figure of speech for feet licking that survives even today.

It is feasible that Defoe was involved after all. The unnamed editor who made the story in a "more agreeable method" may very well have been that famous author. Nevertheless, it is clear that Drury's incredible story was no fiction.

Robert Drury was a man of his era. An irony of his story is that after spending considerable time in his narrative extolling the moral virtues of the natives—even claiming their moral superiority to the white men of Europe—he spent much of his later life trying to return to Madagascar aboard a slaver, determined to make a fortune on the trade in humans. He never managed it, however.

Moral ambiguities aside, what cannot be denied is that Drury's story—*his* story, not Defoe's—is one of the more remarkable to come down through the centuries.

Grosvenor (1782)

The Mariner's Chronicle begins its account of the wreck of the East Indiaman *Grosvenor* this way: "In the melancholy catalogue of human woes, few things appear more eminently disastrous than the general fate of the *Grosvenor's* crew."

Indeed, when Alexander Dalrymple, hydrographer for the East India Company, met four surviving *Grosvenor* sailors in London, what he wrote would resonate through the entire seafaring world for years to come. Published in 1783, Dalrymple's *An Account of the Loss of the Grosvenor Indiaman* presented such a sympathetic portrait of the wretched sailors that the Admiralty was persuaded to send a rescue ship to the far southern shores of Africa, an unprecedented move. It was possible that there were still *Grosvenor* survivors there, long after the ship had gone down.

The previous year, the *Grosvenor*, laden with jewels and treasure, was on its way home from the pestilent shores of the far-flung Indian colony, captained by John Coxon. From Madras, the *Grosvenor* made a call at Trincomalee, on today's Sri Lanka. From there, the route back home to England took the *Grosvenor* through the Outer Passage, passing the Maldives and eventually swinging south of Madagascar, to sweep around the southern coast of Africa, where the Indian and Atlantic oceans meet; the ship left Trincomalee on June 13, 1782. The *Grosvenor* had a crew of 105, plus thirty-five passengers.

The *Grosvenor* sped on; to the consternation of some on board, strange pinpoints of light dotted the near horizon. Much discussion ensued as to what these lights were, and the general consensus was that they were "lights in the air, something similar to the Northern Lights." But they soon disappeared and so no more discussion of them followed.

But the lights then reappeared. The men would later realize that the lights were fires created by natives burning grasses, and the reason for their momentary disappearance was hills temporarily blotting them out. The renewed visions caused a stir. Men on watch argued the dangers. Captain Coxon came on board, declared the ship to be some three hundred miles from land, and told the crew to steer the ship westward—toward land, much nearer than anyone suspected.

But as the hours crawled toward dawn, more and more men declared they could see land. Others, including the captain, dismissed the idea outright, declaring that the mushy outlines on the horizon were merely storm clouds. But one man was undeterred. Quartermaster William Mixon ran to his superior, Third Mate Thomas Beale, and informed him that several men said that land was very near. Beale dismissed him without even bothering to look for himself. According to one of the witnesses to this exchange, "Mr. Beale only laughed at their want of knowledge, and gave not the least credit to their conjuecture." Mixon, now breaking rank, bypassed his superior Beale, and roused the captain himself.

African Hospitality, an aboltionist view of the wreck of the *Grosvenor*.
(1791) John Raphael Smith.

Coxon was decisive. Veer ship, he yelled. But it was too late; land now dimly in view in the breaking day, the *Grosvenor* crashed against a rock and shuddered violently. "Nothing but confusion and dismay prevailed," wrote seaman William Habberly. "[People] running distractedly about the vessel imploring the Almighty to deliver them." It was a desperate situation, indeed. A storm produced pounding rain and thick darkness. Crashing waves swept over the distressed group on the ship. They could make out land, but it was a jumble of precipitous and jagged rocks. Any kind of landing was thought impossible.

But when daylight arrived fully and the men could take stock of their situation, it was agreed that they would probably be able to get the ship off the rocks. They set about cutting masts and changing sails. As the wind was blowing from shore, soon the *Grosvenor* was off the rocks and blowing away from land. However, as the ship changed directions, the stern snagged upon the rocks, creating a breach that caused the *Grosvenor* to begin filling with water. They were barely one hundred yards from shore, but their only chance at survival was finding a way across the violent space where the ocean crashed mightily against the rocks. The obvious next step was to lower the yawl. But the very moment it hit the water, the current carried it and smashed it into the rocks, turning it into pathetic splinters. Two Italian sailors, spurred by the promise of great financial award from the wealthier passengers on board, dove in. After fierce battles with the surf, one of them made his way to shore, holding a rope connected to the ship. The other sailor was dashed against the rocks and never seen again. With someone now ashore, there was hope. The Italian wrapped the rope around a rock. Crewmen attached a hawser to the rope, providing a lifeline, albeit one that could easily lead to death.

The first man to use the hawser made it safely, but the device then became entangled in the rocks and was damaged. It was still attached to the rope, however, and several more crewmen tried their luck. Most were unsuccessful, the hawser having dipped so low that waves broke over it, sending the men into the sea and to their deaths. Some on board, seeing this, broke into the stores and drank themselves into such stupors that they quickly drowned inside the flooded ship. Others constructed a raft, and five men boarded. This flimsy vessel was also smashed against the rocks, dooming four of the men. Those still left on board, numbering more than one hundred, watched in horror and waited for death. The *Grosvenor* looked to be complying, splintering and cracking and rolling over in large chunks into the frothy ocean. One by one, several of those remaining tested the hawser. Some made it, with great help from those already on shore; others did not.

What happened next was extraordinary. The stern, where the remaining eighty or so people had congregated, suddenly split in two. Virtually every passenger managed to scramble onto the starboard deck, which was still afloat. At the same moment, the wind shifted and pushed this portion of the *Grosvenor* toward shore. Still connected by the rope that held the hawser, those on shore began tugging. Soon everyone on board the starboard deck was delivered to waiting and helping hands. Not only that, but other *Grosvenor* passengers and crew who hadn't been aboard the deck began washing ashore, clinging to other sections of the ship.

By full daylight, the crew and passengers on shore took stock: incredibly, 123 made it alive; fifteen were lost and numerous others suffered injuries, ranging from minor to serious.

The able survivors recovered whatever had floated ashore and could be of use: barrels, canvas, iron or other metals. What they didn't have was weapons, and they would soon feel the very real need for them. More accurately, the weapons they did have—small firearms—were useless without gunpowder. When a band of natives on shore came to scavenge, they had a different take. They grabbed the guns and smashed them against rocks, collecting the pieces of metal. Meeting no resistance, some of the natives entered the makeshift tents, where the horrified women had been placed, and helped themselves to whatever was there.

One can only imagine the women's revulsion; this was the latter part of the eighteenth century and the English ideals of civilized behavior and propriety would find their match in the unembarrassed nakedness of the natives standing now before the passengers and crew. They were very dark-skinned, "almost black in color," and had strange hairstyles, pushed up as they were into towering conical shapes. One of the foremastmen, John Hynes, described the natives as "woolly-headed and quite black." Over their subsequent travels across the southern coast of Africa, they would meet with more strange sights: natives painted with copper-red mud, and other natives sporting ostrich feathers.

Many of the crew wanted to protest this taking of their possessions, but Captain Coxon convinced them that being passive was the best bet; otherwise, the men would invite trouble from the natives, armed as they were with spears. Besides, if it was clear that the Europeans meant no harm, perhaps the natives would supply them with aid. The men agreed, but not without grumbling. Several of them found liquor and drank; they were becoming rowdy and disorderly. Technically, because they were no longer on the ship, Coxon had no authority. If the men followed his orders, they did so voluntarily. They had no fear of penalty if they chose otherwise.

But follow him they did; Coxon gave a rousing speech, assuring the men that if they left right away they could make a Dutch or Portuguese settlement—and safety—in sixteen days. Further, they were duty-bound by morality to take everyone with them, and to walk as one single force. Those injured should not be left to wild animals or natives. The men were convinced, and moved. They would set out together. It was an auspicious beginning, but one that constituted the first great mistake of the party: hydrographer Dalrymple later described their decision as a "resolution which involved them in complicated misery." Instead, they "might easily have built a vessel capable of containing them all." In this, they could have hugged the coast until reaching a Dutch settlement. But as Dalrymple pointed out, "Distress . . . sometimes deprives men of all presence of mind."

Dalrymple gives a good accounting of the natives, in this case the Caffres (Kaffirs). He calls them a "humane and inoffensive people." But there must be some accounting for their cruel behavior in stripping the Europeans of their possessions and offering nothing in return. The Englishman pins it on the Dutch; referencing the recent Kaffir War, Dalrymple reminds his readers that the Kaffirs had been "treated with unparalleled cruelty and oppression" by the

Dutch. Seeing the white men marching along the fringes of their land, it is no surprise then that the natives weren't very hospitable.

The *Grosvenor* survivors moved in three close clusters: stout seamen leading the way; followed by the women (one heavily pregnant), children, and sick; and then the captain and other officers. It wasn't long before all of them came to realize the terrible geophysical truth of this portion of South Africa: this was no easy stroll along the beach. In fact, had they known what awaited them, they would have undoubtedly turned back to the wreck site. What stood between them and the nearest settlement was in fact 400 miles of land, pocked with rivers, waterfalls, and desert. Add to this wild animals and hostile tribes, and the groups as currently constituted stood little chance. Not long after leaving the wreck site, they came to Waterfall Bluff, a cliff three miles long and two hundred feet high, with water falling so forcefully that passing under it meant certain death. Instead, they would have to scale the heights and go around. They did get to the top, but there were faced with more formidable barriers. It was also there that they received their first warning. A Malay man, probably an escapee from a Dutch settlement, told Captain Coxon that the trip he was undertaking was impossible: antagonistic natives, raging rivers, wild animals, barren deserts—there was simply no way they could make it.

Nevertheless, they pushed on. And it wasn't long before the first of the Malay's warnings came true: coastal tribesmen, the Pondo, set on the *Grosvenor* survivors. Though they didn't do any bodily harm, they did strip the Europeans of most of their possessions, leaving them only with scant provisions and the tattered remains of the clothing on their backs. The scene must have been horrifying for the sheltered Europeans; seaman Habberly described "a great number of natives who began throwing stones at us and, holding their lances in a threatening manner, seemed desirous of preventing us proceeding." But they did manage on without any serious injury.

One week from the wreck day, the provisions ran out. The healthiest of the sailors, frustrated by the slow pace caused by the sick and injured, declared that they would break off from the rest. Discipline had broken down, and this never boded well for shipwreck survivors. Second mate William Shaw led the separating crew, almost fifty men. Habberly noted that everyone leaving did so "according to their strength . . . Every person was desirous of making the best of their way, saying it was of little use to stay and perish with those they could not give any assistance to. By this we were completely separated, and never after together again."

Years later, it would come to light in survivors' accounts that Coxon, too, eventually abandoned his passengers, including the women, the children, and the infirm. Only repeated promises from the wealthy passengers of great financial rewards could persuade any of the officers to stay. Eventually, Coxon, the officers, and virtually everyone else in this original group perished. One of the few survivors, an Indian maid, reported having later seen Coxon's jacket on one of the natives.

Of those who continued on, a further splintering soon took place. As Shaw's group moved along the coast, a major disagreement broke out as to the best possible route: one side argued inland, where they could maybe gain sustenance from friendly natives; the others argued that they should stick to the coast, where at least they knew they could obtain shellfish. They split: twenty-one inland, twenty-three along the sea. This was now the splintering of the initial separation; once this pattern had been established and accepted, it was inevitable that it would continue. And continue it did. Every time several members of a group lagged behind due to illness, fatigue, or injury, the others simply left them. In Dalrymple's narrative, it is consistently the case that those left behind were "never seen afterwards."

After weeks of hard travel, two factions did in fact meet again, the one overtaking the other and becoming shocked by the state the first group was in. Despite the desperate appearances, the second group didn't offer aid to the first. This would be the theme that would define the aftermath of the wreck of the *Grosvenor*. In Dalrymple's words, "The reflection of their forlorn condition did not rouse them to a sense of the good effects of unanimity, which alone, had it been either a permanent principle or enforced by an authority to which they ought to have submitted, might have saved them many distresses, and would have tended the preservation of numbers." In fact, the very opposite belief and principle was applied—to disastrous results.

At this point in the drama, it is accurate to say that this portion of the southern African coast was dotted with small bands of *Grosvenor* survivors, each making its way toward the Dutch settlements at Algoa Bay, one group often meeting with or overtaking another, and then splitting yet again. William Habberly's journal reflects the sad state of affairs of the desperate passengers originally left behind: "Mrs. Logie's servant informed us that she had remained with Mrs. Logie about five days after the captain, purser, surgeon, third mate and others had left them, which was the same day that the party I was with had done, that Mr. Logie was almost dead when she quitted him, then in company with Mr. and Mrs. Hosea and a few others, that Colonel and Mrs. James had retired from them the next day after the captain did so, likewise that she and the other girl had deserted their mistress with an intention of joining the Lascars, that she had passed Colonel and Mrs. James, and that the colonel was unable to move without assistance." One by one, people began to lie down, declaring they could go no farther. And in each case, the rest moved on.

They came to great rivers, and there some would quit, saying they simply couldn't make it. Others would try to swim for it, often drowning in the swift currents. And others would travel inland, looking for a way across. Those who did make it invariably met with the next imposing obstacle awaiting them: thick, impenetrable forests, great deserts, animals, or hostile natives.

Shaw was the oldest and most senior in rank of his breakaway group. But, on September 18, six weeks after the wreck, Shaw died. William Habberly, who considered Shaw "a father and a friend," was particularly crushed. Shaw's death had another effect on Habberly; it thrust him into the position of leader. It was one he wouldn't have asked for, considering the still desperate situation facing the men. At this point, the original party, which had been twenty-one men, was down to nine. Those remaining, despite earlier scrapes with natives, desperately wanted to come across a band of them, as this would be their only hope. But the previous three weeks of travel had yielded not one encounter.

Then, in the Kei River region, they did finally come across natives. In each case, they appeared initially friendly, offering milk, but seeing that the Europeans had nothing to trade, refused to give any and instead ran them off. This setback was too much for three of the nine, who died "through great weariness."

It was now mid-October, and those remaining were twice attacked by Xhosa warriors, who beat them with sticks and rocks. They barely escaped with their lives. They soon after found a dead dog and ate it, but this wasn't enough for another of the band, who died soon after. Yet another drowned trying to cross the Keiskamma River. Another survivor, set on by more Xhosa, was thrown into the river and pelted with stones. One stone hit him in the head and he drowned. There were now only two left, Habberly and merchant George Taylor. The two men fled the warriors, but Taylor was captured and beaten mercilessly. He managed to survive, but while Habberly nursed him through the next evening, Taylor slowly slipped away. His death was the cruelest blow yet to Habberly: "Not a night since the ship was lost could equal this," he wrote. "Grief overpowering me, I laid myself down."

It was exactly three months to the day that the *Grosvenor* had gone down, and William Habberly was alone. He was by now also completely stricken with scurvy. His skin was black and his frame skeletal. He managed on for another five days, scarcely able to move. When he spotted a kraal, he went to it;

whatever awaited him would be a welcome relief. Indeed, if it was death at the hands of Xhosa warriors, "then my sufferings would be over."

When he presented himself, the women there ran off in terror at the sight of him. One of the alarmed women dropped the baby she was holding. Seeing his chance, Habberly cradled the baby to himself and then gently placed the child in his mother's arms. This did the trick; soon, he was offered meat and milk. Days went by, spent in luxury compared with the privations he had suffered. Once his strength was restored, he was anxious to keep going, but the village chief made it clear that he was still a very long way from white people; he would never make it. But he set off anyway, carrying with him a supply of meat. To his great astonishment, he met other *Grosvenor* survivors at successive kraals. Each had managed to ingratiate himself to the villagers, either by working for them or by providing medical attention to the sick.

No matter how well each man was getting on, he never ceased his dreaming of home. By mid-December, the *Grosvenor* crew ingrained at the kraals and now numbering four, made plans to resume the march. One man, an Irish seaman named Thomas Lewis, couldn't be persuaded to leave. He decided that the life of a coastal tribesman was an extravagance compared to the grind of the sea and hard work back in the industrial north. Besides, he warned, it was preferable to die where they were than "chance traveling the beach again." He managed to persuade Habberly to stay as well, but two others, Italians living at a nearby kraal, set out. One returned weeks later, barely alive and having witnessed his friend's death from want. This confirmed Lewis's assessment of their chances. Habberly was stuck. But soon, three black men dressed like Dutchmen arrived in the kraal and persuaded him to come with them toward the beach. When he did, he was astonished to see a large group of men on horseback, trailing cattle and wagons. When he came close enough, he recognized among the men two of his old shipmates, seamen Jeremiah Evans and Francisco di Lasso.

Evans and Lasso had been part of the group led by carpenter Thomas Page that had split months earlier at the beach. Page's group, staying near shore, managed to subsist on mollusks. But malnutrition took its toll on this band as well, and they began to die one by one. Those remaining acted much like the other groups had: they formed smaller bands, peeled off again, and then dissolved once more. A contemporary writer commented, "I cannot help lamenting that persons in so perilous a situation as these poor shipwrecked wanderers, should be wanting in that unanimity which alone would ensure their preservation." Of that original group of twenty-one, only six survived. These men—Evans, seaman John Hynes, Lasso, landsman Barney Leary, servant and teenager Robert Price, and seaman John Warmington—had made it to the Dutch settlement at Swellendam.

Their arrival was a miracle: "In vain shall we attempt to describe the sensations of the shipwrecked wanderers," wrote Dalrymple. "The joy that instantly filled every bosom produced effects as various as extraordinary; one man laughed, another wept, and a third danced with transport." They had survived 117 days since the wreck. Their arrival stoked the pity of the magistrate, who beseeched the governor for aid. "Their condition is so pitiable that I trust that I may speedily receive orders from Your Honour," he wrote, "To save those unfortunate people from their wretched plight, or to use any other means that may meet with Your Honor's approval to rescue these unhappy people," a reference to those *Grosvenor* crew who were still out there and, presumably, still alive.

The Dutch response found form in the party that Habberly ran into. The total number of survivors now reached seven, not counting the two left behind at their kraals. The Dutch rescue mission carried on. Soon, they ran into ten more survivors: eight lascars (East Indian sailors) and two Indian maids, attendants from Calcutta who were the maids of one of the ladies on board. It brought the final count of survivors to fewer than twenty out of the original 140. Sadly, one of the maids and five of the lascars subsequently drowned when their homeward ship sank. Of the original number, 106 died while on the African shore and only thirteen ever made it back home alive.

Captain Edward Riou, part of an ineffectual rescue attempt launched years after the *Grosvenor* went down, offered his assessment: "What we have most to regret is that, perhaps, the failure of the endeavors of the unfortunate crew to save their lives was owing to their own misconduct . . . It is to be hoped then, that the fatal consequences attending disorderly conduct on these calamitous occasions will impress on the minds of seamen this incontrovertible truth, that their only hope of safety must depend upon obedience."

Of course, the obedience he refers to means to the captain. But Coxon's assessment of his ship's proximity to land was so far off that it caused the wreck in the first place. Then, his approximation of the distance to a settlement was wrong by hundreds of miles as well. The most prudent course would have been to stay at the wreck site. The natives, understandably feared by the Europeans, were in fact friendly. Some accounts even have it that the natives assisted in the original rescue efforts. The only truly hostile tribes the Europeans encountered were those freshly treated with "unparalleled cruelty and oppression" by the Dutch. But the fascinating story of the natives and their part in the tragic saga of the *Grosvenor* doesn't end there.

Even today, the *Grosvenor* wreck site attracts interest because the vast treasure on board was never recovered. But perhaps an even more extraordinary legacy of the *Grosvenor* wreck is the rumored fate of several of the women. In 1905, more than 120 years after the wreck, author Kathleen Blechnyden published *Calcutta: Past and Present;* within is the startling claim: "During the Kaffir war of 1835, a curious incident partly raised the veil of doubt and mystery which enwrapped the fate of the lost lady passengers [the women in Coxon's original group]. A tribe of native warriors offered their services as 'brothers' to the English against their own countrymen, the Kaffirs, saying that their tribe, which numbered six hundred souls, were descendants of the English ladies who had been wrecked in the *Grosvenor*." Blechnyden continued: "Again and yet again came strange rumours of English women being seen in Kaffir *kraals*, dressed in Kaffir fashion, and refusing to leave their savage surroundings, on the pleas that they had become contented mothers of families, and were no longer willing or able to return to their old lives."

Indeed, others familiar with the area confirmed the steady stories of white women living with the natives, either as unwilling concubines or living in positions of high distinction but under impress nonetheless. Almost a decade after the wreck, a Dutchman stood witness to a "kraal of Christian bastards descended from people from a ship wrecked there."

There had been five children in the original group of survivors, none of whom Habberly (or the servant who relayed the information to him about Coxon's crew of women and children) mentioned. It might have been simple propriety that accounts for this omission. Surely no one back home in England would have liked to dwell too long on the death of small children, or the women who had been "cruelly reserved" for the pleasures of the native men. But one of these children was a newborn. It doesn't strain credulity to suggest that the mother went with friendly natives to save the life of her child. Once there, there could really be no way out. Assimilation would follow, and her English child would grow up an African.

Commerce (1815)

The proposed plan and route were fairly straightforward. The *Commerce*, captained by James Riley, would leave Middletown, Connecticut, early May 1815, head to New Orleans to off-load hay and bricks, cross the Atlantic to Gibraltar, and then land at the Cape Verde Islands to load up on salt to bring back to Connecticut. The crew of eleven men could reasonably expect to be back home by November.

Things began well, the *Commerce* making fast progress down the eastern seaboard. But the hazards of the Bahamas—shallow water riddled with coral— marked the first alarm of the journey. The *Commerce* scraped against coral several times, and when Riley ordered anchor dropped, he realized that the ship was sitting in only fifteen feet of water. But by the next morning, the *Commerce* was off again, heading to New Orleans through the Bahama Channel south of the Florida Keys. The first potential crisis had been avoided.

In New Orleans, the crew off-loaded the bricks and hay and took on tobacco and flour for Gibraltar. Two of the ship's crewmen left in New Orleans and were replaced. Riley turned his ship, and the *Commerce* set off toward Africa on June 24. What followed would resonate in American popular culture for years, gripping some of the most influential men in the history of the republic.

The *Commerce* had no trouble across the ocean and arrived at Gibraltar in just six weeks. There, the acting U.S. consul persuaded Riley to bring aboard an old sailor, Antonio Michel, who had been wrecked at the Canary Islands. With his crew now set, Riley turned south for the Cape Verdes, leaving Gibraltar on August 23. Riley's plan was to steer clear of the forbidding African coast, replete with marauding bandits and slaveholding Arab tribes. Instead, he would head west and through the Canaries on the way to the Cape Verdes.

But on the way, and without Riley's knowledge, the *Commerce* was sucked into the Canary Current, a fast-flowing sweep of water that funnels everything southward, toward the African coast. Riley sensed something amiss. He doubted they could have passed Tenerife, with mountains higher than 12,000 feet. But, he figured, the pitch blackness and thick fog that had dogged their trip meant that they must have sailed right past it, and, in fact, were where he thought they were: south of the Canaries. A terrible jolt to the ship in the middle of the night told him otherwise. Dropping their largest anchor proved

From *An Authentic Narrative of the Loss of the American Brig* Commerce. (1818) James Riley

Courtesy of the George Peabody Library, Johns Hopkins University

useless. The ocean waves pounded the ship and continually smashed it against the rocks that seemed to have appeared from nowhere. The ship eventually became wedged. Riley ordered the men to prepare provisions and the two boats on board, readying them for delivery into the pounding surf.

As the slight moonlight allowed, Riley determined that they were not far from shore and ordered the boats filled and lowered. The first, with two crewmen aboard, was immediately taken by the sea, which washed the men out. They fought the surf until they were thrown onto a beach, half drowned but alive. The other men on board set up a hawser and made their way to shore, one by one, each battling the waves that ran over his head as he shimmied to safety. They all made it, but this was a terrible place to be shipwrecked. Once the natives got wind of their presence, the crew's possessions would become fair game. But that was the least of what they faced; they would probably either be taken as slaves or killed.

Realizing their worst fears, the men weren't even on shore a day before they met a native—and he lived up, or down, to all their expectations. His hair and beard were matted and wild; he looked absolutely feral. One of the seamen, Archibald Robbins, called him "a slander upon our species." Riley, remarkably free of the prejudices that ruled the age, nonetheless compared the man to an orangutan. Riley "could not but imagine that those well set teeth were sharpened for the purpose of devouring flesh!" Riley had instructed the men to restrain from any violence, figuring that doing otherwise would be their death sentence. His hope was that the natives would take their possessions and then leave them, satisfied. This native did just that, and then left peaceably. But none of the crew of the *Commerce* dared to think that would be their lone encounter.

Indeed, by the next day, the man was back—this time with more of his people. Again Riley restrained his men, and the natives helped themselves to whatever had washed on shore. But after taking almost everything that had once belonged on the ship, the natives offered the *Commerce* crew a fire. Riley's plan thus far proved the wisest course. The men eventually lay down to sleep, but Riley's mind spun: "I knew I was on a barren and inhospitable coast; a tempestuous ocean lay before me . . . no vessel or boat sufficient for our escape . . . behind us were savage beings, human form indeed, but in its most terrific appearance." Though no violence had yet come, Riley knew better than to hope the harmony would last.

By the next day, after the men had built a crude camp and set about repairing their damaged longboat, the natives returned, and this time they seemed intent on aggression. One of them carried a long spear and held it cocked. He ordered Riley's men back toward the wreck of the ship and made it clear that they should grab whatever else was left on board. Pointing to the east, the man showed that there were many reinforcements; at that very moment, dozens of men on camels were riding toward the scene.

The reinforcements plundered what was left of the sailors' possessions, while the crewmen of the *Commerce* made their way toward the ship in their half-swamped longboat. Once at the ship, the men discussed the possibility of trying to escape in the longboat, but its pitiful condition made that out of the question. So Riley headed back to shore and tried to befriend his nemesis. It didn't work; the man grabbed Riley by the head and put his scimitar to Riley's throat. "I concluded my last moments had come," Riley wrote. "And that my body was doomed to be devoured by these beings, whom I now considered to be none other than Cannibals, that would soon glut their hungry stomachs with my flesh." But Riley was spared; instead, the native ordered him to tell his men to bring all the treasure from the ship. Riley made it known to his men that he wished the passenger from New Orleans, Antonio Michel, to come on shore. Michel dutifully followed; what happened next would haunt Riley forever after. The men on shore ran to Michel, thinking he was bringing treasure with him. When it was clear that he had come with nothing, they began beating him. He managed to make himself understood enough to point the men toward the tent where the crewmen had buried tools and money.

While this was taking place, Riley made a break for the sea. He dove under a wave and only when he thought his lungs would burst did he surface to see his ex-captor behind him, just his head bobbing above water. Next came the spear, piercing the sea foam just inches from Riley's body. A wave crashed into his pursuer, and Riley swam the rest of the way to the longboat. Their nemeses cursed the *Commerce* crewmen and then marched over the dunes with their plunder, which included the battered and stabbed Michel, who in essence had been sacrificed for the others.

The men of the *Commerce* pulled everything they could in the form of drink, food, and tools onto the longboat. They would try to make a sea voyage that way, deciding that going back on land promised certain servitude or death. But it was clear, after only a couple of days in the longboat, that it constituted an impossible dream. The men couldn't even sleep, so busy were they in bailing the leaky boat. When they did have moments of rest, there was certainly no comfort in sitting in ankle-deep saltwater crammed in a space that disallowed unfolding one's legs. The men knew that their only real choices were to continue on in that condition, hoping to hail a passing ship—unlikely so close to shore—or try their luck once again on land. Trying to navigate along the coast would be virtually impossible. Reefs, swells, and the rocks that had doomed the *Commerce* would prove way too formidable obstacles for the longboat they now inhabited.

Days passed and the men's conditions worsened. They had earlier killed a pig that they had retrieved from the *Commerce*. Now, according to Dean King, in his book, *Skeletons on the Zahara* (Little Brown and Company, 2004), "They ate the skin and raw flesh of the pig as it was doled out in precious, rancid-sweet bits. Then they ate its bones. They continued to wet their blistered and festering lips twice a day with water, wine, and urine. Their fiery heads and necks radiated heat. Their skin peeled off in sheets, leaving bleeding sores." They had little choice: they would head for land.

Almost completely lacking the strength to row themselves, nature lent the men a hand. As they approached the coast, a wave took up the longboat and deposited it, with all its contents, on the sand with a thud. The boat's wooden bottom exploded beneath the men. They were now in the Sahara.

One might imagine this meeting of desert and ocean as relatively easy to traverse—a thin line of sand, the petering of the waves slithering and retreating at the men's feet. But the coast where the crew struck was littered with cliffs, slick

From *An Authentic Narrative of the Loss of the American Brig* Commerce, by James Riley (1818)

Courtesy of the George Peabody Library, Johns Hopkins University

rock, and twisting tunnels where the men either had to climb—risking a plunge into the ocean—or wade around, through the seething surf. The space in between was barely tolerable; Riley related that "under those towering cliffs, there was not a breath of air to fan our boiling blood."

The men spent the entire next day and into the night heading east through this forbidding terrain, hoping to flag a passing ship. They searched each rock wall for freshwater, and found none. Bleeding, wiped out, already weak from their trial at sea, the men were reaching their limits. Archibald Robbins wrote, "A harder day's travel was never made by man . . . I had become so inured to misery that she adopted me as her child."

It would get much worse.

The crew came to an imposing rock wall that would require every last reserve to cross. In an extraordinary, and painful, feat of perseverance, all the men made it to the top, only to look out at the empty wilderness before them. An earlier visitor to the western Sahara had described it as a wasteland: "Neither bird, nor insect, is seen in the air: a profound silence, that has something dreadful in it, prevails." The men took it hard; "The little moisture yet left overflowed in our eyes," Riley wrote. It had been two weeks since the wreck, and it was miraculous that all the men were still alive. They carried on, nearing death, and more than willing to take their chances with the natives, if only they could be delivered to fellow human beings, no matter the consequences. They got their wish: peering down over a ledge, they saw firelight.

They steeled themselves for a rendezvous and made their way to what they could now see was a crowd of men and camels. Captain Riley and two other seamen immediately dropped to their knees to show submission, hoping for some humanity. Instead, the Arabs rushed on all the crewmen, pulling and tugging each in a contest over ownership. The Arabs took no mercy on each other either, swinging with their scimitars, slashing clothing and skin. Once it was all sorted out, the men of the *Commerce* were slaves. Worse, their new enslavement didn't bring any relief; their owners had no water or food to give. The option of having simply died on their own now seemed the more attractive. It appeared that they would soon be dead anyway, but this time they would spend their last days in servitude. Riley even searched for a large stone with which to "knock out my own brains."

The men struggled to keep up with their new owners. Inexperienced on the sand, they slipped and tripped and then received blows upon their backs for falling. When it was clear that they could go no further, the men were placed on camelback. This was hardly better. Their thighs stretched wide over the camels' full bellies, and without any saddle underneath, soon the men's legs were rubbed raw and bled profusely. Every sway of the camel, every step, presented a new nadir of pain as their bones were jolted and jarred out of their sockets. That night proved no relief. After the men were given a pint of milk, which did act as a restorative, they lay down to sleep. But the landscape wasn't bare soft sand. Instead, it was littered with small, spiky rocks that prevented rest. Worse, the wind blew all night and, as there is virtually no humidity in the desert, it was freezing cold. The men had nothing to protect them. It was, in Riley's words, "One of the longest and most dismal nights ever passed by any human beings." (Despite this, Riley would describe another night, two weeks later: "I cannot imagine that the tortures of the rack can exceed those we experienced this night.") At the least, they still had one another to share in the misery. But soon this luxury would also pass. Every few days, one or two members of the crew were hauled off by new masters after rounds of feverish arguments and brandishing of weapons. When Archibald Robbins was sold, he was paraded and inspected before being pronounced fit for sale: "I suspected [Mohamet Meaarah, his new owner] was about to open my mouth to judge of my age by my teeth," Robbins recalled.

Riley, too, passed from master to master, once being bought for a blanket. Twice during this period, he had chance meetings with two of his former crewmen. Both were on the verge of death, their skin inflamed and seared. Both gave messages to Riley to deliver to their families before being driven off by unhappy masters who hadn't consented to the Europeans consorting. Riley kept on. Once, as he begged for water, his master Sideullah, after watering his four horses, spilled out the rest on the ground as an offering to Allah. Riley watched as the greedy sand soaked it up instantaneously. The men moved on as if in a haze, completely without the means even to protest. Riley, as their captain, managed to keep a tenuous hold on sanity and tried desperately, at every opportunity, to cheer his remaining men. He stopped them from eating the hanging flesh from their own bodies, so hungry were they for any sustenance. When he saw his camel urinating, he jumped under it and caught its stream to drink. All the while, his masters roamed, searching the vast wastelands for water.

Riley's new master, Hamet, questioned him extensively, trying to glean where he had come from and what he was doing on the shore. The perceptive Riley considered him perhaps a kindred spirit. Hamet had a spark of intelligence in his eyes, but more important to Riley was the absence of wickedness. In the course of trying to answer Hamet's questions, Riley mentioned his wife and children (also claiming that one of the young crewmen, Horace Savage, age fifteen, was his own son). Then Riley cried. This was a terrible breach of masculinity for the Arabs, who considered it a "womanish weakness." But Hamet actually shed a tear as well. Riley wouldn't know it until later, but Hamet, too, had recently left his own wife and three children to take to the desert in an attempt to earn money to pay off debts to his father-in-law, a powerful sheikh who despised him. Riley saw his opportunity. He later approached Hamet again and told him that if he would deliver the *Commerce*'s men to the Sultan of Morocco in the north, he would be rewarded with a tremendous sum of money. No deal, Hamet told him. It was impossible. He would never make it. If for no other reason, his father-in-law, Ali, lived in the north and held dominion over vast regions. There was no way Hamet would be able to pass through unnoticed. Ali would simply take Riley and his men as partial payment, and further humiliations—for all of them—would await.

Riley persisted. He promised extraordinary wealth and repeated his claim of a friend at the sultan's residence; this was an untruth, but it was Riley's only hope. Hamet called his bluff, but Riley kept at it, promising enough money for Hamet to wipe out all his debts and reap a small fortune besides. Hamet eventually agreed, but not without warning Riley that if he was deceiving him, he would cut Riley's throat. Soon, news of the potential riches spread, and other Arabs came with their *Commerce* crewmen, offering to sell their half-dead property. Riley promised exorbitant fees would be paid for each of them once they reached Swearah (today's Essaouira, Morocco). In the end, Riley and four of his shipmates began the journey north. Riley agonized over the fact that the departure meant he was leaving six shipmates behind; he despaired at ever seeing them again. As for one of them, Richard Delisle, the cook, there could be little hope. He was African American, a freeman from a land of slavery, now delivered to a place where men of his color were also slaves.

Riley's anguish grew and did so in unexpected ways. One day, a trader offering goods inquired to Hamet if he'd like to buy a shiny metal piece that he assumed was worth a great amount but, he confessed, he knew not what it was for. Riley immediately recognized it as the new spyglass he had bought in Gibraltar the previous month. It was a tough blow, a palpable reminder of better times. But he was still alive, and Hamet made sure that Riley and his men were fed and given water. It was hardly enough to do anything more than simply keep them going, but the Arabs had little themselves. The privations were too much for at least one man, Aaron Savage, who, against Riley's warnings, picked and ate the leaves of the spiny euphorbia plant. Soon, he was retching blood and struggling to keep up, stopping every few minutes to heave.

Two of the Arabs, Seid (Hamet's brother) and Hassar, began to flog Savage, who was by then unconscious. They claimed that Savage was purposely lagging behind so that he would slow the entire caravan and put them in danger of attack from rival marauders. When Riley arrived, Hassar had his scimitar drawn across Savage's throat. Riley lunged at Hassar and knocked him over; in one swift motion, he turned to Savage, scooped him up in his arms, and pleaded for water to revive him. "I expected to lose my life," Riley wrote. "But had determined to save Mr. Savage's at all hazards." Hassar had only time to restore himself and make for Riley to kill him for the insult before Hamet arrived and ordered everyone to stop. When Hassar calmed down, even he had to admit that he admired Riley's pluck. When they set off again, Hamet told Riley to walk with him. "Leave the camels to the others," he said. "Good Riley, you will see your children again, inshallah."

Within the next few days, the men noticed that the landscape had changed considerably—and in their favor. Gone were the barren stretches of sand punctured only by small stones. Now they saw flowering trees and streams with grass besides. The men plunged their heads in the water and drank greedily until their stomachs seemed ready to burst. They reached encampments where different bands of Arab traders and nomads came and went. The positive result of this was consistent access to goods, food, and water. However, word of Hamet's five Christian slaves spread; their bounty would undoubtedly prove too irresistible for some. So Hamet and his men broke into three groups, each taking a different route north. By doing this, they increased their chances of remaining unseen, but their access to water and food was severely curtailed.

Once, along the beach, Hamet's group came under attack by a group of bandits. One of them followed the typical greeting—"Is it peace?"—with an assent, only to raise a musket toward Hamet's face before pretending the whole affair had merely been a joke after Hassar and two others rode forward with raised muskets themselves. The group moved on, but the bandits trailed them, hoping that one of the slaves would fall behind and suffer a fate like a straggling antelope would to a lion. The close escape rattled Hamet. He believed that Riley had been anointed by Allah as someone special, someone worth fighting for. Hamet told Riley that he considered it Allah's will that they had escaped, that those men were brutal cutthroats. Hamet asked Riley if he would have been willing to fight for him. Riley swore he would, answering, "No one will kill you while I am alive." Hamet placed his hand on Riley's shoulder. Yes, Riley was his property, but he was much more.

But the close call, as well as other near scrapes with locals, greatly disturbed Seid. He felt it was lunacy to continue north. He dismounted his camel, declared that he didn't believe Riley knew anyone in Swearah, and that he would head off with his two slaves—Savage and Horace—and sell them for what he could get here in the desert. The two brothers soon came to blows, culminating in an armed face-off until Hamet threw down his weapon and dared his brother to shoot him in the chest. Only when strangers approached did the men regain their senses, realizing that creating a division within themselves would surely be the death of them all.

When an influential man named Sidi Mohammed visited the men, he told them that he knew many people in Swearah. As they were now close, Hamet declared that Riley would write a letter to his (imaginary) friend in Swearah, and Sidi Mohammed and Hamet would ride there and deliver it. "If your friend will fulfill your engagements," Hamet told Riley, "and pay the money for you and your men, you shall be free; if not, you must die for having deceived me. Your men will be sold for what they will bring."

Riley penned his letter, in English unintelligible to his masters, hoping it would simply fall into the hands of someone capable of reading it and acting quickly; he addressed it to "English, French, Spanish, or American consuls, or any Christian merchants in Mogadore or Swerah":

> Sir,
> The brig Commerce from Gibraltar for America, was wrecked on Cape Bajador, on the 28 August last; myself and four of my crew are here nearly naked in barbarian slavery: I conjure you by

all the ties that bind man to man, by those of kindred blood, and every thing you hold most dear, and by as much as liberty is dearer than life, to advance the money required for our redemption, which is nine hundred and twenty dollars, and two double barreled guns: I can draw for any amount, the moment I am at liberty . . . Should you not relieve me, my life must instantly pay the forfeit. I leave a wife and five helpless children to deplore my death . . . My present master, Sidi Hamet, will hand you this, and tell you where we are— he is a worthy man. Worn down to the bones by the most dreadful of all sufferings—naked and a slave, I implore your pity, and trust that such distress will not be suffered to plead in vain.

Hamet and Mohammed set off to Swearah to deliver the letter. They were gone more than a week, time when Riley had little to do but contemplate the horrors before him; at any moment, his master could come back declaring that no one knew him, and no one offered to pay anything. "I longed for the return of my master," Riley wrote, "And yet I anticipated it with the most fearful and dreadful apprehensions . . . [Hamet's arrival] would either restore me to liberty, or doom me to instant death." But before Hamet came back, his father-in-law, the powerful and malicious Sheik Ali, arrived. He was, in Riley's words, "one of the most fierce and ill-looking men I had ever beheld."

Hamet and Mohammed had in fact made it to Swearah. They had been taken to the British consul-general, William Willshire. Because Riley hadn't stated the nationality of himself or his men, Willshire was unsure if it fell under his dominion, or that of the nearest American in any position to do anything about it, James Simpson, the American consul in Tangier, all the way on Morocco's northern tip. Whatever the case, the sum being asked was exorbitant. If word got out that Riley and his men were bought for such money, the interests in taking American and British slaves would grow exponentially. Further, the entire thing could be a ruse, and Willshire, after going through complicated processes to secure the money, might very well be handing over a huge sum and getting nothing in return. Eventually, it was decided that Hamet would stay as a guest of the consul, and Mohammed would take Rais bel Cossim, one of Willshire's trusted intermediaries, back to see Riley and the men.

Bel Cossim rode all day and night to reach the men. He entered the tent and presented himself to Riley. "How de-do, Capetan. ¿Habla español?" he asked. Riley nodded. "Mr. Willshire will pay your ransom," Bel Cossim reported. He handed Riley a letter that read, in part: "I have agreed to pay the sum of nine hundred and twenty hard dollars to Sidi Hamet on your safe arrival in this town with your fellow sufferers; he remains here as a kind of hostage for your safe appearance." Riley's joy was checked only by the difficulty in believing it was really true. It must be noted that Willshire and Riley were on opposite sides during the recent War of 1812, and while Willshire surely suspected this, perhaps the men's shared cultural heritage trumped everything else.

Hearing of the deal, Sheik Ali castigated his fool son-in-law who, he fumed, had willingly placed himself under the control of the Christian dogs. He also claimed that Hamet could have gotten much more money and, in any case, it was all a trick. Once Riley and his men were delivered to the "villainous Christian" in Swearah, Hamet would be murdered and the money would be taken back.

Bel Cossim claimed that he had already paid a lot of money for the slaves, that they were his property now, and that he would take them to another tent with him. There, he gave the men shoes, clothes, and solid food and tea. The crewmen scarfed down all the food, paying the price all through the night with "violent griping pains in our stomachs and intestines, that we could with great difficulty forbear screaming out with agony."

Heading back to Swearah the next day, Bel Cossim told Riley that he agreed with Hamet's view of him; he was a special man indeed. Never had there been a recorded instance of a Christian who had covered such a long distance in the desert. Hamet and Bel Cossim weren't the only ones with this opinion, it seemed. The next day, Sheik Ali caught the group and tried to persuade Riley to come with him. Ali would make him a chief and offer one of his daughters for marriage. Ali's tactic didn't work. Now full of rage, Ali pressed his case in the next town, ruled by the powerful *Moulay* (Prince) Ibrahim. Here, Ali repeated his claim that he owned the slaves. After all, his son-in-law had paid for them and Hamet owed him much money. Ali was within his rights to seize the slaves as payment on Hamet's debt. Ali, supported by Seid, Hamet's brother, and now by Ibrahim, won the day.

But Bel Cossim continued to plead his case. Finally, Ibrahim declared a cessation: all parties would sit and wait until Hamet could be retrieved from Swearah. Then negotiations would resume. So they sat, the well-fed and comfortable Arabs on one side of the room, the lice-ridden emaciated Americans on the other.

When Riley confessed to Bel Cossim that he finally despaired of ever being delivered, Bel Cossim castigated him. How dare you question God's will, when he has already spared you such trials? he asked. "To hear such sentiments from the mouth of a Moor," Riley reflected. "Whose nation I had been taught to consider the worst of barbarians, I confess, filled my mind with awe and reverence, and I looked up to him as a kind of superior being."

The next day, the clever and resourceful Bel Cossim paid a visit to a nearby market and bought a bull, to be sent to another powerful man, el-Ajjh. When el-Ajjh asked what the gift was for, Bel Cossim told him about the situation at Ibrahim's and asked for el-Ajjh's intercession, which was duly promised. El-Ajjh visited Ali and deceitfully told him that the powerful Berber ruler Sidi Hashem had learned of the Christian slaves and would be arriving any day to claim them. Hashem was one of the few men Ali feared, and so he heeded el-Ajjh's advice to ride north quickly.

The men arrived in the fishing port of Agadir and rested. During the night, Ali went off and sought the governor of Agadir. They made a deal; the governor's men would seize Riley and the others in the morning and demand they pay Hamet's debt. If they couldn't, they would become Ali's property. Bel Cossim warned Riley that they had to leave right away, just after midnight. They set off as quietly as possible and once outside of town, rushed as quickly as they could. Somewhere along the coast, as the caravan sped toward Swearah, they saw another group coming from the north. All the men gripped their weapons and prepared for a showdown, but at the final moment, Riley called out to his old master. "Hamet? Is that you?" It was. "I had the joy of kissing the hand of my old master and benefactor," Riley wrote.

Among this group was Bel Mooden, another emissary of Willshire's. With no wasted moments, Bel Mooden handed the money to Hamet and turned around, the men of the *Commerce* now in his possession. Hamet instructed the men to keep heading north, speedily; he would continue south and try to intercept Ali, sure he would be following soon. The great confrontation between father-in-law and son-in-law loomed.

When Ali awoke in the morning, he found Bel Cossim lying across the threshold to his room. Bel Cossim suggested that he would get Riley to make them coffee. When Bel Cossim "discovered" that the men were missing, he flew into a rage and accused Ali of stealing them. Ibrahim joined Bel Cossim in the scolding. Ali, of course, vigorously defended himself. By this time, the sailors had been gone some seven hours. But it wasn't long before the panicked Ali and the others met Hamet on the desert trail. Ali, no longer in any position of strength, but fuming nonetheless, settled for the money originally owed him. Hamet was in the clear. Riley and the others, meanwhile, approached Swearah, eight weeks after the *Commerce* had run aground. When Riley caught sight of an American flag flying over a distant part of the city, "the little blood remaining in my veins, gushed through my heart with wild impetuosity." Willshire, tears in his eyes, was at the city gate to meet them. He took Riley in his arms. "Come, my friends," he said, "Let us go to the city."

It was Riley's mental strength that had carried him through. He never gave up hope and it had saved him, as well as his men. But his physical body had absorbed a terrible toll; 240 pounds when the ordeal began, Riley was now a skeletal 90. In describing two of his mates, James Clark and Thomas Burns, in his subsequent book, *Sufferings in Africa* (cited by Abraham Lincoln, among others, as singly influential in his life), Riley offered a paralipsis, declining to mention how much they weighed, "for I apprehend it would not be believed, that the bodies of men retaining the vital spark should not weigh forty pounds." Now that he was safe, Riley's mind gave out as well, buckling under the immense strain of keeping himself and his men alive. He lost his senses and often cried and trembled for hours on end until finally recovering after a week.

Eventually, Riley, Savage, Burns, Clark, and Horace Savage sailed for home. Two more crewmen, Robbins and William Porter, also lived through their slavery and made it home. Robbins's saving grace probably stemmed from the fact that he had unwittingly "converted" to Islam there in the burning desert. When his master bathed himself in sand and rose up and called prayers, Robbins did the same, hoping to ingratiate himself to his master, Ganus. It had worked.

Two more crewmen, James Barrett and George Williams, had been spotted in the south, but all attempts to save them failed. The other crewmen of the *Commerce*—Delisle, Hogan, and Michel—were never heard from again. Riley would continue to be haunted by visions of his indenture for the rest of his life, often waking in the night. But he became a staunch abolitionist as a result of his experience, arguing forcefully for the emancipation of blacks "who have been snatched & torn from their native country . . . by professors too of moral & political freedom & christian benevolence."

EXTRAORDINARY SURVIVAL

Finally, there are some success stories, even in the midst of failure. While things had to go horribly wrong for the crews in this chapter to have been stuck when and where they were, all but one man in these three wrecks managed to survive and come back, bringing with them the most extraordinary tales.

Here we have the romantic castaway, "master of all he surveys," reduced to incredible deprivations and pining for a return home. We have teamwork and ingenuity, the flip side of the "incompetence, disorder, and evil" we saw earlier. Here are men who worked toward the common good, who engaged in almost impossible creativity to survive. Here we see great leaders. "Loneliness is the penalty of leadership," Ernest Shackleton once wrote. True, to be followed, one had to disassociate himself a bit, put himself above the others (but not too far as to be unapproachable) and sell the image of his knowledge and trustworthiness to a shaken and frightened crew.

When the ship went down, custom dictated that the captain surrendered his leadership. Crew could still choose to follow his orders, but they didn't have to. No fear of penalty awaited the insubordinate sailor. Leadership, then, was an open affair, available to anyone who seized it and steered its heavy responsibility aright. Sometimes this meant everyone surrendering his particular station and declaring equality for the sake of the common good. Other times, the sailor had no one left to rely upon and had to make a hero of himself, to call upon reserves of strength and inventiveness he hardly knew he possessed.

Here then are the stories of men who survived—against all the odds.

Masters of All They Survey—Castaways: *Serrano* (1540–47), *Selkirk* (1704–09), and *Ashton* (1723–25)

Pedro de Serrano

Many castaway stories have been lost to history. Others linger. The most famous castaway is Alexander Selkirk, for reasons we will see later in this chapter. But Selkirk was certainly not the first. A full century and a half before him, there circulated a story about a Spaniard named Pedro de Serrano. Much of his story may be wildly exaggerated, or even completely invented. For one thing, the two versions of his story place him in very different places: one on an island off the coast of Peru, and the other on a small cay (in what is now known as the Serrana Bank) in the Caribbean. Further, it is alleged that Serrano survived either seven or eight years on an island that had no freshwater, something that strains the bounds of credibility. There is a good probability, however, that there was in fact a real Serrano, and some version of the amazing story later told about him was indeed true.

In the 1550s, a man of mixed Spanish and Incan ancestry named Garcilaso de la Vega wrote a history of the Incas and the Spanish conquest and included Serrano's story. His version, of course, is the Peruvian one. Garcilaso heard the story from a gentleman named Sánchez de Figueroa, who, allegedly, knew Serrano. Garcilaso, a very trustworthy chronicler, deemed the story credible. The discrepancy may be as simple as Garcilaso taking a true story, but moving its geography to Peru so that it fell into the dominion of his ancestors.

In 1540, Serrano's boat sank near the island and he managed to swim ashore with only his clothes and a knife tucked into his waistband. Once he crawled upon the sand, his relief turned to horror; according to Garcilaso, "He was in a state of despair, for he found no water and no fuel nor even grass he could graze on, nor anything else to maintain life till some ship might pass to rescue him before he perished from hunger and thirst." His new home was simply a five-mile round patch of sand. Understandably, he spent his first night and day "bewailing his misfortune." When hunger got the better of him, he ringed the island, finding shellfish, crabs, shrimp, and other creatures, all of which he ate raw for want of a fire. Then he spotted a troop of turtles coming to shore. These would prove to be his lifeline. He caught them easily, turned them on their backs to immobilize them, and then cut their throats to drink their blood. He ate some of the meat, laying out large portions in the sun to dry, and then

Serrano (left) and his visitor flee. (18th century).

cleaned out the shells. These he let dry and then used as rainwater catches. Because some of these turtles were enormous, and Serrano killed so many of them, and because the region received lots of rainfall, he soon had a ready supply of basins of fresh rainwater. All he needed now was fire.

Ever the resourceful mariner, Serrano dived below the surf and collected pebbles, which he then struck together with the flint of his knife until he made sparks. He took threads from his shirt to use as tinder. Soon, he had fire, which he sustained by collecting jetsam on shore. Using the largest of the turtle shells, he constructed a small shelter to protect the fire from rain.

Garcilaso picks up the story: "Within two months or less, he was as naked as when he was born, for the great rain, the heat, and the humidity of the region rotted the few clothes he had." Eventually, "Owing to the harshness of the climate hair grew all over his body till it was like an animal's pelt, and not just any animal's, but a wild boar's. His hair and beard fell below his waist."

Several times he saw a ship sail pass, but each either failed to spot him, or ignored him, too frightened to brave the same shoals that had doomed his vessel. This "so discouraged [Serrano] that he had resigned himself to dying and ending his misery." But he lived for another three years, until something extraordinary happened. He woke one day to find that he wasn't alone. Another castaway, also surviving the sinking of his ship, had come on shore. The two men were not initially happy to see each other; Serrano assumed it was the devil in human form, coming to "tempt him to some desperate act." The stranger assumed that Serrano, "so coated with hair, beard, and hide" was in fact the devil in true form. Serrano supplicated Jesus Christ as the two men fled from each other. So, too, did the stranger, who then turned around and proclaimed, "Flee not, brother, for I am a Christian too."

The two men then agreed to share chores and work toward their mutual survival. Soon, however, they quarreled violently, each accusing the other of shirking. Incredibly, the two men decided to separate and move to opposite ends of the island. But they soon made up and awaited what seemed an impossible rescue. "During this time they saw some ships pass and made their smoke signals, but in vain, and this so depressed them that they all but died." Finally, after four more years passed, they spotted a ship so close that the smoke signal worked and soon a small boat was headed their way. Because Serrano's companion had also grown a pelt and because "they no longer looked like human beings," the two men yelled the Apostles' Creed ("I believe in God, the Father Almighty, the Creator of heaven and earth, and in Jesus Christ, His only Son, our Lord") so loudly that the mariners wouldn't assume they were demons. It worked, and the men were taken on board, "to the greatest wonder of all present, who with admiration beheld their hairy shapes, not like men but beasts" (Robert Marx, "Pedro Serrano: The First Robinson Crusoe," *Oceans*, September 7, 1974).

Unfortunately, Serrano's companion died during the passage, but Serrano made it to Spain, and then went on to Germany, where the Spanish emperor was. Serrano "kept his pelt as it was, as a proof of his wreck and all he had gone through. In every village he passed through on the way he earned much money whenever he chose to exhibit himself." He had to plait his beard at night; otherwise, the hair "disturbed his rest." Serrano eventually died in Panama, on his way to retrieve 4,000 pesos awarded him by the emperor.

Alexander Selkirk

In early 1704, the English pirate ship *Cinque Ports* left the Juan Fernandez Island chain, off the coast of Chile, heading toward Peru with hopes of taking a Spanish treasure ship. Instead, the *Cinque Ports* sank off the coast. Most on board drowned. The others lived a terrible existence on an island, drinking tortoise blood for lack of freshwater. Survivors eventually surrendered to the

Selkirk fired upon by the Spaniards.

Image from *The Life and Adventures of Alexander Selkirk, the Real Robinson Crusoe*. (1850) John Howell.

Courtesy of The Albin O. Kuhn Library, University of Maryland, Baltimore County

Spanish instead of facing the inevitability of starvation. They were taken to shore and marched to Lima, where they suffered dreadful tortures in prison.

One man escaped this terror; before the *Cinque Ports* left Juan Fernandez, he decried the poor condition of the ship and the ignominy of having to sail with its captain, who he felt was an imbecile. Because he stayed, he faced an almost unimaginable ordeal—four years and four months in complete solitude. His story, though not entirely unique, would inspire what many regard as the English language's first novel, *Robinson Crusoe*.

The *Cinque Ports* first arrived at the Juan Fernandez Island chain on August 6, 1703, captained by Charles Pickering, with Alexander Selkirk on as ship's master, or navigator. His name at birth was actually Selcraig, but he changed it upon signing on for a naval journey. Perhaps this revision was his way of distancing himself from what he perceived as the oppressiveness and small-mindedness of his hometown, Largo, Scotland. Selkirk had always been a rough sort, and he paid the price. At age fifteen, he was to be disciplined for "undecent beaiviar" in a church. He failed to appear for punishment, however, sailing off to sea instead. Back home five years later, Selkirk was once again called to a disciplinary panel at the local church, this time for a violent fight in his home, where Selkirk beat his brother and had to be restrained from shooting him. Unwilling to put up with the narrow constraints of his small town and the narrower constraints of the all-powerful church, Selkirk set off again—to the uncomfortable, rough-edged life offered by the sea. He signed on to the two-ship team, *Cinque Ports* and *St. George*, a pirate crew led by the irascible privateer (distinct from "pirate" only in having the patronage of a national government) William Dampier, who, according to one contemporary source, considered discipline to consist of "calling his subordinate officers 'rogues, rascals, or sons of bitches.'"

Prone to drunkenness, Dampier seemed unwilling to engage in fights that would bring big prizes. His crew began to openly revolt. He quashed each attempt. But with each new day at sea, wallowing in filth and pestilence, without any booty, the men wearied. A respite at the remote flyspeck of Más á Tierra in the Juan Fernandez Islands offered the men a chance to revive and set out for raids along the Chilean coast: the great prize would be the treasure-laden Spanish galleon heading back home from Manila.

Más á Tierra is described in William Funnell's *A Voyage Round the World* (1707): "The melancholy howling of innumerable seals on the beach . . . rocky precipices, inhospitable woods, dropping with rain, lofty hills, whose tops were hid by thick and dark clouds, on the one hand, and tempestuous sea on the other." Four million years old, the island hasn't changed much since Funnell's time; it's a ragged piece of land, lashed by rains and creased by ravines running through precipitous slopes. Virtually nowhere on the island is flat.

It was, in short, a forbidding place, despite the fact that it contained food, water, and enjoyed moderate weather year-round. Dampier didn't stay long. He took the *St. George* and headed toward Peru, leaving the *Cinque Ports* in the charge of Thomas Stradling. Selkirk and Stradling simply didn't get along; Stradling was an aristocrat, and he carried a pet monkey on board with him. The rough-and-tumble Selkirk found him incompetent and insufferable. After several months at Juan Fernandez, Stradling ordered the boat loaded and the men ready for sail. Selkirk tried to persuade the men to stay at Juan Fernandez, pointing out not only Stradling's ill personality, but also the sorry state of their boat. It would, he predicted, sink within the month. But Selkirk couldn't persuade any of them, and Stradling obligingly left Selkirk alone, reportedly mocking him as Selkirk charged into the surf, calling after the ship. Selkirk had only his bedding, some clothes, a knife, a gun and powder, a cooking pot, some navigation instruments, and his Bible. He watched the ship sail away. His new island home must have felt at once immense and constrained, twelve by four miles, a circumference of thirty-four miles, and surrounded by an unforgiving and fuming sea.

He found an abandoned hut near the shore, where he stored his possessions.

Three times a day, he climbed to a high point overlooking the bay and scanned the horizon for a passing ship. None came. His misery continued for a full eight months before he reconciled himself to his utter aloneness. During this period, "He grew dejected, languid, and melancholy, scarcely able to refrain from doing himself Violence" (Richard Steele, the *Englishman Magazine*, December 1713). He stopped eating fish "because they occasion'd a Looseness." He turned instead to the many goats that had colonized the island. He kept up his "faculties of speech" only by shouting exhortations to the heavens.

Weeks turned to months, which turned to years. He exhausted his ammunition and became as much animal as the goats, cats, and rats that roamed around him. At night, the rats chewed on his feet and clothes while he attempted sleep. To clear that problem, he lured feral cats into the hut, but as he watched them chase, kill, and eat the rats, he was disturbed by what inevitably awaited him: "After his death, as there would be no one to bury his remains, or to supply the cats with food, his body must be devoured by the very animals which he at present nourished for his convenience" (Steele). He scoured the shoreline for metal implements, castaways from unlucky ships. He fashioned tools, became adept at catching goats—some of them for fornication, others for food and pelts. He made crude forks and spoons out of the goats' horns. He carved a notch in a tree every day, marking the duration of his imprisonment. He fashioned a flute out of a stick and played for the woodland creatures that in turns accepted him as landscape and then fled at his approach, unsure if the sounds he made were of their own species, or something foreign and threatening. The hair on his head met that on his face, twisting into one knotted mat. He used his fingernails to dig and carve.

Selkirk "wore out all his Shoes and Clothes by running thro the Woods; and at last being forc'd to shift without them, his Feet became so hard, that he run every where without Annoyance" (Woodes Rogers, *A Cruising Voyage Round the World*, 1712). Once he almost died. He had pursued a goat with so much eagerness that he caught it "on the brink of a Precipice . . . so that he fell with the Goat down the said Precipice a great height, and was so stun'd and bruis'd with the Fall, that he narrowly escap'd with his Life, and when he came to his Senses, found the Goat dead under him. He lay senseless for the space of three days [it was probably only one day] and was scarce able to crawl to his Hutt, which was about a mile distant, or to stir abroad again in ten days" (Woodes Rogers).

He recovered. He saw a ship. He ran to the shore, waving a burning branch. He saw a Spanish flag fluttering atop. They would take him as a slave, so he ran; they pursued, calling him "savage" and "dog." He climbed a tree and watched as they killed a goat and ate it just below him. They gave up the search, destroying some of his possessions before boarding their boat.

On January 31, 1709, William Dampier was back, near Más á Tierra once again, this time with Woodes Rogers, leading two ships, the *Duke* and the *Duchess*. Selkirk spotted them; seeing a French flag this time, he lit a fire and leapt along the shore. The men in the ships saw the fire and assumed it was the Spanish; they readied for a fight.

When the men came on shore with guns cocked, they didn't get a fight. Instead, they faced what appeared to be a creature half man, half woodland beast. He was dressed in animal pelts; it was difficult to tell where his hair ended and the pelts began. His face was bronzed by the sun, and his feet were blackened and rough. He lifted his hands and muttered incomprehensibly. One of the sailors later remarked, "He had so much forgot his Language for want of Use, that we could scarce understand him, for he seem'd to speak his words by halves." Finally, Selkirk made himself understood: "Marooned," he managed, the tears running down his cheeks.

When Selkirk was brought back to the ship, Rogers wrote that the returning sailors had with them "A Man cloth'd in Goat Skins who look'd wilder than the first Owners of them." Amazingly, there on board was Dampier, the captain of the original expedition from which Selkirk had been marooned. It was a circle then completed. Dampier, knowing Selkirk's abilities and confirming Selkirk's story for the skeptical sailors, recommended that the Goat Man be appointed second mate on the *Duke*.

When Selkirk offered to show the men where to find food and water, they had him perform feats and were mightily impressed at his adaptability; Rogers wrote, "We had a Bull-Dog, which we sent with several of our nimblest Runners, to help him in catching Goats; but he distanc'd and tir'd both the Dog and the Men, catch'd the Goats, and brought 'em to us on his back." The men took to calling Selkirk "the Governour."

There would be more raids along the way, but Selkirk, after more than fifty months alone—and over eight years since he left—was now headed home. A payday of eight hundred pounds, his share of the plunder, was in the process of being sorted out. A few years would pass, but the money eventually became his.

The tale, probably apocryphal, was that Selkirk never could reconcile himself to a "normal" life back home. He got into fights, tired of mealtime conversation, withdrew, eventually built himself a cave behind his father's house, and lived there in solitude. According to Richard Steele, Selkirk lamented his exile from his island, exclaiming, "I am now worth 800 Pounds, but shall never be so happy, as when I was not worth a farthing." It does beg the imagination to assume that a man who just spent two years on board a cloistered ship after his rescue would then suddenly find Scotland and its inhabitants insufferable.

However, his story was a widely disseminated one, and it appealed to all the romantic sentiments of his day. It was little surprise then that Selkirk—in highly fictionalized form—would serve as the model for Defoe's famous character. Two and a half centuries later, Selkirk's fictional incarnation still resonated; in 1966, the government of Chile officially changed his old island home's name to Isla Robinson Crusoe. An uninhabited island nearby now carries the name, Isla Alejandro Selkirk. And in Largo, Scotland, one can see a statue of the old roughneck troublemaker, dressed in goatskins and scanning the horizon for passing ships.

Philip Ashton

Alexander Selkirk's voluntary marooning had nothing to do with objections to the cunning nature of his company's profession. This wasn't the case with Philip Ashton, another voluntary maroon, who fled his captors—ruthless, bloodthirsty pirates under the command of the brutal Ned Low.

Ashton's schooner was boarded by four of Low's men on June 15, 1722, and his crew and everyone on board became captive. The next step was to have the new captives sign articles of agreement, effectively joining the band. Ashton refused and was threatened with death until one of Low's men simply forged his name anyway. Ashton later tried to escape with two men who had gone to retrieve Low's dog, accidentally left behind on an island. Ashton was prevented by the quartermaster, and when the two men failed to return, the quartermaster accused Ashton of being in on the plot. He raised his gun to Ashton's head and pulled the trigger. It misfired. He tried three more times, and misfire was the result each time. Ashton leapt belowdecks and was thus spared.

On March 9, 1723, the crew stopped at Roatán, an island north of Honduras, to reprovision. Ashton strolled along the beach and "on reaching the distance of a musketshot from the party," the cooper yelled at him and asked where he was headed. Ashton replied that he would get some coconuts and continued on along the beach. The moment he was out of view, he ran, "as fast as the thickness of the bushes and my naked feet would admit." The others called after him until the cooper threatened to leave him, knowing full well that this was a fate few sailors wanted. (Selkirk's situation illustrates this—despite an insufferable captain and a leaky boat, none of the dozens of sailors on board the *Cinque Ports* chose to stay with Selkirk.) Ashton was undeterred: "I was left on a desolate island, destitute of all help and remote from the track of navigators; but, compared with the state and society I had quitted, I considered the wilderness hospitable."

Only after the pirates left did Ashton come to understand the full weight of his decision: "I was on an island which I had no means of leaving; I knew of no human being within many miles; my clothing was scanty and it was impossible to procure a supply. I was altogether destitute of provision, nor could tell how my life was to be supported. This melancholy prospect drew a copious flood of tears from my eyes." Without a knife or weapon of any kind, harvesting the island's wild pig and deer was impossible. He had to live solely on the fruit he plucked from trees. An unexpected reward came, however, when Ashton plunged a stick into the sand and came up with encrusted yolk. He dug and found a bounty of tortoise eggs. Without the means to start a fire, he had to eat these raw, but eventually devised a system of hanging them in the trees until the insides hardened from the baking sun.

He built structures that shaded him from the mean sun and "the heavy dews at night." But they did nothing to protect him from the relentless and "pestiferous" mosquitoes and biting flies, which created such an annoyance "that even if a person possessed ever so many comforts his life would be oppressive to him." Ashton wasn't a very good swimmer, so he took a long bamboo pole and tucked it under his shoulders, which buoyed him enough to make his way to a nearby desert island situated within the trade winds, which successfully kept the insects at bay. So he spent his nights there, and returned to his home on Roatán during the day. The journey itself was not without risks; on one occasion, a shovel-nosed shark rammed his leg before getting stuck in the shallows. It hadn't managed to bite him, but it left Ashton with a terribly painful and deep bruise.

He slowly became reconciled to his new life on the island, but not to its discomforts. He complained:

> I suffered very much from being barefoot. So many deep wounds were made in my feet from traversing the woods, where the ground was covered with sticks and stones, and on the hot beach over sharp broken shells, that I was scarce able to walk at all. Often, when treading with all possible caution, a stone or shell on the beach or a pointed stick in the woods would penetrate the old wound and the extreme anguish would strike me down as suddenly as if I had been shot. Then I would remain for hours together with tears gushing from my eyes from the acuteness of the pain.

Ashton began to lose weight, and hope: "As my weakness continued to increase I often fell to the ground insensible and then, as also when I laid myself to sleep, I thought I should never wake again, or rise in life." One day, as Ashton lay insensate on the beach, a man in a canoe startled him. The man stopped, staring at the wild figure on the shore of what he thought to be an uninhabited island. Ashton bade him come forward. The man "knew not what to make of me; my garb and countenance seemed so singular that he looked wild with astonishment." The man, a Brit on the run from the Spanish, eventually did come on shore and he and Ashton lived together for two days before the man declared that he would set off on a hunting trip to a nearby island and be back within a few hours. Barely an hour after the man departed, a violent storm arose; the man never came back. But he had left behind invaluable provisions: "about five pounds of pork, a knife, a bottle of gunpowder, tobacco, tongs, and flint." Now Ashton could make fire.

Three months went by before Ashton found what he thought was his departed friend's canoe washed up on the beach. Turned out it wasn't his but his companions's but no matter—Ashton now had free reign of the nearby islands and cays. In his own words, he was "admiral of the neighboring seas as well as sole possessor and chief commander of the islands." Taking his vessel toward the small island of Bonacco, Ashton spotted a sloop anchored on the eastern side of the island. Wary, he paddled to the western side and laid in there, making a two-day trek through dense undergrowth to spy on the sloop. But when he got to the island's eastern shore, the sloop was gone. Utterly weary, he sat down and fell asleep against a tree stump. He was awakened by the sound of musket fire. He ran, the gunfire and bullets chasing him through the woods. Spanish sailors were after him, shouting down the fleeing Ashton and slicing the foliage around his body as he ran. He made his way unscathed to his canoe, which he quickly paddled back to his home on Roatán.

Another seven months passed alone before Ashton was again visited, this time by two canoes full of seventeen men. After hesitant questioning on both sides, the men came on shore. They were led by a John Hope, and they had been living in the Bay of Honduras. Learning of an impending Spanish raid, the men fled to the neighboring island of Barbarat. It was a fairly sparse place, and they needed to find food, firewood, and water. It was during this foray that they came to Roatán and Ashton.

Hope and his men persuaded Ashton to quit his home on Roatán and come with them to Barbarat. Sensing increased safety in numbers (especially with men who were armed), Ashton agreed. He lived a somewhat better life on Barbarat, comforted at least by the presence of company. But seven months into his stay, the raid came. It wasn't Spaniards, as feared, but pirates; worse, these pirates were led by one of Ned Low's men. If he recognized Ashton, there would be hell to pay. The buccaneers leapt onshore and caught several of Hope's men; they gave chase to the others, promising quarter if they would turn themselves in. Ashton was unconvinced: "Nothing could have been said to discourage me more from putting myself in their power. I had the utmost dread of a pirate; and my original aversion was now enhanced by the apprehension of being sacrificed by my former desertion."

Ashton's aversion was well founded; the pirates killed one of the captured—throwing his body into a canoe and setting it afire—set afloat five others without any provisions, and "shamefully abused" an Indian woman. The pirates left, and after a time, Hope's remaining men decided they would leave, too. But one man, John Symonds, decided to stay, hoping to make money trading with colonists on Jamaica. Symonds convinced Ashton to stay with him, reasoning that he'd be better able to catch an America-bound ship from Jamaica than from where Hope's men were heading in the Bay of Honduras. Symonds was right. English traders soon visited the men, now stationed on Bonacco. One vessel came close to shore and Ashton was able to ascertain that it was part of a convoy headed by the man-o'-war *Diamond*, bound for Jamaica and then New England. The captain of the ship, a Mr. Dove, took Ashton on board and assigned him the position of crewman.

They left the island at the end of March, 1725 and arrived in Salem, Massachusetts, in May. There, just three miles from his father's home, Ashton made the trip home where he "was received as one risen from the dead."

He had been gone two years, ten months, and fifteen days.

Four Russians at Spitsbergen (1743–49)

It was May 1743. Sailors set out from their north Russian hometown of Mezen, about seven hundred miles east of present-day Finland. Mezen provides easy access to the waterway of Beloye More, a tributary of the Barents Sea. Once in the Barents, it's roughly thirteen hundred miles northwest to Svalbard, currently administered by Norway. Svalbard is made up of many islands, with Spitsbergen being the largest and in the shape of a splintered arrowhead pointing toward northern Scandinavia. Svalbard's southernmost point is still well above the Arctic Circle. It's a bleak place, and not somewhere anyone would ever want to be stranded. There are two large islands to the east of Spitsbergen, Barentsøya and the larger, more southerly Edgeøya. And just to the east of Edgeøya's southern tip is Halvmåneøya (Halfmoon Island), where,

Spitsbergen

Courtesy of Julia Kolodko

as best as can be figured, four Russians endured for almost six and a half years.

In its day, the story excited much interest, though its dissemination was limited because of eighteenth-century Russia's restricted communication outlets. Nevertheless, the story did reach Queen Catherine the Great. Her interest in the sailors' ordeal fueled her subsequent inspiration toward further Arctic exploration, including discovery of the Northwest Passage. One Russian historian, writing in 1821, remarked: "By chance there came to this Great Sovereign's attention a modest book under the title 'Adventures of Four Sailors on the Island Spitsbergen'. Their grim existence on that sterile land touched the sensitive heart of the Monarch." Despite interest in the tale from the highest levels, the story eventually lapsed into obscurity. Part of the reason for the tale's anonymity is its lack of sources. Not one of the sailors penned a memoir, and for the next two and a half centuries, only one book was ever written about it: *A Narrative of the Singular Adventures of Four Russian Soldiers, Who Were Cast Away on the Desert Island of East-Spitzbergen,* written by history professor and member of Russian Imperial Academy of Sciences, P. L. Le Roy.

The survivors of the ordeal sat down for an interview with Le Roy four months after their arrival in Russia. He wrote *A Narrative* in German. It was later translated into English in 1774; subsequently, a significant portion of Le

Roy's account was published by Andrus and Starr of Hartford, Connecticut, in the book *Remarkable Shipwrecks; Or, A Collection of Interesting Accounts of Naval Disasters* in 1813. Thereafter, the story essentially disappeared. By the twentieth century, it was known almost exclusively by the small communities of ethnic Pomori living around Mezen who had passed down the tale from generation to generation. Today it remains one of the most extraordinary, yet unknown stories of survival.

Part of what makes piecing together the true story of these four men so difficult is that Le Roy's account is virtually all that has appeared in print, aside from a scant few references, which often used Le Roy's account as primary. Le Roy, however, didn't speak Russian and had to rely upon interpreters. The survivors telling their tale in Russian (and, no doubt, not sufficiently distant from the events to be terribly objective about the details) to a man who wrote it in German and then had it later translated into French and English, presents obvious problems. Worse, a period of sixteen years elapsed (for reasons unknown) between Le Roy's interview and his actual publication of the book.

But the basic story goes this way: Fourteen sailors set out for Svalbard to hunt walruses, whose ivory tusks would then be traded all over the world. At least two of the men, Aleksei and Khrisanf Inkov, had a great-grandfather who had also undertaken the trip in the 1670s. The resolve for such a punishing journey to one of the world's most inhospitable climes was something that flowed through their blood.

The ship that carried the men was a *kotch*, a north Russian specialty designed to work within the particular demands created by delta tides in northern Russian rivers. A kotch's planks were lashed together with juniper roots, meaning that without nails or spikes, the wooden ships could actually flex and bend with the currents. As a result, they were incredibly adaptable boats singularly suited for the difficult conditions near and above the Arctic Circle. A typical kotch carried six oars, had a massive sail in the middle of the boat, and contained living quarters underneath the main deck, with storage in the middle of the boat.

The sailors enjoyed eight straight days of good and steady progress, but a gale on the ninth day blew them off course. Instead of the established settlements on West Spitsbergen, they came instead to an island called Edgeøya, a godforsaken place that saw pack ice in its waters for almost the entire year. Its surface, too, was forbidding, covered by a large ice cap, Edgeøyjøkulen.

The boat was soon trapped by ice. The crew began to despair until first mate Aleksei Inkov declared that he knew preceding Russian seamen had once wintered on this very island. In fact, they had carried timber with them from

Russia for the purpose of erecting a hut. Inkov went with three other seamen to find the hut; accompanying the first mate were his godson, Khrisanf (Ivan) Inkov, Stepan Sharapov, and Fedor Verigin. The men set off without a load of provisions, knowing full well that added weight could mean a plunge through thin ice. They had between one and two miles to cover, if they could find the hut at all. According to Le Roy, the men carried with them only the following items: "a musket, a powder-horn, containing twelve charges of powder, with as many balls; an axe, a small kettle, a bag with about twenty pounds of flour, a knife, a tinder box with tinder, a bladder filled with tobacco, and every man his wooden pipe."

Remarkably, the men did discover the hut, about a mile and a half from the shore. Their joy at finding it was great; it would mean that they could winter here and hope to return home in the spring when the ice began to break up. Without that hut, they reasoned, they would not survive. It might be miserable, but certainly the prospect of having to spend months here wasn't the worst thing in the world. Indeed, they might even consider themselves lucky that they had managed to avoid being overturned in the gale.

It's important here to define "hut," which carries a connotation of a small structure. In fact, this one was rather large: roughly thirty-six feet by eighteen feet. Inside was an antechamber roughly twelve feet across. This had two doors, one leading to the interior room and the other to shut out trapped exterior air. Also inside was a samovar, a large stove that could double as a sleeping area during extreme cold snaps.

The hut, however, was weathered and while it would certainly suffice as a shelter for a night or two, it needed reinforcement. The men hunkered down for a cold evening and then proceeded back to shore to tell the rest of the crew about their discovery. When they got there, however, "Their astonishment and agony of mind, when on reaching the place where they had landed, they saw nothing but an open sea, free from ice, which but the day before had covered the ocean, may more easily be conceived than descried," wrote Le Roy. Either the kotch had been smashed to pieces by sheets of ice driven by high winds from a gale the previous evening or the vessel had been carried out to sea, the men's efforts at keeping her near shore futile against the power of the currents. In either case, the kotch was gone, and none of the four men would ever see any trace of her, or the rest of the men, again. "This unfortunate event deprived the wretched mariners of all hope of ever being able to quit the island, and they returned to the hut full of horror and despair." The men had barely two days' worth of gear on their backs.

Spending a winter anywhere on Svalbard was a dicey proposition at best. In the first record of overwinterers, eight English sailors were accidentally marooned at Svalbard in 1630. One of them, Edward Pellham, later recorded their ordeal, describing their deflated reaction to the abandonment this way: "We thought that no other thing could be looked for but a miserable and pining death, seeing there appeared no possibility of inhabiting there . . . [W]e knew that neither Christian or Heathen people had ever before inhabited those desolate and untemperate climates." In fact, the English sailors' prospects, though dire, didn't come close to matching the desperateness of the Russians' in the next century. The British had at their disposal the detritus of many past Dutch and English whaling expeditions, and they were able to cobble together scores of supplies. For example, old abandoned shallops were broken apart and used for firewood.

The Englishmen ate what they could, prayed daily, and tried to keep their thoughts from drifting to their families; the thought of their wives and children hearing of their demise was too much for them to endure. They saw the last of the sun in mid-October, and thereafter suffered in darkness for three and a half months until early February. Though welcome, the sun's reappearance did nothing for their chances of rescue; the sea ice was still frozen thick. It wouldn't be until the last week of May that the ice would break up and the seas become free. Amazingly, the English crew was rescued the very day after the sea ice finally broke. They did have to endure another season on the island, helping in the whaling slaughter that their rescue ship had come for, but they did eventually make it back home in August. The entire crew had survived. It meant that spending a winter in that "untemperate climate" was possible, if terrible.

But how could one do it for six consecutive years, plus three months in addition to that? Mental stress alone should have been enough to doom any prospect of survival.

Gloomily, and in despaired silence, the four Russians walked back to the hut and set about making necessary repairs. This meant mostly filling in the cracks and splits in the wood where the icy Arctic air whistled through. Large clumps of moss grew abundantly on the island, and they were able to collect copious amounts and jam it in the crevices. They also used their ax to cut at cross boards to cover holes. They did the work with great deliberateness and care. It was clear to the four Russian sailors that this rudimentary hut, ingenious as it was, would be their home through a long and bitter winter. That prospect must have been supremely deflating.

Spitsbergen

Courtesy of Julia Kolodko

Halfmoon Island was (and still is) a forbidding landscape. The closest island looked even more unwelcoming. Its approach was marked by tall outcrops and mountains lining the coast like sentinels, all covered with ice and snow. From where the men stood, it was this view in one direction, frozen sea in the other, and desolation all around. The brutally cold climate ensured that no trees or shrubs of any kind grew there. This meant they would have no wood, no fire, and no ready source of heat. But it wasn't as if the place was devoid of life; after all, the men had come in search of walrus. However, another animal roamed these parts; Halfmoon Island sat in the migratory route for polar bears.

Fortunately for the sailors, their first interactions with animals were not with polar bears, but with reindeer. In fact, over the next few weeks, the men managed to fell twelve reindeer with the twelve musket balls they had with them. Their extraordinary accuracy can be explained in part by Svalbard reindeers' unfamiliarity with humans; even today, they tend to allow people to approach within twenty yards or so before they take off. Nevertheless, a one hundred percent hit rate is impressive no matter the circumstances. However, once that twelfth shot found its mark, the musket became superfluous.

The men had to eat their reindeer meat raw due to their want of fire. The same currents that brought the sailors unintentionally to that shore also pushed the wood of shipwrecks and even whole trees from far away on the Russian mainland; floods often carried entire swaths of uprooted forest to the Arctic, where they made the almost one thousand-mile journey to Svalbard's islands. In short, a daily collection of driftwood should have provided the men with the fuel they needed. However, in a cruel blow, the driftwood was always waterlogged, and without fire, and with frequent rain, snow, and humidity, the men had no quick or easy way to dry it out.

But among the driftwood were long pieces of board, many of them impaled with long nails and iron hooks, "the melancholy relics of some vessels cast away in those remote parts." They also found a fir tree branch that nearly approximated a bow. The ingenious Russians, down to their last bits of reindeer meat, fashioned crude but effective weapons out of this cache. Using large stones, deer antlers, and long iron hooks, they made hammers and ultimately spears. They attacked a polar bear, killing it as the great *Ursus maritimus* lashed at them with six-inch-long talons and bared teeth. The men's conquest was significant; it meant that they could feed themselves even without the aid of the musket, and it also meant that they had just kept themselves in food for a good long while; Svalbard polar bears often exceed one thousand pounds in weight, and, when fully grown, hardly ever remain below six hundred pounds. One bear kill meant sustenance for the foreseeable future.

After devouring the meat, the men stripped and cleaned the bear's elastic tendons. Now they had string for their bow. All that was left now was a surplus of arrows. For these, they repeated the process for the spears, only a bit smaller, and thus armed themselves with a complete bow and arrow arsenal. Ultimately, this effective weaponry was used to kill no fewer than 250 reindeer during the men's time on the island. They also killed and ate blue and white foxes, and used the skins of all to fashion new clothing and bedding for themselves.

When their exile would end more than six years later, the men counted ten polar bears among their kills. The astonishing fact about this number is that only one—the first—resulted from a premeditated attack on the part of the men. The nine other bear deaths were a result of the men fending off attacks. This points to another important element of the men's survival that makes it all the more amazing. They lived in constant fear of a bear attack. This meant that the simplest activity—going outside the hut to relieve oneself, for example—always had to be undertaken at least in pairs. In fact, every excursion outside—to collect driftwood, to search the horizon for approaching ships, to check conditions of the ice—had to be done under extreme stress because of the imminent attack. Add to this constant fright the fact that for almost four months of every year, the men labored in complete darkness, the sun failing to show over the horizon from mid-October to early February. It wasn't just the cold and darkness that made winter the worst time; snowfalls were heavy. Le Roy reports, "The snow fell on this island in such great quantities during the winter, that it wholly covered their hut, and left them no way of getting out of it, but through a hole they had made in the upper part of the roof of their anti-chamber."

As indicated, the sailors' first attempts at producing fire proved fruitless. However, they eventually achieved the production of a flame with another amazing feat of ingenuity. According to Le Roy's account, the men "fashioned a kind of lamp, they filled it with some rein-deer's fat, and stuck in it some linen twisted to the shape of a wick." Unfortunately, when the fat melted, it soaked the clay and ran through all sides, extinguishing the flame. "They made another one, dried it thoroughly in the air, then heated it red hot, and afterwards quenched it in their kettle, in which they had boiled down a quantity of flour to the consistence of starch. The lamp being then dried and filled with melted fat, they now found to their great joy that it did not leak. But for greater security, they dipped linen rags in their paste, and with them covered it all over on the outside. Having succeeded in this attempt, they immediately made another lamp for fear of an accident, that at all events they might not be destitute of a light; upon which they determined to reserve the remainder of their flour for similar purposes." As a result, the men had an eternal flame for the entire duration of their forced exile. The men's decision to forsake food—the flour— for the sake of a flame indicates the importance of fire not only for warmth, but also for its simple psychological boost.

When they failed to collect enough fuel for their fires—rope or oakum from the shoreline—they used their clothing, slowly substituting what they had carried on their backs with the furs of killed animals. They sewed these together by fashioning a needle from wire and animal tendons. With fire, they were able to keep a "stove" in the hut; this contraption wasn't strong enough to cook meat, however, and the men continued to eat their reindeer raw until they hit upon the idea of hanging the meat above the stove's output, thereby smoking it and preserving it for later use. Of course, in such a hostile environment, one solution often begat a new problem. The store of meat attracted polar bears, and the men, already tense with the possibility of an attack, often had to chase away bears with loud shouting and brandishing of their homemade lances. Usually, such a display of offense was enough to drive the bears away. However, when one wouldn't budge, or if it went on the attack, the men were forced to kill it. The chance of the bear inflicting a grievous injury on one of the men was great.

Amazingly, none of the men ever suffered a serious injury from bear attack, and there would be nine such instances in all.

The men kept daily watches on the horizon, hoping beyond hope to see the appearance of a sail. And day after day (almost twenty-three hundred in all), month after month, season after season, and year after year, they saw nothing.

Of course, it would be ludicrous to suggest that because these ingenious men had found ways to meet all their needs for basic survival, they were left happy or even content. Le Roy, in perhaps the only portion of his narrative in which he makes any attempt to delve into the psychology of the men, writes, "Excepting an uneasiness which generally accompanies an involuntary solitude, these people having thus, by their ingenuity, so far overcome their wants, might have had reason to be contented with what Providence had done for them in their distressful situation. But that melancholy reflection, to which each of these forlorn persons could not help giving way, that perhaps he might survive his companions, and then perish for want of subsistence, or become a prey to the wild beasts, incessantly disturbed their minds."

After surviving for six long years, each summer holding out hope of rescue until the shortening days of September brought back the pack ice and eliminated all chance, one of the men finally succumbed. In a very telling comment, Le Roy relates that after Feodor Verigin died, the other men "wished to be the next to follow him." This, despite the fact that Verigin's death increased the other men's chances of survival by simple virtue of lessening their numbers. Indeed, it's nothing short of a miracle that Verigin managed to survive so long, and his continued presence was certainly a weight on the others, for Verigin had been ill from the start. His steadfast refusal to drink warm reindeer blood no doubt contributed to his worsening illness. Le Roy describes Verigin's agonies thus: "He passed almost six years under the greatest sufferings: in the latter part of that time, he became so weak that he could no longer sit erect, nor even raise his hand to his mouth; so that his humane companions were obliged to feed and tend him, like a new-born infant, to the hour of his death." The survivors buried Verigin as best they could in the deep snow and frozen ground. This may have plunged the remaining men into the depths of despair, as the prospect of a seventh year on the island loomed. In fact, almost half a year would pass again before, on August 15, 1749, a Russian ship appeared on the horizon. If they hadn't seen a ship by the end of that month, they faced yet another dark, dismal, trapped winter before next year's renewed chance of rescue.

The same conditions that had sent the Russians onto East Spitsbergen more than six years earlier now did the same to this Russian vessel, which also was attempting to get to West Spitsbergen. Spotting the vessel, the marooned sailors lit fires and ran toward the beach waving a pole with a reindeer skin attached. They were spotted, and saved. But not without a bit of negotiation first.

Though the ship would be their rescue, it hadn't set off from Russia with that intention. The crew were traders and trappers, and they, too, were out to make money. The marooned sailors offered to work on board during the whole of the passage back home and to pay the captain, Amos Kornilov, eighty rubles upon arrival. It was agreed, and the men were, at last, after a period of six years and three months, headed home. As Le Roy wrote, "It would be in vain to attempt to describe the joy of these poor people, at seeing the moment of their deliverance so near."

They arrived home at Archangelsk on September 28. The initial greeting at their surprising homecoming was almost tragic: "The moment of their landing was near proving fatal to the loving and beloved wife of Alexis Himkoff [Aleksei Inkov], who being present when the vessel came into port, immediately knew her husband, and ran with such eagerness to his embraces, that she slipped into the water and very narrowly escaped being drowned!"

The final postscript to their story: all that Le Roy recorded of their lives after returning home, was an odd one: "All three on their arrival were strong and healthy; but having lived so long without bread, they could not reconcile themselves to the use of it, and complained that it filled them with wind; nor could they bear any spirituous liquors, and therefore never drank anything but water afterwards."

Back in Russia, the men met such suspicion that they were subjected to repeated retellings, sometimes hostile, to see if their stories began to unsynch. In short, what they had pulled off simply couldn't be believed. They had been gone so long that they had been listed as dead on a subsequent Mezen census. Even the author of their story, P. L. Le Roy, remarked, "I myself was, in the beginning, at a loss what opinion to form." According to his suspicions, Le Roy interviewed the men with a certain dubiousness: "I examined them with all the circumspection and care I was master of; proposing to them such questions as I thought necessary to satisfy me of the truth of this relation."

But it was all true—the men had pulled off the impossible. But even more amazing when considering the men's survival is the fact that three out of the four—excepting Khrisanf Inkov—were at least in their midforties, an advanced age in the mid-eighteenth century. More incredible still, the extraordinary hardships the three returning men endured were not enough to dissuade them from undertaking the same trip again. Local tradition has it that all three men returned to Spitsbergen numerous times. Perhaps they felt an even greater sense of security in undertaking the trip, knowing that they had already seen the worst, had already survived the outer limits of human deprivation, and made it through. Sadly, records indicate that Khrisanf Inkov died on one of these subsequent trips, most probably of scurvy.

Endurance (1915–16)

Twenty-eight men (and one hundred Canadian Husky sledge dogs) led by Sir Ernest Shackleton—the "Boss"—constituted the Imperial Trans-Antarctic Expedition. If successful, the members of the expedition would be the first to cross the entire Antarctic peninsula; it was an audacious plan (and one that wouldn't be successfully completed until 1958). Shackleton's advertisement calling for volunteers made no attempt to hide the daring: "The distance will be roughly 1800 miles, and the first half of this, from the Weddell Sea to the Pole, will be over unknown ground." Out of almost five thousand applications, Shackleton chose just fifty-six men (only half this number would eventually go). He chose his members as much for their expertise as for their compatibility— good thing, too, because their character would be sorely tested. The Boss was a master at moving men—he could be stern when the time called for it, but he could be just as flexible if need be. "Shackleton had a genius," one of the expedition members remembered, "for keeping those about him in high spirits. We loved him." He was, in short, a great leader. And he would need to be.

Shackleton's choice of captain for the expedition's ship, the *Endurance*, was a good one: Frank Worsley was a New Zealander who, at the age of forty-two, had already spent almost three decades at sea. Worsley guided the *Endurance* from Buenos Aires on October 26, 1914, and brought her to South Georgia Island, off the southern tip of South America, stopping her at the Grytviken whaling station. Bad news awaited the men there: Norwegian whalers reported that the ice in the Weddell Sea was the worst they'd ever seen. But Shackleton was eager to get on, despite the warnings. England's primacy in exploration and national pride were at stake. And with World War I looming, these ideals took on added importance. The men of the expedition had volunteered, in a body, to fight the war in Europe. But the Admiralty telegraphed its response with one clear message: "Proceed." So the expedition forged ahead. The men would be engaged in what Shackleton called "The White Warfare of the South."

It wasn't long before they met the thick ice. But the *Endurance* was up to the task, speeding through and pushing aside large chunks. But by the

Endurance Crushed

Courtesy of the Royal Geographic Society, London

end of January, the middle of the Antarctic summer, the *Endurance* became trapped by the pack. Tough conditions—northerly gales, and then periods of calm, mixed with temperatures well below zero—created a perfect storm. The result was a thick pack that wouldn't melt. They were frozen in. As the season wore on, inching closer to winter, the *Endurance* hardly stood a chance. The men got on the ice, picking and clawing in front of the ship, trying to open a lead where she could ram herself. They put forth incredible efforts, but to no avail. After three weeks, they were ready to give it up. First Officer Lionel Greenstreet could take comfort only in the fact that should the *Endurance* have to winter where she was, "We shall have the satisfaction of knowing that we did our darndest to try & get out." But the *Endurance* was stuck fast, floating with the clockwise current of the sea. Shackleton noted, "The men had worked long hours without thought of rest, and they deserved success. But the task was beyond our powers."

Resigning themselves to wintering where they were, the men at least took some relief from the cessation of backbreaking labor. They made their shipboard home as comfortable as possible, took exercise on the ice, and generally kept in a fine mood. Food was no problem, either. Seals and penguins decorated the landscape and because they had never encountered humans before, they were easy to catch and kill. Indeed, the men could simply walk up to them and club them to death, laying in fresh stores of meat as a result. By mid-April, they had stored some 500 pounds of meat. Within three weeks, the sun would disappear and the long Antarctic winter would begin. Still, the men took it with good humor. They could keep themselves warm in the ship, they had collegial company, and they had food. They moved the stores from the hold and turned it instead into a gathering place to talk, sing, and drink. The quarter was roughly thirty-five by twenty-five feet and was dubbed "The Ritz."

As relatively comfortable as the men might be, they could not ignore the sounds of the groaning and snapping ice, nor the darkening season. And the pressure was working against the *Endurance*; at least one hundred tons of snow was piled against the bow and port side. The ship would have to live up to its name against the extraordinary pressure, which was capable of snapping her like a peanut shell. Shackleton described the pack ice as a giant jigsaw puzzle. "The opposing edges of heavy floes," he wrote, "Rear up in slow and almost silent conflict, till high 'hedgerows' are formed round each part of the puzzle." The result was a "winding canyon" of "icy walls 6 ft. to 10 ft. high." It was the deep of the winter—cold, dark, lifeless. The animals disappeared, as had the sun. The monotony of it was almost as maddening as the constant ice pressure. Worsley lamented in his journal: "No animal life observed—no land—no nothing!!!" But Worsley also marveled at the staunchness of their home, surviving numerous breaking floes against her; he commented: "Undoubtedly she is the finest little wooden vessel ever built." On three occasions, the *Endurance* looked to be on the verge of breaking up, only to survive the onslaught of pressure. But her luck wouldn't hold indefinitely. Shackleton had often noted, "What the ice gets, the ice keeps."

On October 27, 1915, one year and one day after she left Buenos Aires, the *Endurance* finally began to succumb. The pressure had been enormous, and rising in the previous days. Surgeon Alexander Macklin noted that the force "was of something colossal, of something in nature too big to grasp." The ship's plankings bowed inward several inches and the steel plates ground against each other, buckling and overriding one another with loud shearing. Toward the bow, ice rose higher and higher against the ship, eventually spilling over the decks and pushing her head farther into the water below. The men worked feverishly at the pumps. But they took pause when they became aware of some ghostly sound outside the ship. Worsley recalled, "I'll swear that we each had the idea that this eerie lament came from some wandering ghost." They looked out to witness a spectacle that none of them had ever seen before. Eight emperor penguins had waddled toward the ship and were singing some sort of strange dirge. No one had ever seen these solitary animals in such a large group before, and none had ever heard them sing. It seemed a bad omen. Seaman Tom McLeod spoke what all of them were thinking: "We'll none of us get back to our homes again."

The *Endurance* offered its best fight—it had survived onslaughts before. But it was obvious to all the men, now on a large ice floe nearby where they had created a makeshift camp, that this time would be different. Several observers later remarked that the *Endurance* took on the characteristics of a large dying animal, gasping for breath and straining for life. At one point, one of the floes sheared into a spear and impaled the deck of the *Endurance*, temporarily keeping her afloat.

The men kept vigil close over their beloved ship, foundering and threatening to go under any moment. It was a precarious position; land was more than two hundred miles away—and that forbidding patch of terrain was a windswept, snowy, and uninhabited spit called the Palmer Peninsula. But where they stood was risky, at best. At any moment, their large floe could spilt and send the men plunging into the icy depths of the freezing water below. In fact, they had to move their tents three times that first night after the floe cracked beneath them.

The men soon abandoned the dying *Endurance* and set out for Palmer, sledging rations, the three saved rescue boats from the *Endurance*, and a few personal effects with them. But the progress was torturously slow, and conditions ahead seemed even worse. Shackleton decided they would do better to head back to their old camp aside the *Endurance* and hope that the flow of the currents would take them closer to their destination.

By mid-November the temperatures began to rise. Inside the tents, with the lamps and body heat, it was stifling, sometimes reaching into the 80s. The conditions on the ice floe became correspondingly treacherous; the entire surface was pocked with little pools of water and melting snow and ice. It was easy to take a false step, and the men had to constantly be on guard against falling through a weak spot. Incredibly, the *Endurance* was still afloat, though uninhabitable. She finally went down on November 21, disappearing under the ice. During a last observation, an electrical light had been left on. As the *Endurance* buckled and was finally overcome, the light snapped off. "The connexion had been cut," Shackleton wrote. It had an obviously deflating effect on the men. One of them recalled, "She then gave one quick dive and the ice closed over her for ever. It gave one a sickening sensation to see it, for, mastless and useless as she was, she seemed to be a link with the outer world." In his journal, the stoic Boss noted, "It is hard to write what I feel."

Shackleton announced a revised plan; they would begin the march toward land and once the ice broke up enough, the men would split into three different teams, one for each boat: the *James Caird*, the *Dudley Docker*, and the *Stancomb Wills*, each named after one of the expedition's sponsors. They left two days before Christmas, after a feast that rendered each man "feeling full as a tick." The men pulled sledges and dragged the boats. It was a miserable exercise. The first day, they covered less than half a mile in five hours. The final tally: seven days hard marching and less than ten miles from the ship. At that rate, it would take them more than two hundred days to reach land. But it was an impossible prospect in any case; the conditions ahead offered no chance for better progress. Once again, they had to retreat to a large floe and reestablish camp. New Year's Eve arrived, and it was not a happy occasion; surgeon Alexander Macklin wrote in his journal: "Tomorrow 1916 begins: I wonder what it will bring forth for us. This time last year we prophesied that just now we would be well across the Continent." Things looked bleak; the absence of seals and penguins meant that food stores were dwindling. Rationing began. The men were soaking wet inside their tents, and the constant wind, snow, and freezing temperatures meant that they couldn't get dry. At night, they would crawl into their wet sleeping bags and try to ignore the desperate conditions. But good news did arrive; when the sun finally broke through and the men were able to get a position reading, they realized that the drifting pack had taken them more than seventy miles toward land and north of the Antarctic Circle. Plus, the reappearance of Adélie penguins meant more meat.

But the ice still hadn't broken for the men to make the trip by boat. And if they couldn't take to the sea, the chances were very good that the northward drift would take them right past Paulet Island, now the nearest land at ninety miles away. More than just simple delivery onto land, the men needed to get off the floe for the sake of their sanity. Macklin summed up their attitudes: "We have been over 4 months on the floe—a time of absolute utter inutility to anyone. There is absolutely nothing to do but kill time as best one may. Even at home, with theatres and all sorts of amusements, changes of scene and people, four months idleness would be tedious: One can then imagine how much worse it is for us." The meat, too, was becoming tedious. The rations from the ship had virtually disappeared, and every meal was meat, to everyone's increasing disgust. And when the meat, too, began to dwindle, the men felt the acute pangs of hunger and the lassitude inevitable in not having their caloric needs met. The time came to kill their dogs. They were eating, too, of course, and the men could no longer spare a morsel.

All the while, the floe upon which they had made their camp continued to crack and shrink. It had once been a mile in diameter, and it was now less than two hundred yards. The men had to constantly shift their materials for fear of losing them. Soon, they had no choice but to abandon it. The floe broke and then broke again, measuring now no more than fifty yards across. One of the men even fell through the ice as it cracked below him. Encased inside his sleeping bag, he escaped death only by Shackleton's quick reaction and extraordinary strength in pulling him out. Seconds after he was rescued, the two floes of ice smashed shut where he had been. It was just one more reason for the men to have complete faith in their leader. Worsley recalled, "They bore toward him the love of sons for a singularly noble father . . . His attitude was almost patriarchal."

Though the sea was still full of ice, Shackleton gave the order to push out. The three boats carried eight, nine, and eleven men respectively. But only the *Caird* carried sails, and it alone could utilize the wind. The men in the other boats were dependent upon their own power alone. During the day, killer whales surfaced in leads and threatened to overturn the boats. When darkness came, the extreme cold prevented sleep. And the men could not keep warm by strenuous rowing; unable to see what lay ahead, speed could be deadly.

They decided to stop for the night at the largest iceberg they saw—roughly thirty-five yards square and rising some fifteen feet above the waterline. They tethered the boats to the berg and spent an uneasy night on top. By morning, the light revealed a horror: as far as they could see, the once relatively clear water was now chockablock with bergs and floes, which made passage impossible. The men were stunned, and terrified. Worse, the berg upon which they stood was being eaten away little by little by the ice, pressure, and constant bombardment of the many floes. But salvation came; with Shackleton on vigil for any open lead that might be caught, a freak current suddenly opened up a wide lane just in front of them. The men wasted no time; they threw their stores onto their boats and jumped in. Behind them their iceberg home calved into the ocean. Huge sheets of ice closed behind; they had taken advantage of their only chance.

But the subsequent boat voyage was dreadful. Constant spray and freezing temperatures meant that the men's clothes were perpetually wet and frozen. Only the men's lips and throats were dry. Sleep was virtually out of the question. On one particularly bad evening, the temperature dropped well below zero, and the winds continued to howl, tearing the tent sheeting under which the men had huddled. It was so cold that when waves broke over the side of the boats, they literally crashed and shattered onto the wood. When the men had to relieve themselves—several of them were suffering from diarrhea—it was a terrible and dangerous ordeal to hang over the side of the boat.

But the three boats managed to stay with one another. And finally, after almost a week, the men at last reached land. The ragged cliffs of Elephant Island were clearly outlined on the horizon. But the Antarctic had taught these men that nothing gave itself up easily. Ahead of them lay rough breakers that would easily destroy the little wooden vessels. They had to spend yet another night on the water and wait for first light to try another route. The boats split up. By morning, many of the men were battling frostbite; several appeared to be losing. And they all were suffering badly from saltwater boils. Their hair was frozen and matted and their eyes were sunken and gray. If they had to spend one more evening on the water, some of them would surely die.

The *Caird* and *Wills* managed to make a safe landing (the very first ever recorded on Elephant Island), but the *Docker* was nowhere to be seen. When it came bobbing over the horizon, after traveling the same fourteen miles the other boats had traveled in looking for a suitable place to land, there was a joyous reunion. They were all in bad shape, but they were all, miraculously, alive.

Where they landed was barely one hundred by fifty feet. But it was land, something they hadn't set foot on in almost five hundred days. According to Shackleton, the first arrivals began "picking up stones and letting handfuls of pebbles trickle between their fingers like misers gloating over hoarded gold." Their bags were still soaking wet, but no matter. They slept soundly and could barely contain their glee when they awoke. Photographer Frank Hurley wrote, "How delicious . . . To fall asleep and awaken again and feel this is real. We have reached the land!!"

What a crushing blow, then, when the men realized that they couldn't stay. A quick look at the cliffs behind them revealed a high water line that reached well beyond where they lay. They had been lucky to land; now they would have to go before conditions changed and swept them out to sea. They rowed to the next available spot, but this proved not much better. Macklin noted, "A more inhospitable place could scarcely be imagined. The gusts increased in violence and became so strong that we could hardly walk against them, and there was not a lee or scrap of shelter anywhere." Worsley echoed Macklin's sentiments: "It is impossible to describe accurately the violence of the atmosphere of Elephant Island, the screech of the wind and the driving storms, the cannon-like reports of the glaciers 'calving' masses of ice as big as the dome of St. Paul's." They could stay without fear of the water reaching them, however. Shackleton decided that he and five other men would set sail in the *Caird* for the whaling stations at South Georgia Island. If they made it, they could send a relief ship back in a month. The others had nothing to do but wait, and survive. The prospects weren't good for any of them; South Georgia was barely twenty-five miles across, and eight hundred miles away. It would take some extraordinary navigating. For this reason, Shackleton brought with him Captain Worsley, the ace navigator. As for those staying behind, their little cove created a perfect funnel for the vicious winds. When they whipped up, they exceeded one hundred miles an hour and hurled rocks—and anything else not tied down—at the men's heads. When Shackleton left, he penned a letter and gave it to second-in-command Frank Wild; it concluded, "You can convey my love to my people and say I tried my best." From the boat, Shackleton looked back; the heavy weight of delivering all his men to safety was almost too much to bear. "The men who were staying behind made a pathetic little group on the beach," he noted, "With the grim heights of the island behind them and the sea seething at their feet." Later, he confided to Worsley: "If things went wrong, it might be said that I had abandoned them."

The twenty-two men on Elephant Island gathered stones and built the walls of their shelter. Then they took the other two boats, upended them, and placed them on top for the roof. The hut's highest point was less than five feet. They lashed everything together with canvas. But the wind made a mockery of their efforts, whistling through every crack and dragging snow and ice with it, so it felt like they were sleeping outside. Hurley wrote that "Life here without a hut and equipment is almost beyond endurance." But by degrees, the men managed to plug the leaks and create something resembling comfort. However, it was already May, and the Antarctic winter was fast approaching. Soon, the ice would be so thick that a relief ship would be prevented from getting in. But any ship coming was first dependent upon Shackleton and the others reaching South Georgia—no easy task. By the end of the month, the men grew discouraged. Hurley wrote, "Our wintry environment embodies the most inhospitable and desolate prospect imaginable. All are resigned now and fully anticipate wintering."

But Shackleton and the others were still alive, and still on course—fully aware that at any moment, one collision with a large block of ice could splinter the boat and end it all. Inside the boat, the constant freeze and water conspired against the men. They suffered from frostbite and Worsley's navigational books were soaked and rendered almost useless. Their reindeer hair sleeping bags were soaked through and the hairs began to loosen and spread themselves like plaster over everything. Worsley lamented: "Reindeer bags in such a hopeless sloppy slimy mess, smelling badly & weighting so heavily that we throw two of the worst overboard." Years later, even with distance, he remembered specifically the torment caused by the reindeer hairs as amongst the worst sensations of the entire ordeal: "Each [hair] seemed to me to assume a baleful entity of its own and crawl like a live thing, with malice aforethought, into everything I touched, ate, or wore, until we landed."

By early May, the nights were so cold that the men woke each morning to find a thick coat of ice covering their entire boat. They had to get at the task of chipping it off for fear of the excess weight. Their bodies were covered with painful boils, and their water was running out. By their calculations, they were ninety miles from South Georgia. But they had little room for error; beyond

South Georgia was just open ocean, all the way to Africa. If they sailed by it, all were doomed—the six on the *Caird* and the twenty-two left behind.

But they did reach it. Again, nothing was ever easy—like before, they couldn't simply try for land; ahead of them lay dangerous breakers that would dash them to pieces. They had to swing back into the water and spend yet another wretched night out there before searching for a suitable place to land. By morning a terrible storm was blowing. All morning and afternoon, the weakened men fought the storm with everything they had. But the winds took the *Caird* directly into the path of Annenkov Island, a towering collection of formidable cliffs and rock. A collision meant sure death. In fact, Worsley resigned himself to it; a crash seemed inevitable, with Annenkov creeping ever closer during the approaching night. "What a pity. We have made this great boat journey and nobody will ever know," he thought. "We might just as well have foundered immediately after leaving Elephant Island."

But somehow they managed to clear the island, so close that they could see its cliffs straight up in front of them; they could hear the booming echoes of surf against her sides. They managed to avoid the island, but it meant yet another evening on the boat. But the next day, May 10, they landed on South Georgia, the very island from which they had sailed more than seventeen months earlier.

But all wasn't secure yet. The men were on the other side of the island from the whaling station at Grytviken. The distance in sailing around the island was 130 miles, but during the evening, the heavy sea took the *Caird*'s rudder—the men had been too exhausted to properly pull her onto shore. Shackleton proposed an overland trek; it was just twenty-nine miles that way. But it had never been done. The middle of South Georgia is an imposing collection of peaks and valleys, with glaciers pocked by wide crevasses often hidden in deep snow. One wrong move meant death. Plus, the men had little equipment with them, tossing even their sleeping bags to lighten their burden. It was virtually suicidal. But they had little choice, and they had already defied the odds a hundred times over. What was one more? Three of the men—Shackleton, Tom Crean, and Worsley—set off, leaving the other three behind (John Vincent, Timothy McCarthy, and Harry McNeish) to recover from illness and injury.

The trip was extraordinary. The men climbed mountains, slid down precipitous edges, marched through darkness, retraced miles of steps when they miscalculated, trudged through snow, circled unclimbable peaks, and eventually heard the tinny shrill steam whistle calling the whalers to work at seven in the morning—"Never had any one of us heard sweeter music," Shackleton remembered. "It was the first signal of civilization that we had heard for nearly two years." The three men tumbled down the last slope, shimmied through an icy waterfall, flung down the adze they had carried, and readied to present themselves at the whaling station, after thirty-six hours of continual and hard travel on desperately weakened frames in an impossible landscape under punishing weather. All that was left at that moment of the Imperial Trans-Antarctic Expedition was three men in wet and tattered clothes; this out of a colossal dream originally stocked with "a well-found ship, full equipment, and high hopes." But they had made it, and rescues could begin.

In 1955, the next successful traverse of South Georgia was accomplished—by men fully decked with gear. The leader, Duncan Carse, marveled at the accomplishments of Shackleton and his men: "I do not know how they did it, except that they had to . . . three men of the heroic age of Antarctic exploration."

The old Norwegian whalers at Grytviken station were amazed. In turn, they each shook Worsley's hand. Had they not met the man who did it, none of them would have believed that a 22-foot open boat could be taken the distance it had to South Georgia over the most violent, storm-tossed ocean on the planet. A whaler soon rounded the island to pick up Vincent, McCarthy, and McNeish. And rescue efforts for those back on Elephant Island were immediately set into motion. But the fates were cruel. The first three attempts were turned back by thick ice. Shackleton was "in an acute fever of mind about the condition of his men away in the south." Only the fourth rescue attempt, on August 30, long after the men had given up hope—was successful.

It had been more than four months since the Boss departed, and no one on Elephant Island still believed that the *Caird* had made it.

There, the men had scratched out a miserable existence. Food was harvested, but was monotonous: penguin steaks and seal blubber day and night. At night, the men huddled together for warmth and tried desperately to snatch sleep. When they had to pee, they used a large can, which had to be emptied when full—no matter the screeching winds and subzero temperatures. Doctor James McIlroy performed two surgeries. One of the men, steward (originally a stowaway) Perce Blackboro had to have all fives toes on one foot amputated in the grimy, soot-blackened, and stinking confines of the shelter. The only anesthetic available was a bit of chloroform. The other case was that of navigator Hubert Hudson, who developed a painful and enormous abscess on his buttocks. When McIlroy performed the surgery, he removed two pints of fluid. The terrain that was their home left little opportunity to exercise; their only physical exertion was, in Hurley's words, when they would "promenade up and down the 80 yards of the spit, or climb to the lookout and scan the misty skyline for a mast."

But despite the daily ritual, they invariably saw nothing. May passed. Then June. Next July. By August (and the two-year anniversary of the *Endurance's* leaving London) the men had given up hope of any ship coming before the spring thaw, which could be half a year away. As the early days of August passed, the men began tentatively planning their own boat journey to Deception Island, where there were stores for shipwrecked mariners. Storekeeper Thomas Orde-Lees wrote in his journal, "Sir Ernest's nonreturn is now openly discussed." By the nineteenth, he confided, "There is no good in deceiving ourselves any longer." But eleven days later, the heroic Shackleton appeared in the Chilean tug, the *Yelcho.* The men hailed him down and left everything behind; they wanted no reminders. As Shackleton approached, he yelled, "Are you all right?"

"All well," they said. Everyone was alive. All twenty-eight of them, after more than two years in an environment that promised death at any moment—and by a thousand different methods.

When the newly rescued men left their desolate residence, some of them turned their faces toward the ocean—and home. Others couldn't help themselves; they stole one last glance at the terrible place that had housed them. Macklin recorded the moment this way: "I stayed on deck to watch Elephant Island recede in the distance . . . I could still see my [jacket] flapping in the breeze on the hillside—no doubt it will flap there to the wonderment of the gulls and penguins till one of our familiar [storms] blows it all to ribbons." It was an ephemeral reminder of the men's existence in that place, one where men, even those with the biggest dreams, could scarcely leave a trace.

The members of the expedition—despite all they had been through—didn't shy from their duties as Englishmen. When they learned that World War I was still raging, they "took their places in the wider field of battle, and the percentage of casualties amongst the members" of the expedition was, sadly, quite high.

Bibliography

Alexander, Michael. *Mrs. Fraser on the Fatal Shore.* London: Phoenix Press, 2001.

Amundsen, Roald. *My Life as an Explorer.* Garden City, NY: Doubleday, Page & Co, 1927.

Ashton, Philip. *Ashton's Memorial: An History of the Strange Adventures and Signal Deliverances of Mr. Philip Ashton.* Boston: Samuel Gerrish, 1725.

Bartlett, Robert. *The Karluk's Last Voyage.* New York: Cooper Square Press, 2001.

Blechnyden, Kathleen. *Calcutta, Past and Present.* London: W. Thacker & Co, 1905.

Brandt, Anthony. *The Tragic History of the Sea: Shipwrecks from the Bible to Titanic.* Washington, D.C.: National Geographic Society, 2007.

Buchana, Neil and Barry Dwyer. *The Rescue of Eliza Fraser.* Noosaville, Queensland: Noosa Graphica, 1986.

Chase, Owen and Thomas Nickerson. *The Loss of the Ship Essex, Sunk by a Whale.* Nathaniel Philbrick and Thomas Philbrick, eds. New York: Penguin Classics, 2000.

Constructions of Colonialism: Perspectives on Eliza Fraser's Shipwreck. Ian J. McNiven, Lynette Russell, and Kay Schaffer, eds. London: Leicester University Press, 1999.

Corréard, Alexandre and Jean Baptiste Henri Savigny. *Narrative of a Voyage to Senegal in 1816. Undertaken by Order of the French Government, Comprising an Account of the Shipwreck of the Medusa, the Sufferings of the Crew, and the Various Occurrences on Board the Raft, in the Desert of Zaara, at St. Louis, and at the Camp of Daccard. To Which Are Subjoined Observations Respecting the Agriculture of the Western Coast of Africa, from Cape Blanco to the Mouth of the Gambia.* London: H. Colburn, 1818.

Curtis, John. *Shipwreck of the Stirling Castle: Containing a faithful narrative of the dreadful sufferings of the crew and the cruel murder of Captain Fraser by the cannibals inflicted upon the captain's widow.* London: G. Virtue, 1838.

Dampier, William. *A New Voyage Round the World.* New York: Dover Publications, 1968.

Dash, Mike. *Batavia's Graveyard: The True Story of the Mad Heretic Who Led History's Bloodiest Mutiny.* New York: Three Rivers Press, 2002.

Drake-Brockman, Henrietta. *Voyage to Disaster, with translations of the Journals of Francisco Pelsaert.* Sydney: Angus and Robertson, 1964.

Drury, Robert. *Madagascar: or Robert Drury's Journal during fifteen years captivity on that island.* London: Fisher Unwin, 1729.

Duncan, Archibald. *The Mariner's Chronicle: Containing Narratives of the Most Remarkable Disasters at Sea, Such as Shipwrecks, Storms, Fires and Famines. Also Naval Engagements, Piratical Adventures, Incidents of Discovery, And Other Extraordinary and Interesting Occurrences.* New Haven, CT: Durrie and Peck, 1834.

Edwards, Hugh. *Islands of Angry Ghosts.* New York: William Morrow, 1966.

Ellms, Charles. *The Tragedy of the Seas; Or, Sorrow on the Ocean, Lake, and River, from Shipwreck, Plague, Fire, and Famine.* Philadelphia: Carey & Hart, 1841.

Foley, Shawn. *The Badijala People.* Hervey Bay, Queensland: Thoorgine Educational and Cultural Centre Aboriginal Corporation, Inc., 1927.

Funnell, William, *A Voyage around the world Containing an Account of Captain Dampier's Expedition into the South Sea in the St. George, 1703-04.* London: J. Knapton, 1707

Gaiarbau, Gerrs Langeuad, and LP Winterbotham. *Some Original Views Around Kilcoy.* Brisbane: Archaeology Branch, Queensland, 1982.

Garcilaso de la Vega. *Royal Commentaries of the Incas and General History of Peru.* Harold V. Livermore, trans. Austin: University of Texas Press, 1966.

Gavron, Jeremy. "Late Rescue for History's Castaway." *Guardian,* January 30, 1999.

Hanson, Neil. *The Custom of the Sea.* New York : Wiley, 1999.

Harrison, David. *The Melancholy Narrative of The Distressful Voyage and Miraculous Deliverance of Captain David Harrison.* London: James Harrison, 1766.

Heffernan, Thomas Farel. *Stove by a Whale: Owen Chase and the Essex.* Hanover, NH: Wesleyan, 1990.

Huntress, Keith Gibson. *Narratives of Shipwrecks and Disasters, 1586-1860.* Ames, IA: Iowa State Press, 1974.

Hynes, John and George Carter. *A Narrative of the Loss of the Grosvenor East Indiaman: Which was Unfortunately Wrecked on the Coast of Caffraria, Somewhere Between the 27th and 32nd Degrees of Southern Latitude, on the 4th of August, 1782, Compiled From the Examination of John Hynes, One of the Unfortunate Survivors.* London: Minerva Press, 1791.

King, Dean. *Skeletons on the Zahara: A True Story of Survival.* New York: Little Brown and Company, 2004.

Kirby, Percival. *The True Story of the Grosvenor East Indiaman.* Cape Town: Oxford University Press, 1960.

— *A Source Book on the Wreck of the Grosvenor East Indiaman.* Cape Town: Van Riebeeck Society, 1953.

Lansing, Alfred. *Endurance. Shackleton's Incredible Voyage.* New York: Carroll & Graf, 1959.

Le Roy, Pierre Louis. *Narrative of the Singular Adventures of Four Russian Soldiers, Who Were Cast Away on the Desert Island of East-Spitzbergen.* London: Collier and Copp, 1785

Leslie, Edward E. *Desperate Journeys, Abandoned Souls: True Stories of Castaways and Other Survivors.* Boston: Mariner Books, 1998.

Leys, Simon. *The Wreck of the Batavia: A True Story.* New York: Thunder's Mouth Press, 2005.

Marx, Robert. "Pedro Serrano: The First Robinson Crusoe." *Oceans,* vol. 7 no. 5, 1974: 50–55.

McKee, Alexander. *Wreck of the Medusa: The Tragic Story of the Death Raft.* New York: Signet, 2000.

McKinlay, William Laird. *The Last Voyage of the Karluk: A Survivor's Memoir of Arctic Disaster.* New York: St. Martin's Griffin, 1999.

Neider, Charles. *Great Shipwrecks and Castaways.* New York: Dorset Press, 1952.

Niven, Jennifer. *The Ice Master: A True Story of Adventure, Betrayal, and Survival in the Arctic.* London: Pan Books, 2001.

Parker Pearson, Mark. "Re-appraising Robert Drury's Journal as a Historical Source." *History in Africa* vol. 23, 1996: 1–23.

Philbrick, Nathaniel. *In the Heart of the Sea: The Tragedy of the Whaleship Essex*. New York: Penguin, 2001.

Riley, James. *Sufferings in Africa: The Astonishing Account of a New England Sea Captain Enslaved by North African Arabs*. New York: Skyhorse Publishing, 2007.

Robbins, Archibald. *Journal, Comprising an Account of the Loss of the Brig Commerce, of Hartford, (Con.) James Riley, Master, upon the Western Coast of Africa, August 28th, 1815; also of the Slavery and Sufferings of the Author and the Rest of the Crew, upon the Desert of Zahara, in the Years 1815, 1816, 1817; with Accounts of the Manners, Customs, and Habits of the Wandering Arabs; also, a Brief Historical and Geographical View of the Continent of Africa*. Hartford, CT: Judd, Loomis & Company, 1836.

Roberts, David. *Four Against the Arctic: Shipwrecked for Six Years at the Top of the World*. New York: Simon & Schuster, 2003.

Roberts, Kenneth. *Boon Island: Including Contemporary Accounts of the Wreck of the Nottingham Galley*. Jack Bales and Richard Warner, eds. Hanover, NH: University Press of New England, 1996.

Rogers, Woodes. *A Crusing Voyage Round the World*. New York: Longmans, Green & Co., 1928.

Russell, Henry Stuart. *The Genesis of Queensland*. Sydney: Turner & Henderson, 1888.

Saunders, Ann. *Narrative of the Shipwreck and Sufferings of Miss Ann Saunders*. Providence: Z.S. Crossmon, 1827.

Severin, Timothy. *In Search of Robinson Crusoe*. New York: Basic Books, 2002.

Shackleton, Ernest. *South: The Last Antarctic Expedition of Shackleton and the Endurance*. Guilford, CT: The Lyons Press, 1998.

Simpson, A.W. Brian. *Cannibalism and the Common Law: A Victorian Yachting Tragedy*. Chicago: The University of Chicago Press, 1984.

Souhami, Diana. *Selkirk's Island: The True and Strange Adventures of the Real Robinson Crusoe*. London: Phoenix Press, 2002.

Stanley, David. *South Pacific Handbook* (6th ed.). Berkeley, CA: Avalon, 1986.

Steele, Richard. *The Englishman Magazine.* Vol. 26. December 3, 1713.

Stefánsson, Vilhjálmur. *The Friendly Arctic: The Story of Five Years in Polar Regions.* New York: Macmillan, 1927.

Taylor, Stephen. *Caliban's Shore: The Wreck of the Grosvenor and the Strange Fate of Her Survivors.* New York: W. W. Norton, 2004.

Worsley, Frank Arthur. *Endurance: An Epic of Polar Adventure.* New York: W. W. Norton, 2000.

Index